Image and Power

in the Archaeology of Early Medieval Britain

Essays in honour of Rosemary Cramp

Edited by

Helena Hamerow and Arthur MacGregor

Oxbow Books

First published in the United Kingdom in 2001. Reprinted in 2016 by
OXBOW BOOKS
The Old Music Hall, 106–108 Cowley Road, Oxford OX4 1JE

and in the United States by
OXBOW BOOKS
1950 Lawrence Road, Havertown, PA 19083

Paperback Edition: ISBN 978-1-78570-465-9
Digital Edition: ISBN 978-1-78570-466-6

A CIP record for this book is available from the British Library

For a complete list of Oxbow titles, please contact:

UNITED KINGDOM
Oxbow Books
Telephone (01865) 241249, Fax (01865) 794449
Email: oxbow@oxbowbooks.com
www.oxbowbooks.com

UNITED STATES OF AMERICA
Oxbow Books
Telephone (800) 791-9354, Fax (610) 853-9146
Email: queries@casemateacademic.com
www.casemateacademic.com/oxbow

Oxbow Books is part of the Casemate Group

The photograph of Rosemary Cramp used as a frontispiece is by T. Woods.
The cover illustration shows the Flixborough brooch.

Contributors

Professor Richard Bailey, FSA. Pro-Vice-Chancellors' Office, University of Newcastle upon Tyne. (BA, Durham, 1954–57; PhD, Durham, 1957–60)

Professor Martin Carver, FSA. Department of Archaeology, University of York. (Diploma in Anglo-Saxon Studies, Durham, 1973–74)

Dr Derek Craig. Department of Archaeology, University of Durham. (PhD, Durham, 1992)

Dr Nancy Edwards, FSA. School of History and Welsh History, University of Wales, Bangor. (PhD, Durham, 1976–79)

Dr Helena Hamerow, FSA. Institute of Archaeology, University of Oxford. (Lecturer in archaeology, Durham, 1990–96)

Mr Peter Hill, FSA. Whithorn Archaeological Trust.

Dr Catherine Hills, FSA. Department of Archaeology, University of Cambridge. (BA, Durham, 1966–69)

Dr Chris Loveluck, Department of Archaeology, University of Southampton. (BA, Durham, 1987–90; PhD, Durham, 1990–94)

Dr Arthur MacGregor, FSA. Ashmolean Museum, University of Oxford. (MPhil, Durham, 1981; DLitt, Durham, 1999)

Professor Chris Morris, FSA. Department of Archaeology, University of Glasgow. (BA, Durham, 1964–67; lecturer, senior lecturer in Viking archaeology, Durham, 1972–90)

Ms Deirdre O'Sullivan. School of Archaeological Studies, University of Leicester. (MPhil, Durham, 1974–76; Research Assistant, Durham, 1977–79)

Foreword

On 23–24 April 1999 some two hundred friends, colleagues and former students – including many pleased to count themselves under more than one of those headings – gathered in Durham to celebrate the seventieth birthday of their doyenne, Professor Rosemary Cramp. As on all such occasions, many of the pleasures shared by the participants were light-hearted, informal and unconducive to permanent record. To draw too rigid a distinction with the more formal proceedings of the weekend, however, would be to commit an injustice to the speakers who together presented a series of papers that honoured their dedicatee with wit and affection, as well as an impressive array of scholarship reflecting Rosemary's lifelong archaeological preoccupations. Nonetheless, their contributions proved more susceptible to capture in permanent form and constitute the basis of the present volume.

Not all of the papers that comprised 'The View from Durham' as presented on that occasion are included here, such omissions as there are being entirely due to external circumstances, without sinister significance and certainly not on account of editorial fiat. In drawing together these papers we have trodden the narrow line that all editors must follow in imposing a necessary degree of coherence on the whole without unduly infringing the integrity of the individual contributions. This modest undertaking represents our own act of homage to our distinguished colleague, mentor and friend.

In undertaking this task we have been fortunate to preserve the goodwill of all the contributors and indeed have benefited from continuing dialogue with them throughout. We have had cause to be grateful too for the word-processing skills of Liz Strange, Lynda Smithson and David Berry and for the support of the School of Archaeology, University of Oxford. Our publisher, David Brown at Oxbow Books, has been a source of creative intervention, enthusiasm and meticulous time-keeping throughout the production process.

Several of our authors stress the interim nature of this token of respect and the confidence with which they anticipate Rosemary's continuing involvement in many aspects of archaeology. As if to vindicate these expectations, she was elected President of the Society of Antiquaries while the present volume was in press. The Society's apartments at Burlington House provided a fitting setting for the presentation of these essays on 28 June 2001.

Helena Hamerow
Arthur MacGregor

Rosemary Cramp as Professor of Archaeology and Head of Department in Durham, 1990

Image and Power
in the Archaeology of Early Medieval Britain
Essays in honour of Rosemary Cramp

Contents

Preface

Richard N. Bailey

Scene 1: Monkwearmouth 1959. 'I will not have scurvy on one of my digs!' A bag of tomatoes was thrust into my hand to supplement a vitamin-deficient lunch and Rosemary Cramp strode away to solve the delicate problem posed by a local resident who had become marooned alongside her netty by a trench filled with skeletons.

Scene 2: Ripon 1974. 'Well, Mr Dean, this is just not good enough, is it?' And the distinguished cleric, confronted by the steely gaze of Durham's Professor of Archaeology and the demolished remains of part of St. Wilfrid's crypt, experienced that sense of inadequacy familiar to generations of undergraduates who failed convincingly to distinguish between Trewhiddle and Jelling styles.

Rosemary Cramp's students and friends – and the one group encompasses the other – will easily be able to write similar scenes and dialogue. All will recall her characteristic combination of personal kindness, academic rigour, and outrageous sense of fun. It was therefore no surprise that the seminar held at the University of Durham marking her 70th birthday in 1999 was so well attended; nor that it was an occasion which bubbled with ideas and laughter. This volume contains some of the papers given on that day. Some of the jokes may, very properly, have been edited out, but what remains is clearly a great affection for an inspiring teacher and a loyal friend.

Many of Rosemary's academic preoccupations are reflected here, and the frequent footnotes to her work are no obsequious acts of *pietas*. The monuments and the spirituality of monasticism, unlocking information from sculpture, the inter-action of Mediterranean and Anglo-Saxon worlds, the validity and limitations of archaeological deductions – all these inter-connected themes have been central to her work, and her own discussions of them are natural reference-points for these papers.

Martin Carver opens the collection with a contribution which sweeps across time and space, arguing that monuments have a political meaning and can be used to write political as well as cultural history. Beginning with an interpretation of the larger barrows of the late sixth and seventh centuries outside Kent as expressions of the political insecurity triggered by Christianity, he astutely points to the 'monumental hiatus' of 625–675 in Anglo-Saxon England before focusing on the fact that the Christian conversion failed to produce a homogeneous culture in Britain – indeed even within Northumbria. In partial explanation he points to different kinds of Christian organization and politics – episcopal, monastic and 'secular Christianity', each with their own archaeological markers and all attested by the documentary evidence. Mapping these political markers offers a route into local intellectual history and a closer definition of political programmes and alliances. This leads him to muse on the significance of Viking-age sculpture in Yorkshire in a manner which will delight the general editor of the *Corpus of Anglo-Saxon Stone Sculpture*.

Peter Hill pays tribute through Whithorn, on whose excavation programme (and associated politics) Rosemary spent much energy. Here he focuses on the early Christian phase of that remarkable site, seizing on Charles Thomas's interpretation of the Latinus stone as a highly sophisticated literary cryptogram. In seeking an audience for such an inscription, Hill finds it in the intelligentsia of a Pelagian diaspora, fleeing Britannia in the wake of the Germanus mission. Whithorn, he argues, would have provided an appropriate refuge for a group of religious exiles, settling with the agreement of a local (even royal) ruler, based on the triple-ringed defences of the Isle of Whithorn. With them came the technology of making lime, perhaps reflected in the *'Ad Candidam Casam'* of Bede, and in the adoption of mouldboard ploughs. Documentary history and archaeology are here brought together in a provocative thesis.

Deirdre O'Sullivan's paper is also concerned with monasteries and with the need, so often argued by Rosemary, to acknowledge the contribution of documentary evidence to our understanding of the period. In particular she draws attention to the manner in which the landscape, its divisions and the flanking tidal ocean of Lindisfarne would be spiritually perceived by those familiar with exegetical texts; the very choice of the island site itself reflected those perceptions. Economic determinism is not, she demonstrates, an adequate theoretical tool with which to approach the archaeology of monasticism – an assertion underlined by the revelation that Green Shiel was a specialized production site processing juvenile cattle, whose skins may well have been used in the *scriptorium* of Eadfrith and his successors.

Chris Loveluck is also concerned with monasticism, though in the context of Flixborough this proves an elusive entity. Here he gives us the first extended post-excavation treatment of this fascinating Lincolnshire settlement, but his main purpose is to raise problems of interpretation. How, crucially, can one distinguish a monastic from a secular site? The very success of the study of high-status monasteries like Jarrow and Monkwearmouth, which Rosemary has spearheaded, has inadvertently coloured interpretations of other settlements. Yet many of the markers of such monasticism are shared with secular sites (location and lay-out, building and food types, craft production

– and even literacy and mortuary chapels). In similar questioning vein, as he reviews the evidence for the changing character of the settlement's economy and status, he emphasises how some phases are more archaeologically visible than others, and how selective interpretation from a limited range of material, combined with insensitivity to changing discard patterns, can seriously mislead.

Rosemary's achievement in launching the British Academy's *Corpus of Anglo-Saxon Stone Sculpture* represented the successful realization of an idea whose history was littered by a century of previous failures. Her contribution to this field is marked by Nancy Edwards, whose Durham work on Irish material first carried *Corpus* approaches into the Celtic west. Here she offers a preliminary view of the sculpture from St David's and its vicinity in a period running from the late fifth through to the early twelfth centuries. Influences from the Mediterranean and Gaul are clear in the earliest phase and contacts around and across the Irish Sea are evident in most of the carvings. The impact of Anglo-Saxon tastes in the eighth or early ninth century is also thoughtfully traced, though it is intriguing to notice that they are not present in the Alfredian period when Asser's activities might have led us to expect them. The majority of the monuments from St David's itself date to the century before the installation of the first Norman bishop, and its increasing prestige in the eleventh century is signalled by the influence of its sculpture on other carvings in Pembrokeshire. This is a paper which whets the appetite for the new corpus of early medieval Welsh sculpture which is now in the final stages of preparation.

Rosemary is not normally associated with the archaeology of the pagan period, but those who search through her bibliography will find ground-breaking studies of the early Northumbrian material. Catherine Hills's paper on the ivory rings found in graves of the fifth to seventh centuries is thus highly appropriate, particularly since it involves an aspect of the Mediteranean links of Anglo-Saxon England which have been a constant theme of Rosemary's writings. She demonstrates that these rings were made from African elephant ivory and were probably parts of bags. Much of the ivory originated in the kingdom of Aksum in Ethiopia and the continental distribution of the rings suggests that the material was traded up the Rhine, and then east to the German and Frisian coast or west to Anglo-Saxon England. This trade followed routes quite distinct from the more westerly Frankish/Kentish axis on which so much stress has hitherto been laid in relation to the transmission of luxury goods.

The final two sections are personal: a list of Rosemary's publications compiled by Derek Craig and a memoir by Chris Morris which captures the impact of her teaching on several generations of undergraduates and post-graduates. Both as a student and, later, as an academic colleague, Chris was well placed to record Rosemary's political skills as she fought internal University battles for her Department and, nationally, ensured a significant archaeological position for Durham in the ruthlessly competitive world of the 1970s and 1980s. Happily, he was also in a position to see her energetic contribution to regional societies and her encouragement of non-academics as they struggled to engage with the subject. Those (now) very professional amateurs are not the least among the range of individuals and institutions whose lives she has changed. And that process is far from ended.

1

Why that? Why there? Why then? The Politics of Early Medieval Monumentality

Martin Carver

The hypothesis presented in this paper has already appeared in various fragmentary forms (Carver 1986, 1993, 1998b), but has not hitherto been drawn together, so it is fitting that I should try to do this in honour of my best teacher and most telling critic. After all, it would not do for Professor Cramp's *Festschrift* to be too burdened by flattering emulation; it should contain something exasperating as well. So I look forward to her leafing through these pages with growing despair, culminating in the tart response familiar from my carefree student days: 'really Mr Carver, I have no idea what you are talking about', meaning: 'actually, I know perfectly well; you on the other hand...'

In brief, the hypothesis concerns the history of the early medieval period in north-west Europe and our ability to read it from archaeology, or more specifically from its major investments such as burial mounds, churches, illuminated manuscripts and sculpture: the word 'monumentality' of my title is intended as shorthand for all these things. Confidence in the idea that monuments had (and have) a meaning beyond some vague celebration of an individual or propitiation of an unseen omnipotence has been growing among prehistorians (e.g. Bradley 1993), and is an accepted feature of the historic period. We know that monuments are more than passive memorials because written commentaries, poetry and inscriptions declare their active purposes for us. Monuments comprise the vocabulary of a political language, fossilized versions of arguments that were continuous and may have related more to what was desired than what had occurred (Carver 1993). At the same time, we need not suppose that the expression is necessarily so subtle, sceptical or to use a fashionable word, ironical, as to lose all hope of making equations between a society and its ideas. That architecture, sculpture, burial mounds and brooches have messages beyond the functional which are dependant on their social, economic and above all their ideological context was never an issue: to understand their real meaning is the goal and the aim of each generation that studies them. It is very likely that the motives I attach to the construction of the monuments to be discussed are equally inadequate characterizations of the profound stresses that motivated and were concealed by their makers. That said, the monuments are what survive, and *our* story must temporarily keep the candle burning until *their* story can be told.

Some assumptions

The argument requires a number of assumptions to be declared. First, all archaeologists are obliged to acknowledge that whereas their efforts have the advantage of generating new evidence, there is never a good moment to argue from it; even newer evidence can quickly take the shine off too detailed a model. Reasoning from documents has the disadvantage that so few survive, but the advantage that no new sources are likely to appear suddenly in the midst of the six-year-long composition of a major synthesis. Archaeological reasoning and historical reasoning have naturally different rhythms, and the world is a more interesting place because of it. But, in order to offer a historically acceptable model, the archaeologist is obliged to assume that it is legitimate to argue from the material culture we have; to assert that in certain matters, such as the occurrence of churches and burial mounds, the distribution will not now alter markedly: that what we have is not exactly what there was, but is an acceptable representation of what there was. Having declared this assumption, the archaeologist should be permitted to develop a model on evidence that is partial; the documentary evidence is partial too, but it is legitimate to attempt to write history from it.

A second assumption is that the repertoire of material culture at our disposal is heterogeneous and cannot be interpreted through a single theoretical exegesis. Not every object or site has an equal claim to be treated as intentionally expressive. If the Sutton Hoo mound 1 burial or the Lindisfarne Gospels can be seen as having agency, representing material culture in its active voice, there is no need to impute the same intentions to a spade or a spindle whorl. The old definition of a 'culture', pulled this way and that since Gordon Childe used it the preface to *The Danube in Prehistory* (1929), can be seen as neither all cultural, nor always seeking identity, status or affiliation, but multi-purposed, a set of different statements addressing different audiences or none. If economic information is incorporated in the layers of midden heap, political meaning is most likely to be embedded in sites and objects of high investment and public access. In our period, the prominent candidates are burial mounds, jewellery, churches, illuminated manuscripts and sculpture. These appear not only in a single place at successive times, but at the same time in different places. If assumption number 1 is tenable this variation has a meaning and was intended to have one.

If the choice of the vehicle of expression is intentional, how far is it *sui generis* and how far is it owed to the emulation of the neighbours? This depends firstly on whether the neighbours are visible, and the third assumption I make is that in early medieval northern Europe they were. The Anglo-Saxons knew about the Romans, the Irish, the Picts, the British, the Franks, the Swedes, the Danes and the Norwegians at both a general and a personal level, and we can infer this both from books (Bede) and from graves (see, for example, Hines 1984). It is these contacts and the transmissions between them that allow us to suppose that the commissioners of seventh-century monuments could fish in a large reservoir of ideas. George Henderson invokes the broad range of stimuli available to the composers of the Book of Durrow in AD 680: 'Discrete national traits, in design, technique and the selection of motifs, came into conjunction in the peculiar, small-scale, packed circumstances of the British Isles, with its ever-changing political scene, under the constant cohesive influence of the internationally active Christian church, writing and speaking Latin to all ears' (Henderson 1999, 53). But to these same people, the local traits of Scandinavia and Saxony were also visible or at least were known – the patterns on cremation urns, the wrist clasps and square-headed brooches which had been worn by East Anglian nobles. The bracteates or *guldgubbe* made in Fyn are sources for Insular Art potentially no more obscure than Coptic bowls or stamped Mediterranean pottery. So why were their ideas not recycled on the pages of the gospel books? The animals of the Sutton Hoo shoulder clasps and purse lid and of the Durrow carpet pages are links in the same technician's chain. But a great deal more of the Sutton Hoo menagerie, on helmet, sceptre, and sword was not adopted by the Christian artisans. Eastern Christian figurative art was known to the kings of East Anglia, as can be seen from a sixth-century bucket found in a field a few hundred metres north of Sutton Hoo (Mango *et al.* 1989). But it was not incorporated into the Sutton Hoo jewellery. The point is an obvious one. The Anglo-Saxons were not 'eclectic' in the sense of taking motifs at random from some workshop floor or exotic street scene. They were not indiscriminately 'influenced' by things they had seen in the halls of Danish relatives or on trips to Rome. They were creative and selective, not eclectic, but choosy. There was, potentially, a broad range of accessible options and since the different options were equally available, the choice which was actually made must have a meaning.

The next assumption is that the repertoire of possible choices does not need to be contemporary; in other words the maker of expressive artefacts and monuments can also fish in the pool of the past. The metal-smiths of later Celtic Britain and Ireland can revive La Tène styles after an interval of 500 years, just as Roman motifs, lettering, ornament and pottery are reintroduced in seventh-century Northumbria, the courts of Offa and Charlemagne, the *burhs* of Alfred, and in numerous subsequent renaissances (Carver 1993). It was recently argued that the notched shield seen on the St Andrews Sarcophagus derived from something last seen (so far as we are aware) in the Iron Age of southern Britain (Carver 1999a). There are two ways in which this transmission can be achieved, the most easily acknowledged being survival of the object or site itself. Bailey (1992) suggests a 'conservatism' to account for the gap between Sutton Hoo and Durrow (see below), while Henderson prefers to see the transmission occurring via surviving pattern books (Henderson 1999, 50). Roman things no doubt turned up or were dug up from time to time, certainly when former Roman sites were being redeveloped from the tenth-century onwards; this easily explains why the form of late Saxon pottery was drawn from Roman, not Frankish models (Carver 1999b, 42). The argument has been extended to sites; former prehistoric ceremonial centres being commandeered by later authorities for their own legitimation (Bradley 1988), and it is likely that the Anglo-Saxons had quite a sophisticated knowledge of 'landscape archaeology'. Bronze Age burial mounds were suitable places for the emulation of Pagan status, while Christian missionaries should be assigned old Roman forts like Burgh Castle (Johnson 1988).

It is more difficult to use the 'survival' argument to explain the readoption of certain other practices such as ship burial, arguably seen previously in that form neither in Scandinavia nor Britain when it was practised at seventh-century Sutton Hoo and Snape. Here the assumption required is that the idea of ship-burial was present in the previous century and perhaps long before, but not then practised. The archaeologist cannot excavate these ethereal images, which are transmitted through unrecorded space like children's rituals in the playground (Opie and Opie 1977). Unless we suppose an early archaeological expedition to the Pyramid city at Gizeh, the idea of ship-burial came out of the heads of people and became archaeologically visible only when it was reified in some moment of exceptional stress. Ship-burial is therefore not a custom but a statement in context, and our interest in it is not so much in the innate meaning of the ritual as the meaning it had for seventh-century East Anglia: why that, why there, why then? (Carver 1995).

The contextual explanation may be thought to deserve precedence over the cultural. For example, there were burial mounds in the fifth, sixth, and seventh centuries in Britain, but this is not simply a 'burial custom' that evolves or endures. The style and location of seventh-century mounds is different from their Anglo-Saxon predecessors, being larger and more solitary (Shephard 1979). In any case, the burial mound does not have to carry exactly the same significance in the seventh century as in the sixth: it depends what else was happening. At Sutton Hoo the use of burial mounds can be deemed 'expressive' or even polemical on two counts: first they represent a higher level of investment than the mounds of previous centuries, and second, they are constructed at a time at which quite different monuments are being constructed in adjacent lands, for example in Kent. By contrast, Kent, rich in burial mounds in the sixth century, is investing in a new repertoire in the seventh – the apsidal churches of Canterbury.

If this is merely to say that monuments have political meaning, and the choice of monument reflects a political agenda, that is already a great deal for some to accept. But it is axiomatic for what follows. I want to propose that early medieval investments, prestige buildings and artefacts, can be used to write political as well as cultural history, and that if this is acceptable, we can paint a picture of confronted polities pursuing different agendas during the fifth to the eighth centuries both within the island of Britain and beyond.

Fig. 1.1. Monumental mound-burial in Britain in the sixth and seventh centuries AD (Carver 1986, after Shephard 1979).

Reactionary mound-building

The conflated version of Shephard's map (Fig. 1.1; Carver 1986) shows a trend: cemeteries with numerous small burial mounds are present in sixth-century Kent, and larger more solitary barrows are built in the late sixth into the seventh century outside Kent. We should seek some explanation for this

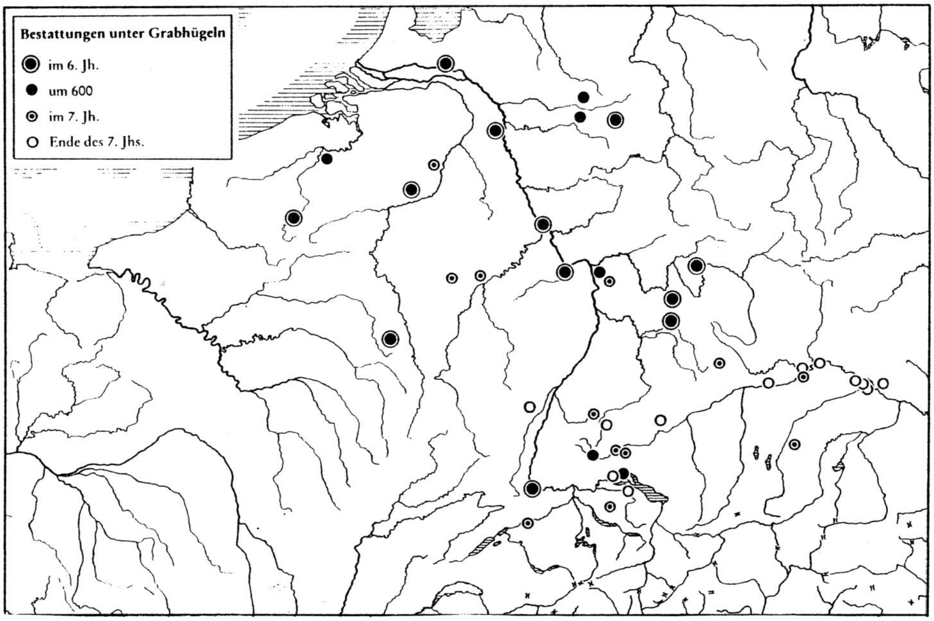

Fig. 1.2. Burial under large mounds, sixth to late seventh century AD in the Rhineland (Böhme 1993, Abb. 101).

apparent contrast, and can easily find one in the pivotal ideological event of the period – the documented arrival of the Christian mission from Rome in 597. If Christianity depressed barrow-building in Kent, it provoked it among the unconverted neighbours in a more militant form. Taplow, Sutton Hoo, and many other monumental constructions of around 600 in Saxon lands, can be read as reactions against the Christian mission (Carver 1986, 1998a, 1998b).

The work of H. W. Böhme enables us to propose a similar process for the Rhineland (Böhme 1993; Müller-Wille 1998), where the building of monumental mounds begins at the Rhine mouth in the fifth century and moves steadily upstream, arriving in Switzerland by the eighth (Fig. 1.2). In an equally thorough census, Böhme has also tracked the building of early churches in the same area; this second kind of monument can be seen to shadow the first – the earliest churches replacing the earliest barrows and the latest churches following the later barrows (Fig. 1.3). This should mean not just that churches replaced monumental barrows: they provoked their construction in the first place. We can imagine this 'bow-wave' effect taking many forms. When the mission of Adam of Bremen arrived at the ceremonial centre of Gamla Uppsala in Sweden, the grotesque sacrificial practices were noted: animals and men were hung on a great tree – and it was naturally assumed that this was a first encounter with an annual barbaric custom. Such it may have been, but the practice of sacrifice has been hard to find archaeologically, except on a small

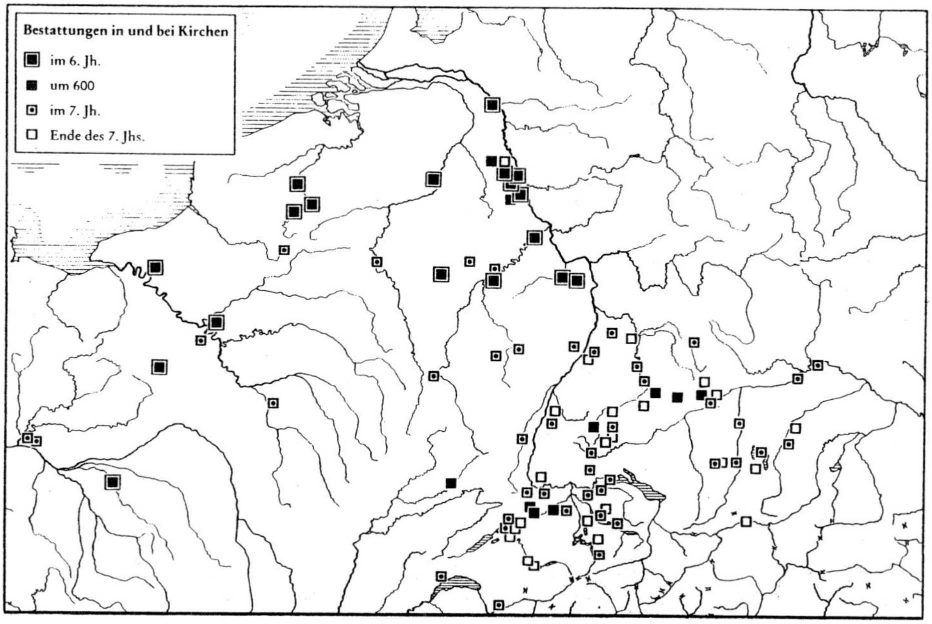

Fig. 1.3. Burial in or in association with churches, sixth to late seventh century, in the Rhineland (Böhme 1993, Abb. 99).

scale – for example animals slaughtered and included in graves. Possibly the text is intended to exaggerate the barbarity and justify the incursion. But if the event really took place, it might have done so out of the insecurity and anxiety caused by the Christian presence itself. The sacrificial practices were not so much discovered by the Christians as provoked by them. The same might have been true of Cortés in Mexico; the increasing orgy of Aztec sacrifice being caused by fear of the alien adventurers who denounced it.

Leslek Pawel Słupecki (1997) argues for similar processes in a study of the impact of Christianity on the eastern Slavs, and cites earlier work along the same lines (for example H. Lowmianski in 1979): the observed surge in Pagan religion was an ideological response to the advances of Christianity. Human sacrifice increases, temples are built and the role of the priest develops. There was even an example of altars to pagan and Christian gods being placed in the same temple, as had been notoriously perpetrated by the East Anglian king Raedwald in similar circumstances two centuries earlier and a few thousand miles westwards (Słupecki 1997, 186). The proximity of Christianity provoked opposition to its ritual power, a menace occasionally molified by dressing in its clothes.

It would not do to ascribe every monumental burial mound in north-west Europe to anti-Christian anxiety; but it must have played an important role. The general map produced by Robert van de Noort (1993; now amended Lutovsky

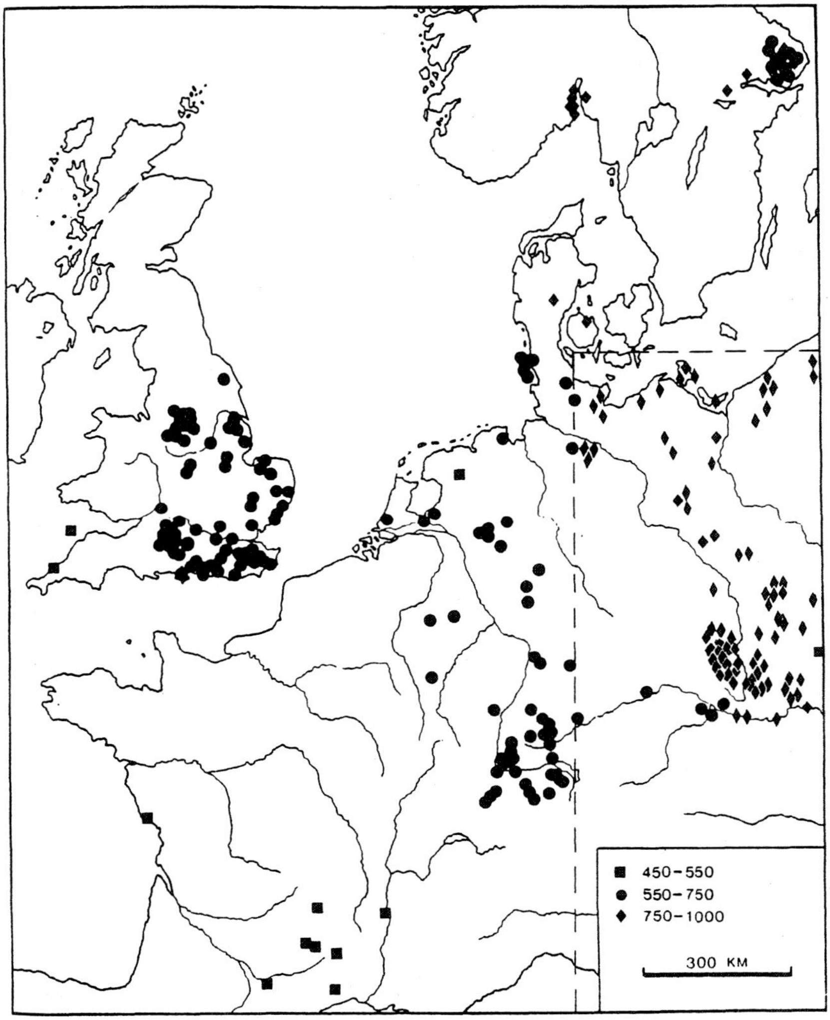

Fig. 1.4. Distribution of dated burial mounds and barrow cemeteries (including some graves with ring ditches, thought to have been mounds) (Lutovsky 1996, fig 1b).

1996) shows a chronological trend which for the most part pre-echoes conversion (Fig. 1.4), but not every case fits the model. The mounds at Högom in Medelpad, Sweden (Ramquist 1992) are too early (at fifth or sixth century) to be reacting to a Christian menace. But that is not to say that no equally stressful circumstances were involved; for every monument we need to seek both the impetus and the motive.

This argument suggests that the building of a monumental burial-mound is best regarded as a historical event, the result of the conjuncture between a set of beliefs and the circumstances of the time. The circumstance most likely to provoke these monuments is political insecurity, and Christianity with its declared programme of conversion and Roman imperial associations must be counted among the provocative forces of the age. Is it right to regard the signals of barrow-burial as 'political' (in that they are seen as mainly expressing power, alignment and allegiance), rather than ethnic, customary or religious? They *could* be seen as ethnic in the sense that a certain group of people who regard themselves as related might act together; or customary, in that barrow burial had existed previously amongst those people as a small-scale ritual ready for political inflation when needed; or religious in the sense that a common set of beliefs might be implied in order for similar events to provoke a similar response. But these factors are neither necessary nor sufficient for monumentality, and they do not explain why monumentality is intermittent. Only politics are sensitive to events, so politics should lie behind change. If political motivation has primacy, this would help to explain why people living in different lands can use the same signals in emulation of each other, without claiming ethnic affiliation or acknowledging the same gods. So to explain Sutton Hoo, for example, we do not need to claim that East Angles worshipped Odin or were Swedes; only that they well understood the philosophies of Pagan thinking and the language of its monumentality. In the sixth century the East Angles muttered their allegiance to the ideology, but in the seventh they felt obliged to shout it.

A monumental hiatus

Sutton Hoo ceased to be used as a high-status burial ground about AD 625, and became for the next 200 to 300 years a place of execution: the ideological struggle had been resolved in favour of rigorous Christian kingship (Carver 1998a). In the aftermath to the documented conversion, however, and not just in East Anglia, there is a curious lull in material expression of nearly half a century from about 625 to 675, when society seems to be holding its breath. Furnished graves have proved difficult to assign to this period (Geake 1997, 124), as have churches (Taylor and Taylor 1965), sculpture (e.g. Hawkes 1999, 404) and illuminated manuscripts (Alexander 1978). It is has to be assumed, nevertheless, that churches were being built and monasteries founded, because the documentary record tells us so. The sixth-century monasteries of Iona and Whithorn were active in the north and the episcopal centre at Canterbury active in the south. A church of wood was built at York in 626 and a bigger one planned in stone. Aidan was in Lindisfarne and Birinus at Dorchester in 635. Ceanwealh built the church of St Peter at Winchester in 648. Christianity became compulsory in Kent in 640; temples were destroyed in Essex in 665. Barrows may also have been built: Penda kept the pagan flag flying until his death at The Winwaed in 655. But investment in objects and constructions on the monumental scale are difficult to find on the ground, and maybe material expression was deliberately modest. Perhaps this was a period in which the actual message of Christian purism was briefly effective, and even the aristocracy lived briefly by precepts of generosity towards others and reserve in celebrating themselves.

On the boundaries, as we have seen from the case of the Rhineland, a more lively monumental confrontation may take place. A British example seems to have been discovered by Edwina Proudfoot in the course of her work at the Hallow Hill and amplified in a brilliant paper by the late Ian Smith (Proudfoot 1996; Smith 1996). Here a range of different monument types – square-ditched barrows and Class I symbol stones in the north and long cist graves and stone crosses in the south are confronted across a seventh-century boundary running across Fife. Objections have been raised that long-cist burials do not have to be diagnostic of Christianity, because they are found in prehistoric variants and are distributed further north. But they certainly resemble the Christian cist graves of the Alpine region (Carver 1987) more closely than any Bronze Age predecessor. If it were an attribute of Christianity, the long-cist would be found to move over Scotland revealing the itinerary of successful conversion. The early Christian pressure on the Picts intimated by Bede (*HE* III.4) is persuasively captured in Smith's snapshot of a monumental frontier (Fig. 1.5)

The Northumbrian forum

Further south, the monumental machine seems to start up again at the end of the seventh-century. Ripon and Monkwearmouth are founded, Brixworth built, the Book of Durrow and Durham A II 10 illuminated. It is of the greatest interest that, in Northumbria and the other English kingdoms, furnished burial also restarts in the later seventh century and continues into the early eighth (Geake 1997, 124). It is furnishing of a very particular kind: necklaces and ornaments of a marked Roman and Byzantine (rather than Frankish) character are found predominantly in female graves. One burial with a purseful of *sceattas* at Garton-on-the-Wolds, is certainly as late as 720. By this time, plain incised grave-markers were being erected at Whitby and Hartlepool, the Lindisfarne Gospels with its virtuoso insular ornament had been completed at Lindisfarne, at Jarrow Bede was writing his history and the immense *Codex Amiatinus* with its meticulous adherence to Cassiodorus' classical prototype had been lost on its way to Rome. Northumbria in the early eighth century was not only a hive of creative endeavour; it was also a mass of alternative expressions, the re-ified ideas of clerics and warriors, northerners and southerners, men and women, those who live on the Wolds and those who lived in the Vale of York or by the Tees, the Wear or the Tyne. The society was presumably stable enough to allow differing opinions and the distribution of

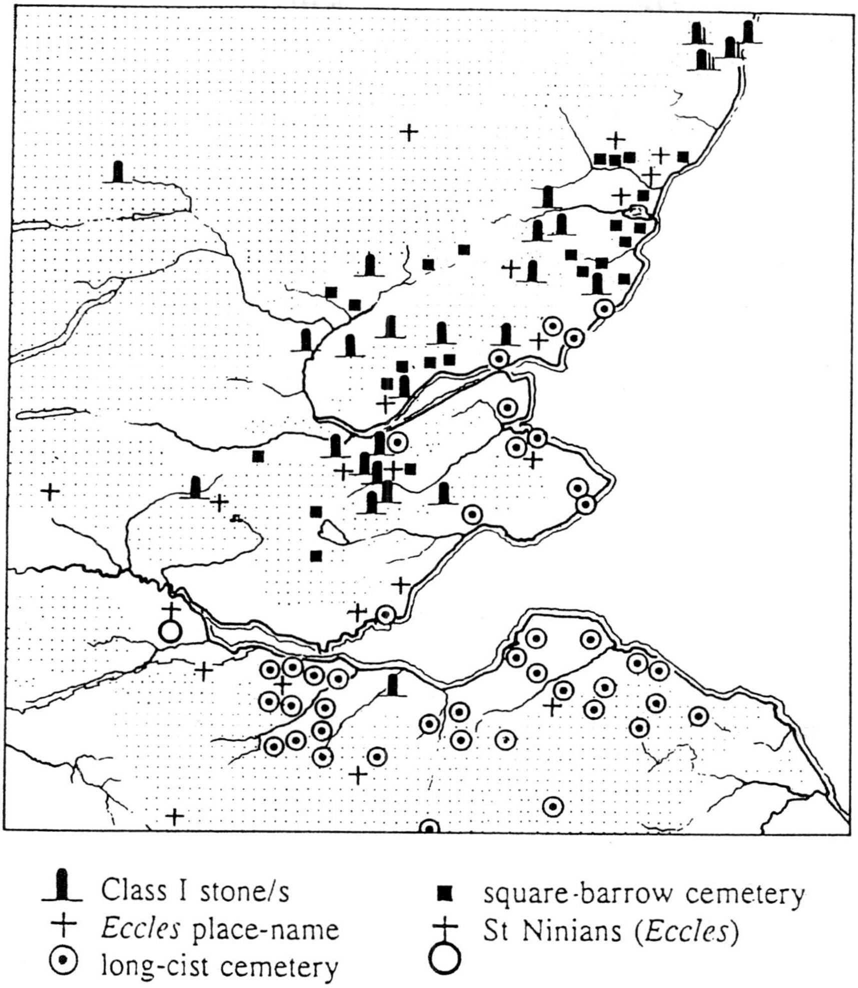

Fig. 1.5. The seventh-century argument in Fife. Map prepared by Ian Smith (Smith 1996, fig 2.5).

resources was generous enough to allow plural and varied expressions in stone and vellum.

In 710, Nechtan, King of the Picts, sent to Ceolfrid, abbot of Wearmouth/Jarrow for advice on the expression of Christianity in the Northumbrian manner: not just how to calculate the date of Easter, but the correct form of the tonsure, and how to build a 'Roman' church (*HE* V.21). And yet the consequences of his initiative seem to have resulted in no network of monastic *scriptoria* producing Pictish gospels and hagiographies. What they have left us is something very different: scores of monumental slabs, carrying Pictish symbols as well as Christian motifs that were familiar in the local repertoire of Iona or Northumbria.

It is hard to resist the conclusion that Canterbury, Jarrow, Iona, the Garton burials, the *Codex Amiatinus*, the Lindisfarne Gospels, and the Class II Pictish stones on Tayside actually represent different reactions to Christianization. Was this because the peoples concerned were ethnically distinguished, or felt they were? Angles, Britons, Scots and Picts spoke a different language, Bede tells us, so why should the language of their art and material investment not differ too? Yet it seems strange that a shared ideology should take so many different forms between neighbours, and in the case of the Garton burials and the *Codex Amiatinus*, the same linguistic group was presumably involved. Do the late seventh- and early eighth-century burials proclaim an enclave of dissident women, resentful of the Christian project? Or are some women guarding their family claims by imitating the imperial ornaments of Theodora, in order to express aristocratic membership of a Roman 'folk', as opposed to the illiberal clerical alliances of Wilfrid?

On the supposition that material culture is meaningful, and that the style of investment is deliberately chosen, we are entitled, I think, to read into it different political stances. There seems no good reason to allow these forms of expression to be simply local, cultural, vague, ill-informed, confused or 'syncretic' (Fletcher 1997, 126–153). That seems a negative way to view a people who emerge from the pages of Bede as predatory, extravagant and fiercely opinionated, just as likely to express themselves forcefully in words and material culture as any other privileged class through the ages. Conversion did not, it seems, produce a homogeneous culture for us to find, but appears to have expressed itself in very different ways – differences here ascribed to politics. How could such political stances be defined? The archaeology has a pattern to it, and the documents give us hints of inter-Christian dissent, so as a first step we could set out to seek correlations between them.

Different roads to Christianity

Since we are concerned here with political signals within communities that have adopted Christianity in some form, we should be searching for a model that distinguishes between the different kinds of Christian organization and economics. At least three varieties of Christian organization or socio-economic control are well known and provide us with a starting point. In the episcopal system, a bishop holds authority over a territory (the diocese) and draws revenue from it. This is the system that most closely echoes Roman imperial administration and requires a similar method of taxation to run it. The archaeological correlate is the episcopal centre of which the finest example has been given by Charles Bonnet's excavation of the episcopal group at Geneva (1993). The attributes are the basilica, itself a type of Roman government building, the baptistery and the pulpit. At Geneva, the baptistery, initially a small tank, developed with the increasing demand until it acquired its own supply of piped water. The trappings of an episcopal church, with its imperial aura, can be contrasted with a materially more elusive but intellectually more influential variant, the monastic church. Whatever the detailed circumstances of early monasticism, it has the general appearance of an autonomous movement, if not exactly dissident then at least less a creature of state than the hierarchy of bishops (Chitty 1977). Whatever else drove the earliest eremitic monks to the desert, an economic consequence would be a freedom from tax or tythe. When the hermits clubbed together in the coenobitic communities, the seeking of independent non-taxable endowment would have been an early method of survival, one which was later adopted in northern Europe. Columba received Iona from the Picts and King Oswald 'gave lands and endowments to establish monasteries' including Lindisfarne (*HE* III.3) and Jarrow was supported by lands on which Bede was born (*HE*, see autobiographical note, p 336).

The Christianity practised by the monasteries of Egypt would not have been organized and delivered in the same way as the imperial Christianity at Geneva or Hagia Sophia, and it seems highly likely that there was confrontation. Such a confrontation has been postulated as endemic in the late Roman town, where the 'episcopal group' is situated inside the official city and grafted into the late Roman administration, while the 'monastic centre' grows up in the extra-mural cemetery around the person of a martyr (Perinetti 1989). Either or both these centres may then act as a kernel for the growth of the early medieval town, providing two nucleii which each presumably had its declared and fiercely argued rationale. This phenonemon, which Perinetti terms 'bipolarity', can be seen at Aosta and Salona. At Geneva, the episcopal centre within the walls wins the battle for hearts and minds and town lay-out, while at Tours the monastery proved to have the greater magnetic force.

The archaeological correlates for northern monasteries earlier than the St Gall plan in the ninth century are notoriously hard to define. The remains in the Egyptian desert invite us to look for simple cells of hermits, perhaps clustered together, a vision which has influenced the identification of Skellig Michel and Tintagel as monasteries. There has long been an assumption that early insular monasteries should be sited in an oval or circular or curvilinear enclosure, the British *lan* of Wales and Cornwall. Few of these have been dated: at Whithorn, a ditch 10m long and 1m wide containing an undated sherd of glass was extrapolated into a monastic boundary enclosing half a hectare (Hill 1997, 29, 77). At Hoddom, the *vallum* and pallisade, traced on the ground as a D-shaped enclosure, gave five radiocarbon dates in the seventh century, prompting the excavator to suggest a date of construction between 600 and 680 (Lowe, in press). The sites of some documented Irish monasteries (for example that at Kiltiernan) are found in association with circular banked enclosures (Mytum 1992, 80); but in so far as they resemble the prehistoric *rath*, they might represent the recycling of a local idea (Ryan and Mitchell 1998,

260), while other forms of monastic enclosure, such as that at Clonmacnoise, are apparently rectangular. The site of the present monastery on Iona is enclosed by a penannular bank, but this has lately yielded a prehistoric radiocarbon date (Fisher 1996). The possibility must be considered that monastic communities took whatever disused fort they were offered by the king, as did Fursa when he moved into the redundant Saxon Shore fort at Burgh Castle, courtesy of King Sigebert of East Anglia (above).

Inside the enclosures, we look for ways of distinguishing the monastic from any other kind of estate centre in which there has been educated investment at a high level. In the north, a number of the documented monastic sites are signed by grave markers with simple crosses and inscriptions: for example Jarrow, Monkwearmouth and Hartlepool. Whitby has 41 (Hawkes 1999) and Iona has numerous examples (Fisher 1996), although many of these may have accrued during the lingering aftermath of the early Christian period. Monasteries use and produce books, so that vellum production or finds of styli ought to be diagnostic. But accepting that the middle Saxon aristocracy provided leadership both for those who fight and those who pray, it would not be impossible for attributes of the literate sector to appear on a seigneurial estate (see Loveluck, this volume). As we can so far see them, the markers of monastic centres, while they echo those of a secular estate, at least differ from those of episcopal centres. Since the peoples of Britain and Ireland potentially had access to the full range of Christian models, we are entitled to deduce that such a difference had a meaning behind it and was deliberately chosen.

A people unused to taxation would find the endowment of monasteries preferable to the imposition of a permanent revenue required to support bishops. But another tendency has long been present in Christian practice, and there seems good reason for supposing that it would have been an option as early as the conversion period; it would moreover require far less of an organizational upheaval in a pagan people. In this adoption of the Christian structure, the faith is administered neither by bishops or monks, but directly by the landowner or local aristocrat who can appoint and pay his own priest. Such a 'secular' or 'private' option should be signalled by individual and decentralized investment, so is bound to be harder to see. The most persuasive examples are provided by those communities that erect monuments in dispersed patterns – patterns which prompt an association with estates. The impression of secularity is reinforced if the iconography is varied and features everyday life, rather than being merely iconographic, repetitive and orthodox. The Pictish Class II and the Anglo-Scandinavian monuments seem to be strong candidates in this respect (Carver 1998c).

A less visible but equally telling example is offered by the small personal funerary crosses found in central Europe, and recently studied by Müller-Wille (1998b; Fig 1.6). In fifth- to seventh-century Trentino, cross-shaped brooches were deposited with females; in the central Rhine/Mosel area, cross-shaped brooches of the late seventh century were also found in the graves of females;

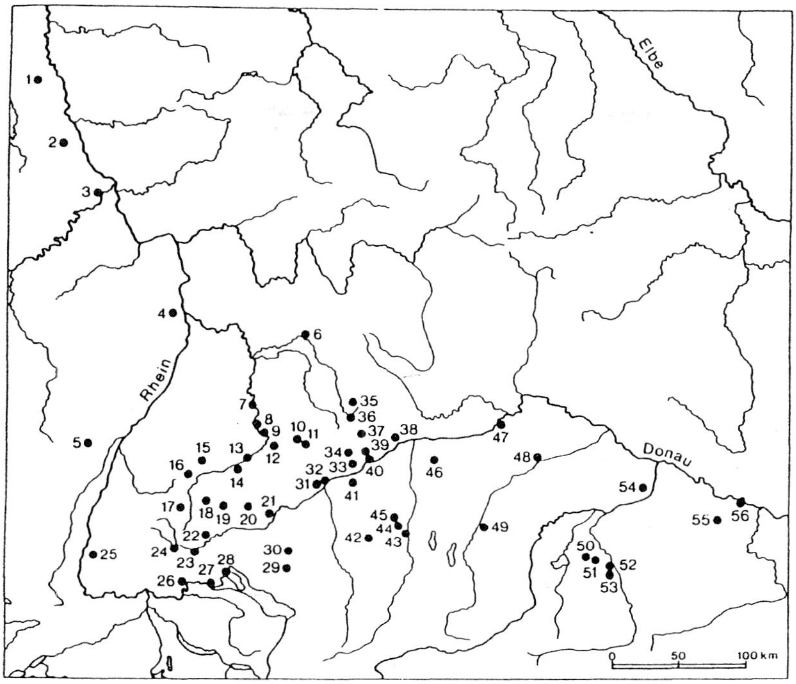

Fig. 1.6. Distribution of sixth- to eighth-century gold foil crosses in the Alamannic area between the Rhine and Danube (Müller-Wille 1998b, fig 6).

while in the Alamannic district between Rhine and Danube, both sexes were buried with gold foil crosses from the sixth to the eighth century. In each case, the cross was the main Christian signal. It is specifically noted that in Alamannia none of the gold-foil crosses was found in connection with the earliest churches; moreover this is not an imitation of an earlier Christian practice, since no grave with a cross is known from the period from the first to the fourth century in the Mediterranean. One reasonable interpretation of this pattern is that the date and distribution of the burials accurately reflect the progress of a gradual conversion northwards (ibid., fig 3); but without having to challenge that general picture, it can be noted at least that the acceptance of Christianity was signalled in these territories in different ways. If the converted landlords of the Rhineland replaced their barrows with churches, and the citizens of Geneva expanded and improved their massive episcopal centre, the people of Alamannia, sandwiched between them, indulged in the less extravagant practice of sewing small gold crosses on to the tunics of their dead. Was this modesty, poverty or ignorance? Or does the chosen signal represent a non-centralized economy and a belief in maintaining authority at community level – in short a different political stance?

This case for a confrontation between Christian prescriptions depends on the archaeological identification of their correlates and their distribution. But some support can also be found in the sparse documentation, for example as was revealed in Wilhelm Levison's classic essay of 1946, which records instances of tension between bishop and monastery and Christianized aristocrats in the eighth century. Already in 672 the Hertford Canons state 'No Bishop is to disturb a monastery or take its property by force' the implication being that they might be tempted to do so (Levison 1946, 23), while the Synod of Cloveshoe in 747 was aimed at restoring 'the hierarchical order and a regular church administration – provinces under an archbishop in direct contact with Rome, dioceses with a monarchical bishop supervised by the archbishop and controlling the whole clergy of his district' (ibid. 86). The Bishop was sacramentally necessary but their function was sometimes exercised by 'wandering bishops and other bishops without dioceses but attached to monasteries' (ibid. 97). Politically powerful converts preferring the secular option could apparently operate in a similar way. Cuthbert and seven continental bishops of English origin sent a letter to King Ethelbald of Mercia to admonish him and reprove him for his dissolute life and his encroachments on possessions and privileges of monasteries (ibid. 92) – a glimpse of an alternative secular church which probably delivered more satisfactorily the economic and political interests of the Mercian aristocracy. Levison summarized the tendency of landowners to form their own 'proprietary' churches and monasteries (*Eigenkirchen, Eigenkloster*) and reminds us that 'such tendencies might be a source of danger to the monastic ideals' (ibid. 28). It is clear that bishop, abbot and lord had a discourse in which much was claimed and definitions were blurred. It would have been in the interests of Bishops to claim jurisdiction although they had none, and for landlords to acknowledge Rome but to pay nothing and do nothing which would encourage Roman control of their affairs. Wandering bishops would have been useful in ordaining priests and giving them liturgical authority and sacred powers, but they would have brought no necessary allegiance to an archbishop or to the whole Roman apparatus – of which the northern Europeans were (and still are) endemically suspicious. We should expect ideological difference to be denied in documents even while it was practised or proclaimed on the ground. This suggests that the search for expressions of local political resistance or alignment through the study of monuments is a legitimate quest.

In Britain, perhaps the object of investment most sensitive to the local Christian prescription is the standing stone monument, a field to which Rosemary Cramp has made an immeasurable contribution. Like barrows, the stone crosses may have started as memorials to an individual ancestor, whose descendants continued to profess control of the same land. Like barrows, they may have acted as places to meet and dispense justice. If family and power are signalled in cross-slabs such as those from St Vigeans or Aberlemno roadside, so are the elements of Christian doctrine; enough at least to merit the benefits of the Christian commercial network without sacrificing autonomy to either king, bishop, abbot or pope. At a later date the cross might have been joined by a church and this too might have been a local or private commission. If we can make its social label stick, the standing stone monument is going to be a powerful tool with which to write history – because we have plenty of them (see Edwards, this volume). Anna Ritchie (1995) has made the case that centres such as Meigle produced monuments, especially the widely distributed standing cross-slabs, through lay patronage in the ninth and tenth centuries. Such monuments, bearing a cross and other icons, were surely estate-markers that reflected the taste and aspirations of the landlords, but also satisfied the need for a ritual focus for a community accustomed to associate spiritual orthodoxy with a local war-leader. George Henderson (1999, 209) observes: 'According to the *Hodoeporicon* or guide book, taken down from the verbal report of St Willibald, the English missionary who died as Bishop of Eichstadt in Germany in 785, it was the custom on nobleman's estates to have the standard of the holy cross set up as a focus for daily prayer... The cross monument was evidently a place of resort in time of crisis.'

The newly-converted Vikings seem to have preferred the secular mode of Christian control to the monastic or episcopal model (Fig. 1.7). Jim Lang's survey of East Yorkshire (1991) showed that the grave-markers of the seventh and eighth centuries were distributed among a handful of monastic sites, a point reinforced by Jane Hawkes (1999, 405) with reference to northern Northumbria: of 'approximately 230 pieces of carved stone associated with pre-Viking contexts north of the Tees, nearly 180 come from just five sites: Lindisfarne, Hartlepool, Hexham, Wearmouth and Jarrow'. But this distribution changes radically in the ninth century. In East Yorkshire, the monuments are more numerous and more dispersed, as well as displaying a more individual iconography. It was Rosemary Cramp's observation, made many years ago (1980, 18), that 'the Vikings secularised art just as they secularised landholding', that set me thinking (in the context of the politics of our own day) that perhaps the Scandinavian hostility was not to Christianity but towards state control, taxation and the alienation of land to non-wealth creators. The Vikings, by dissolving the monastic system and substituting a secular alternative, had succeeded in effecting a conversion of their own (Carver 1998c).

Conclusion

These case studies, briefly expounded, are held to imply that the episcopal, the monastic and the secular church represented three different strategies for developing a Christian kingdom which has shed paganism. Each mode of religious control had very different implications for the people – especially the aristocracy – in terms of self-determination, inheritance, prosperity and alliance. A fly on the wall of a Dark Age hall must have heard the argument over and over again: loss of sovereignty and increased taxation is the penalty, heaven and an expanded market the reward. A soft strategy for the king (who had most to gain from the church's protection of his dynasty) was to endow some of his own land and encourage others to do the same, in the hope of qualifying for the Christian alliance, while avoiding the alienation of his own peerage. But some leaders would not be strong enough to achieve even this compromise. Landowners resist an irreversible commitment to extreme and *dirigiste* doctrines, preferring to cherish the northerner's ancestral ethos: every man his own lord, in control of his own land and with his own link to God. But there would be no harm in adding Christ's escutcheon to one's shield, especially if it earned useful contacts and warded off the threat of a take-over or conquest on trumped-up ideological grounds.

How likely is this picture? Was the eighth-century inhabitant of Britain really capable of such ingenious decision-making? How far does this model superimpose on early Christianity the intellectual fragmentation of all that has happened since that time? Does it urge a particular version of Christianity to which certain local politics of our own day inclines? William Frend (1996, 61) uses the term 'confessional interests' to describe scholarship driven by a particular branch of Christian ideology, showing how loyalty to the success of the Roman imperial past had inhibited the archaeological recognition and rediscovery of the Donatists. But Donatism was a Christian variant which most certainly existed, was professed, debated, opposed, championed and expressed in monuments. The native inhabitants of Numidia (now Libya) had under Rome adopted a religion ruled by a sacrifice-hungry god ('Saturn') which demanded human victims. In 260–290 'the religion of the great majority of the Numidians swung irreversibly towards a biblically-inspired form of Christianity in which the blood-sacrifice of martyrdom replaced the blood-sacrifice to Saturn. This was central and southern Numidia, the heartland of the Donatist movement' (ibid. 118). On the ground Donatism was traced through inscriptions which carried 'recognizably Donatist formulae' and by association sculptural themes, such as martyrdom (ibid. 69, 231). For Frend himself (1996, 168), one of the duties of archaeology is to release some of those alternative voices long suppressed by orthodoxy: 'Donatists, Montanists, Manicheans and Coptic and Nubian Monophysites at last could begin to speak for themselves through inscriptions, papyri and the steady accumulation of material evidence'.

A number of Frend's great French North African predecessors had asserted that the roots of Donatism lay in Berber (i.e. indigenous) nationalism. A 'local rebuilding' of the incoming doctrine happened again under Islam when the Maghreb produced a number of sects culminating in that of the Fatimids which was to spread far and wide. It is certainly tempting to see all the monumental variations cited here as due to an endemic, indigenous viewpoint. On this interpretation, the Scots, Picts, Northumbrians and Saxons would not be expressing their differing politics, but adapting the incoming

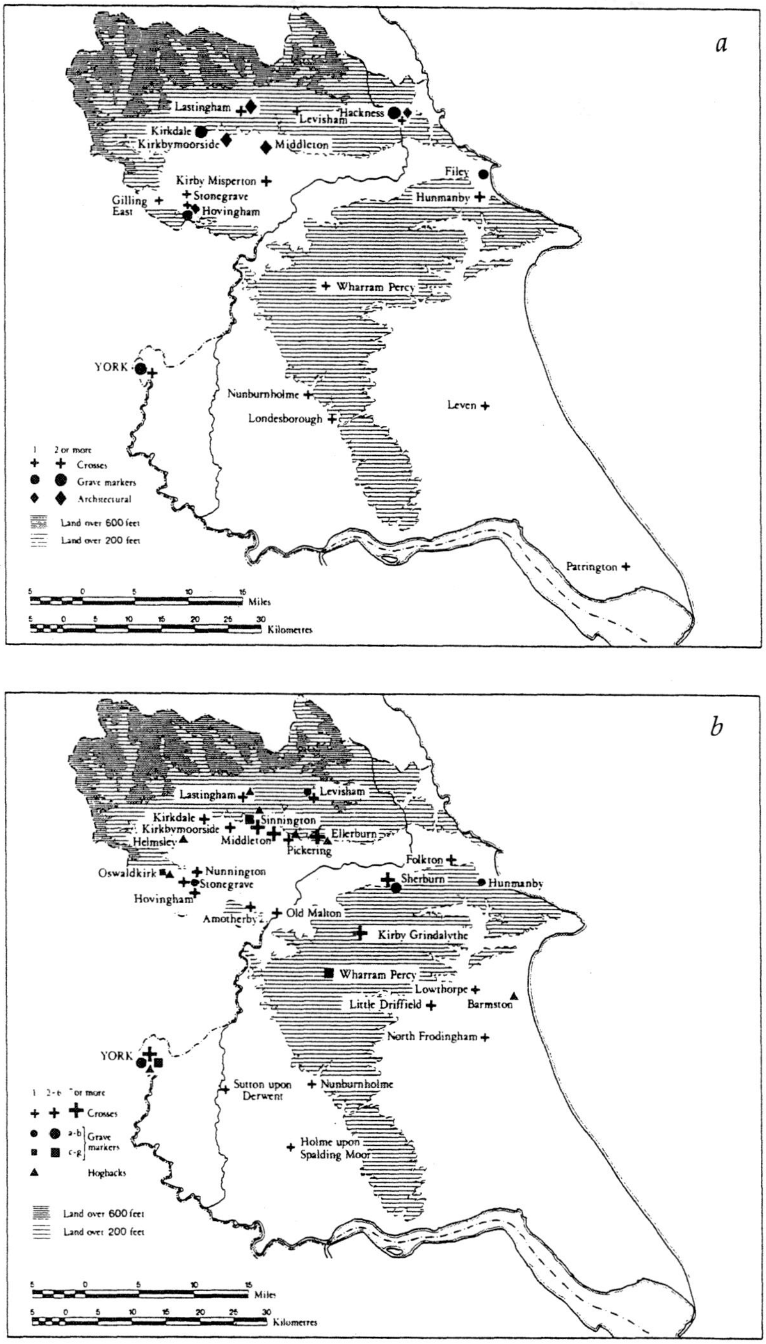

Fig. 1.7. Distribution of sculpture in East Yorkshire (Lang 1991): a) seventh to eighth centuries; b) ninth to eleventh centuries.

doctrines to an unchanging and inevitable individual preference. This is an ethnically determinist argument which, instead of arguing for immigration of new ethnic groups to explain cultural change (e.g. the Anglo-Saxons) attributes the change to the different reactions of permanently rooted native groups occupying adjacent territories. For Northumbria at least, this could be questioned: here within a territory that extended from York to Lindisfarne, were produced in the same decade the Lindisfarne Gospels, the *Codex Amiatinus* and the Garton-on-the-Wolds burials (above). This is an era of experiment rather than adaptation.

Recent scholars have gone out of their way to diminish the differences between any 'Celtic' church and others (Fletcher 1997, 92; Blair 1996, 6; Blair and Sharpe 1992). My thesis is intended to bring into focus and interpret such differences as we can find, and to suggest that behind them lay real conflict. But it should be noted that I have attempted to explain these differences not on ethnic or even cultural grounds, but on the basis of politics. I have nothing to say about a 'Celtic' church either, only that during the seventh and eighth centuries, some of those living in the west appear to have adopted a different monumental programme to those living in the east, and that this must indicate something. That something, in my view, would not be an incorrigible ethnicity but a different way of thinking and a different approach to power. It would probably be sensible at this stage to allow the possibility that deep-rooted local culture might have an effect on whatever monumentality was practised. But the facility of communication and awareness of pressure should have allowed the big issues to be debated in a communal forum. With the variation of political stance known from North Africa, we can hardly doubt that such variations were also manifested in the north of Europe, both in the seventh century and over the next 1,000 years.

References

Alexander, J. G. 1978. *Insular Manuscripts, 6th to the 9th Century* (A Survey of Manuscripts illuminated in the British Isles), London: Harvey Miller

Bailey, R. N. 1992. Sutton Hoo and seventh-century art, in R. T. Farrell and C. Neuman de Vegvar (eds), *Sutton Hoo: fifty years after*, 31–34, Oxford, Ohio: Miami University

Bede. *Historia Ecclesiastica Gentis Anglorum*, B. Colgrave and R. Mynors (eds and trans), Oxford: Clarendon Press

Blair, J. 1996. Churches in the early English landscape: social and cultural contexts, in J. Blair and C. Pyrah (eds), *Church Archaeology: Research directions for the future* (CBA Res Rep 104), 6–18, York: CBA

Blair, J. and Pyrah, C (eds) 1996. *Church Archaeology: Research directions for the future* (CBA Res Rep 104), York: CBA

Blair, J. and Sharpe, R. (eds) 1992. *Pastoral Care before the Parish*, Leicester: Leicester University Press

Böhme, H. W. 1993. Adelsgräber im Frankenreich. Archäologische Zeugnisse zur Herausbildung einer Herrenschicht unter dem merowingischen Königen, *Jahrbuch des Römisch-Germanischen Zetralmuseums Mainz*, 40, 397–534

Bonnet, C. 1993. *Les fouilles de l'ancien groupe épiscopal de Genève (1976–1993)* (Cahiers d'archéologie genèvoise 1), Geneva

Bradley, R. 1988. Time regained: the creation of continuity, *J Brit Archaeol Assoc*, 140, 1–17

Bradley, R. 1993. *Altering the Earth: the origins of monuments in Britain and continental Europe: the Rhind Lectures, 1991–92*, Edinburgh: Society of Antiquaries of Scotland

Carver, M. O. H. 1986. Sutton Hoo in context, *Settimane di Studio*, 32, Spoleto: Centro Italiano di Studi sull'Alto Medioevo, 77–123

Carver, M. O. H. 1987. Santa Maria foris Portas at Castel Seprio: a famous church in a new context, *World Archaeology*, 18 (3), 312–29

Carver, M. O. H. 1993. *Arguments in Stone: Archaeological research and the European town in the first millennium AD*, Oxford: Oxbow Books

Carver, M. O. H. 1995. Boat burial in Britain: ancient custom or political signal?, in O. Crumlin-Pedersen (ed), *The Ship as Symbol in Prehistoric and Medieval Scandinavia*, 111–24, Copenhagen: National Museum of Denmark

Carver, M. O. H. 1998(a). *Sutton Hoo. Burial ground of Kings?*, London: British Museum Press

Carver, M. O. H. 1998(b). Überlegungen zür Bedeutung angel-sächsischer Grabhügel, in A. Wesse (ed), *Studien zür Archäologie des Ostseeraumes von der Eisenzeit zum Mittelalter. Festschrift für Michael Müller-Wille*, 259–68, Neumünster: Wachholtz

Carver, M. O. H. 1998(c). Conversion and politics on the eastern seaboard of Britain: some archaeological indicators, in B. E. Crawford (ed), *Conversion and Christianity in the North Sea World*, 11–40, St Andrews: University of St Andrews

Carver, M. O. H. 1999(a). Review of Ian Stead, *The Salisbury Hoard*, *British Museum Magazine*, (Spring 1999), 39

Carver, M. O. H. 1999(b). Exploring, explaining, imagining: Anglo-Saxon archaeology 1998, in C. Karkov (ed), *The Archaeology of Anglo-Saxon England: basic readings*, 25–52, New York and London: Garland

Carver, M. O. H. in press. Burial as poetry: the case of Sutton Hoo, in E. Tyler (ed), *Anglo-Saxon Treasure*, York: Centre for Medieval Studies

Childe, V. G. 1929. *The Danube in Prehistory*, Oxford: Clarendon Press

Chitty, D. J. 1977. *The Desert a City: Egyptian and Palestinian monasticism under a Christian empire*

Cramp, R. J. 1980. The Viking image, in R. Farrell (ed), *The Vikings*, 8–19, London: Phillimore

Fisher, I. 1996. The west of Scotland, in Blair and Pyrah, 37–41

Fletcher, R. 1997. *The Conversion of Europe*, Berkeley: University of California Press

Frend, W. H. C. 1996. *The Archaeology of Early Christianity. A history*, London: Chapman

Foot, S. 1990. What was an early Anglo-Saxon monastery?, in J. Loades (ed), *Monastic Studies: the continuity of a tradition*, 48–57, Bangor: Headstart History

Geake, H. 1997. *The Use of Grave Goods in Conversion-period England c.600-c.850* (Brit Archaeol Rep 261), Oxford: BAR

Hawkes, J. 1999. Statements in stone. Anglo-Saxon sculpture, Whitby and the Christianization of the North, in C. Karkov (ed), *The Archaeology of Anglo-Saxon England: basic readings*, 403–21, New York and London: Garland

Henderson, G. 1999. *Vision and Image in Early Christian England*, Cambridge: Cambridge University Press

Hill, P. 1997. *Whithorn and St Ninian: the excavation of a monastic town 1984–1991*, Whithorn and Stroud: Whithorn Trust and Sutton Publishing

Hines, J. 1984. *The Scandinavian Character of Anglian England in the Pre-Viking Period* (Brit Archaeol Rep 124), Oxford: BAR

Johnson, S. 1983. *Burgh Castle: Excavations by Charles Green 1958–61* (East Anglian Archaeol Rep 20), Gressenhall: Norfolk Museum Service

Lang, J. 1991. *Corpus of Anglo-Saxon Sculpture, 3, York and Yorkshire*, Oxford: British Academy / Oxford University Press

Levison, W. 1946. *England and the Continent in the Eighth Century*, Oxford: Oxford University Press

Lowe, C. forthcoming. *Excavations at Hoddom, Dumfriesshire: An enclosed holy place of the late first millennium AD*, Edinburgh: Historic Scotland

Lutovsky, M. 1996. Between Sutton Hoo and Chernaya Mogila: barrows in eastern and western early medieval Europe, *Antiquity*, 70, 671–6

Mango, M. M., Mango, C., Evans, A. and Hughes, M. 1989. A 6th century Mediterranean bucket from Bromeswell parish, Suffolk, *Antiquity*, 63, 295–311

Mitchell, F. and Ryan, M. 1998. *Reading the Irish Landscape*, Dublin: Town House

Müller-Wille, M. 1998(a). Zwei reliogiöse Welten: Bestattungen der fränkischen Könige Childerich und Chlodwig, *Abhandlung der Akademie der Wissenschaften und der Literatur*, Mainz: Steiner Verlag

Müller-Wille, M. 1998(b). The Cross as a symbol of personal Christian belief in a changing religious world. Examples from selected areas in Merovingian and Carolingian Europe, *KVHAA Konferenser* 40, 179–200, Stockholm: KVHAA

Mytum, H. 1992. *The Origins of Early Christian Ireland*, London: Routledge

Opie, I. and Opie, P. 1977. *The Lore and Language of School Children*, London: Granada

Perinetti, R. 1989. Augusta Praetoria. Le necropoli christiane, *Actes du XI Congrès International d'archéologie Chrétienne*, 1215–26, Vatican City

Proudfoot, E. 1996. Excavations at the long-cist cemetery on the Hallow Hill, St Andrews, Fife 1975–7, *Proc Soc Antiq Scot*, 126, 387–454

Proudfoot, E. 1998. The Hallowhill and the origins of Christianity in Scotland, in B. E. Crawford (ed), *Conversion and Christianity in the North Sea World*, 57–74, St Andrews: University of St Andrews

Ramquist, P. H. 1992. *Högom. The excavations 1949–1984*, Umeå: University of Umeå

Ritchie, A. 1995. Meigle and lay patronage in the 9th and 10th centuries AD, *Tayside and Fife Archaeological Journal*, 1, 1–10

Sharpe, R. (trans) 1995. *Adomnan of Iona. Life of St Columba*, Harmondsworth: Penguin

Shephard, J. 1979. The social identity of the individual in isolated barrows and barrow cemeteries in Anglo-Saxon England, in B. Burnham and J. Kingsbury (eds), *Space, Hierarchy and Society: interdisciplinary studies in social area analysis* (Brit Archaeol Rep, Int Ser, 59), 47–79, Oxford: BAR

Smith, I. 1996. The archaeology of the early Christian church in Scotland and Man AD 400–1200, in Blair and Pyrah, 19–37

Słupecki, L. P. 1997. Einflüsse des Christentums auf die heidnische Religion der Ostseeslawen im 8.–12. Jahrhundert: Tempel – Gottbilder – Kult, in M. Müller-Wille (ed), *Rom und Byzanz im Norden. Mission und Glaubenswechsel im Ostseeraum während des 8–14. Jahrhunderts*, 177–89, Mainz: Akademie der Wissenschaften und der Literatur

Taylor, H. M. and Taylor, J. 1965. *Anglo-Saxon Architecture*, Cambridge: Cambridge University Press

van de Noort, R. 1993. The context of early medieval barrows in Western Europe, *Antiquity*, 67, 66–73

2

Whithorn, Latinus and the Origins of Christianity in Northern Britain

Peter Hill

Rosemary Cramp was a founding member of the Whithorn Trust, and has been one of its staunchest supporters over the years. The publication of *Whithorn and St Ninian: the Excavation of a Monastic Town* in 1997 was a particular triumph for us both, justifying all the investment of time and energy in a remarkable medieval site. The Trust's excavations did not reveal the origins of the settlement with any degree of clarity, and my contribution to Rosemary's *Festschrift* forms some small attempt to redress the situation.

The claim of Whithorn to be the cradle of Scottish Christianity relies heavily, though not exclusively, upon a brief passage in Bede's *Ecclesiastical History* (*HE* III.iv) which records the conversion of the southern Picts by Nynia, a Bishop 'of the British nation'. Nynia, or Ninian, ruled a diocese in Galloway, and had built a stone church 'in a manner to which the British were unaccustomed', in which he was eventually buried. According to Bede the church and diocese were dedicated to St Martin, but the 'place' (*locus*, presumably the settlement associated with the church) was known as *Candida Casa* or *Hwit Aerne* in Old English, the latter giving rise to modern Whithorn. This early episode in the envangelization of the north is undated, and almost every aspect of Bede's account has attracted controversy. Popular opinion, for example, accepts the authority of a twelfth-century life of St Ninian ascribed to Aelred of Rievaulx, which portrays him as a contemporary and disciple of St Martin, and dates the building of *Candida Casa* to the years immediately after Martin's death in AD 397. Many scholars (e.g. Thomas 1992) have ascribed St Ninian to the mid-fifth century, while a recent study argues for a sixth-century date (MacQuarrie 1987, 1997). The chronological evidence is inadequate and there are even grounds for questioning the historicity of Ninian himself: Thomas Owen Clancy has argued that Ninian is a 'typographical error' produced by mis-transcribing Bishop Finian (Uinniau) as Ninian (Ninniau). David Dumville holds that the sources used to interpret the early history of Whithorn are literary, and of greatly-circumscribed historical value.

From this viewpoint, Ninianic 'history' has much the same quality as studies of the geography of Ruritania (Gregory 1983, 261–70) or the pathology of Dr Watson's battle scars from the Afghan War, and should be similarly treated. The archaeology of Whithorn is rather more concrete: and this paper focuses upon the earliest archaeological and epigraphic evidence, and suggests a coherent historical context for it.

There is one text, the inscription on the *Latinus* stone, which is of immediate relevance to the early Christian community at Whithorn. The text has been treated commonly as a Christian funerary inscription recording the burial of Latinus and his four-year-old daughter (e.g. Macquarrie 1997, 24), but a series of papers by Professor Charles Thomas has concluded firstly that the inscription records the making of a *sinus* (a place of safety, possibly a church), secondly that it contains an unequivocal numerological reference to the Temple of Solomon, thirdly that it represents a plan of the Temple itself, and fourthly that it can be dated to between 420 and 450 (Thomas 1998, 106–8). These ideas offer exciting new possibilities for interpreting the early development of Whithorn, and I can confirm that the inscription does indeed contain the numbers he identifies. My enthusiasm for his thesis seems not to have been widely shared, and I have heard his ideas dismissed as numerological nonsense and as Templar mythology. While raising valid doubts, his critics have failed to refute Thomas's arguments, although Professor MacQueen's suggestion that it records a fifth-century martyrdom provides an equally stimulating thesis (1999). It now seems clear that the *Latinus* stone is not a simple memorial in inaccurate provincial Latin as was once supposed, but a sophisticated and enigmatic statement composed by a scholar and intended for a literate audience. The quest for this scholar and his audience has led me down (or up!) the path I have followed in this paper.

The *Latinus* stone seems to have been found near the north transept of the medieval cathedral (Craig 1997), and may have occupied a focal position in the early settlement (e.g. Hill 1997, figs. 2.2–6). Apart from a small collection of Roman artefacts which could have been displaced from an earlier occupation horizon, the first well-stratified and datable finds were some fifty or more years later than the *Latinus* stone. There is nevertheless clear evidence of earlier occupation, which could have been contemporary with it. The principal features were a broad metalled road and a curving ditch, neither of which produced dateable finds. The road heads eastwards towards the early stone building to the east of the medieval cathedral (Fig. 2.1), which was formerly identified as *Candida Casa* (Radford 1950, 119) or some other building of the early establishment (Radford 1957, 181). The ditch was cut through the road, and may have served as the boundary of a later enclosure (Fig. 2.2). It was still functioning as an internal division in the early sixth century. The most surprising finds were lumps of concreted lime which had been displaced from an unlocated (but necessarily early) context (Hill 1997, fig. 3.5). The nearest limestone deposits are some 22 miles away, and there is no earlier evidence for

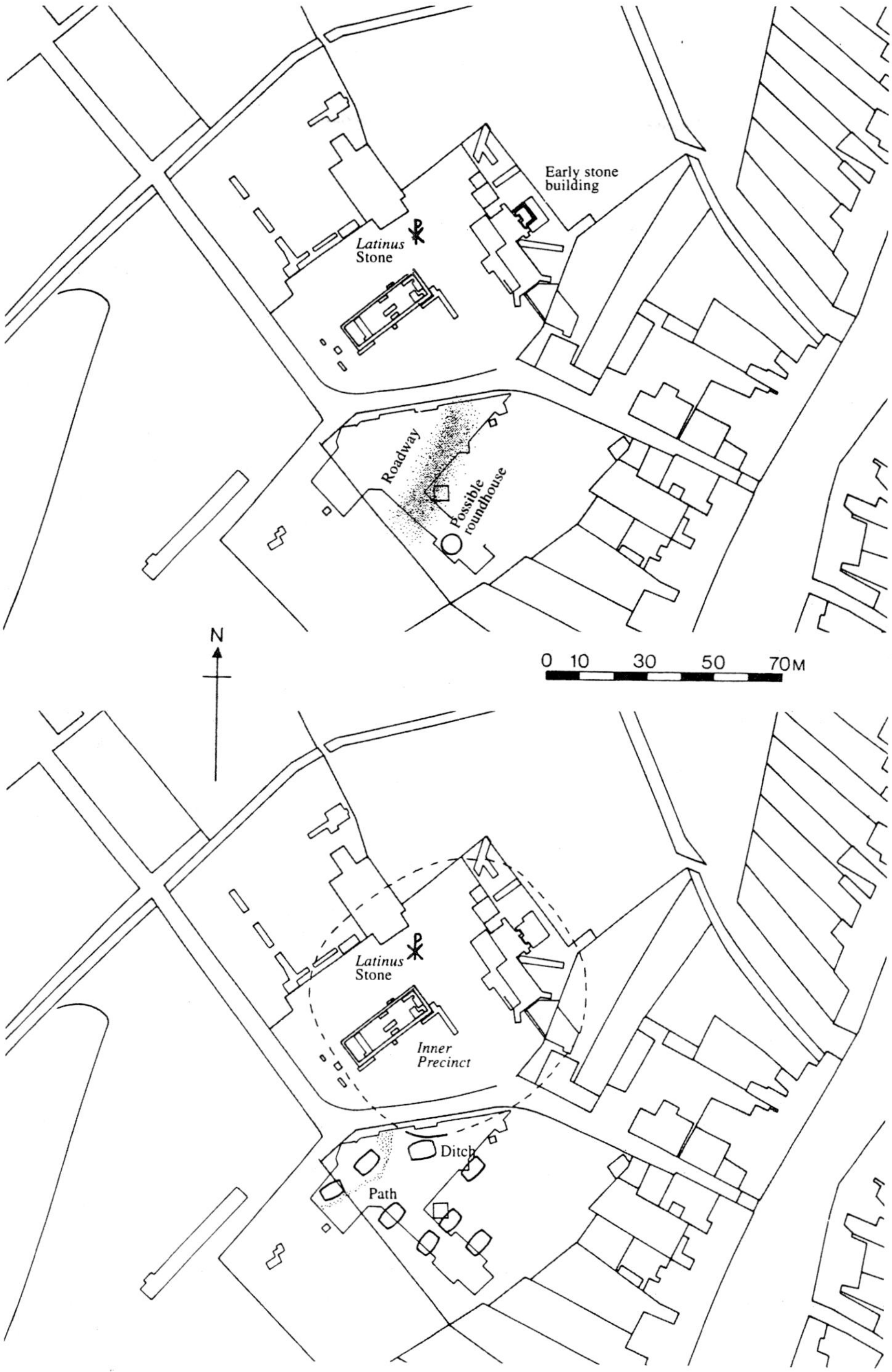

Early phases at Whithorn. Fig. 2.1: the early roadway. Fig. 2.2: the early enclosure.

the use of lime in the area. The lime may have been debris from the construction of a plastered or mortared building, supporting the traditional account of a 'shining' stone church. This hypothetical building, the roadway and the enclosure could all have been elements of a fifth-century settlement contemporary with the *Latinus* stone. Other early finds included plough-pebbles and haematite, both materials of great significance to the early development of the site.

There are hints of an earlier phase of activity. Excavation on the north side of the hill revealed a massive prostrate slab that could have been part of an early prehistoric monument cast down during the early years of the Christian community (Pollock 1995, 2–3). Two further stones to the south could have been part of the same setting. We should not be unduly surprised to find a pagan cult centre preceding the Christian foundation at Whithorn. It has long been supposed that St Medan, who had a following in the Rhins and Machars, had an earlier existence as a Celtic deity associated with healing wells, and Daphne Brooke's Whithorn Lecture (1999) identifies other pagan cult centres absorbed and transformed by the early Christian church. The posthumous miracles of St Ninian related in the eighth-century *Miracula Nynie Episcopi* (MacQueen 1961) reveal a healing regime of sacred sleep and miraculous visions. This incubation or dormition emulates Aesklapian practice, and may have been introduced from the classical world (Levison 1940, 286; Hill 1997, 20), but dormition was also known at Celtic shrines (Green 1986, 138–66), and the therapy offered at Anglian Whithorn could have originated in a pagan Celtic cult centre on the site.

The missionary tradition is so strong in recent history that many consider it would have been a consistent imperative from the earliest days of the church. This sentiment underlies many interpretative accounts of Whithorn as a missionary centre for the conversion of the north. It is, however, anachronistic. There are of course New Testament precedents for the conversion of gentiles, but in the fourth century Eusebius had equated the bounds of Christendom with those of the Roman Empire, and in the fifth century the prevailing Augustinian view was that Divine Grace did not extend to those in ignorance of Christ. An evangelical mission from an established church to a pagan region beyond the empire – say from Carlisle to Whithorn would not merely be unprecedented, but unorthodox and possibly heretical. This helps to explain the appointment in 431 of Palladius as bishop to the believers (*ad credentes*) in Ireland, and so for the earliest recorded expansion of organized Christianity beyond the confines of the Western Empire. Palladius was not sent to convert pagan people, but to minister to an extant Christian population. The catalyst for this remarkable initiative seems to have been the Pelagian heresy and the administrative measures taken to suppress it (Charles-Edwards 1993).

The Pelagian heresy originated in theological debates in the closing years of the fourth century, in which Pelagius and his adherents proposed a doctrine of free will as an alternative to the predestination preached by Augustine. The Pelagians, for example, were prepared to admit the possible goodness of non-Christians, while Augustine held that Divine Grace – the prerequisite of salvation – was withheld from those without knowledge of Christ. The issues were debated in 416 at the Council of Carthage where the Augustinian party prevailed. It became a civil issue in 418 when the Emperor Honorius made a law that anyone expressing Pelagian opinions should be brought before the civil authorities and sent into exile. This was some fifteen or more years after the Roman province of Britannia had freed herself from the authority of the empire, and Britannia would have been an unusually comfortable destination for Pelagian exiles, despite the widespread decay of the infrastructure of civilization (Esmonde Cleary 1989). Pelagius was of British origin, and others of his persuasion may also have been Britons. Prosper states that '...[Pope Celestine] had been no less energetic in freeing the British provinces from this same disease [the Pelagian heresy]; he removed from that hiding place certain enemies of grace who had occupied the land of their origin...' (*Contra Collatorem* 21), suggesting that British heretics had returned to Britannia. Their arrival may have precipitated the crisis of heretical opinion that persuaded an orthodox faction in the British church to seek Papal assistance, resulting in the mission of Bishop Germanus of Auxerre in 429. Germanus was an aristocrat with a background in civil administration, and he adopted an administrative solution to the problem, exiling the Pelagians from Britannia. Already banned from areas controlled from Ravenna, the most convenient destinations for these new exiles would have been the adjacent parts of northern Britain and Ireland. Palladius's appointment as Bishop only two years later was probably intended to protect 'the believers' in Ireland from theological contamination by Pelagian exiles. Palladius's venture seems to have been successful, and continuing papal interest in this enterprise beyond the former imperial bounds, is evidenced in Prosper's *Contra Collatorem* and *De uocatione omnium gentium*, and also in Pope Leo's sermon on the feast of SS Peter and Paul in 441 (Charles-Edwards 1993).

The evidence can be summarized thus. Pelagius was an educated Briton whose career took him to the heart of the empire. His adherents included other Britons, and their doctrine of freewill may represent the intellectual climate prevailing in Britannia during his youth. The act of Honorius in 418 led some of them to seek exile in Britannia, and there may have been a second diaspora following St Germanus's mission of 429. Palladius may have been appointed to preserve Christians living in Ireland from contamination by émigré Pelagians. This mission remained in contact with the papacy until at least 441.

What then of Whithorn? The *Latinus* stone now seems to be earlier than *c.* 465, and possibly later than *c.* 410. Thomas (1998, 106, 108) postulates a tighter date of between 420 and 450. This corresponds closely to the period of the Pelagian diaspora and Palladius' mission to Ireland (Fig. 2.3), and related circumstances may have obtained at Whithorn. I have long felt uneasy with the idea that there was a large literate, Latinate, Christian, late-Roman community

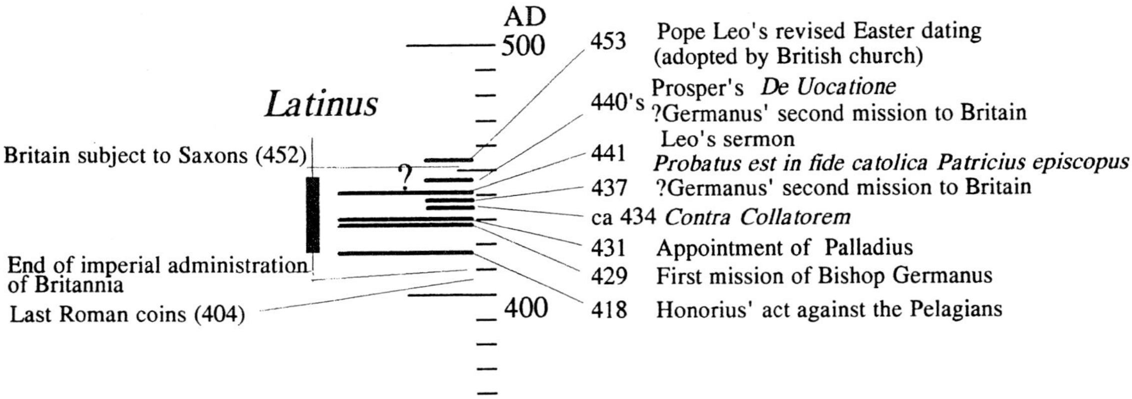

Fig. 2.3. The chronology of the Latinus stone and the Pelagian diaspora.

at Whithorn, necessary to explain the appointment of Ninian as bishop; the stream of papers emanating from Charles Thomas in the spring of 1997 gave me new insight into this problem. The *Latinus* stone had been treated unimaginatively as a memorial in bad Latin, and it is still displayed unimaginatively without interpretation or adequate lighting. It has now been exposed as a highly literate cryptogram replete with hidden meaning. Who was the scholar who composed it, and – equally important – what was the audience that would have appreciated its sophisticated message? The obvious candidates are the intelligentsia of the Pelagian diaspora.

It does not truly matter whether the *Latinus* stone displays an encrypted ground-plan of the Temple of Solomon, and it need not even be the dedication slab of a church (Thomas 1992). The *sinus* of the inscription might be a 'place of safety', and this meaning is better attested in antiquity than 'church', preferred by Thomas. The ecclesiastical site at Whithorn is secreted in a hollow and is virtually invisible from a distance (Fig. 2.4). It is nevertheless convenient to the sea-lanes of the Irish Sea, and the high ground immediately to the south commands a view of the Solway coast, Cumbria and the Isle of Man. It would have been an ideal refuge for a group of religious exiles, secure and obscure, but not too remote from the civilized world.

Our notional émigrés cannot have settled at Whithorn without the agreement of the local ruler, but we do not know what size of territory he would have controlled. We might look for a large area, such as the tribal lands of the Novantae, but I favour smaller territories on the scale of the *plebs* or *tuath* of early medieval Ireland (Charles-Edwards 1992, 64–5), the kindred lands of Dál Riata (Campbell 1999, 17), or the early provinces of the Picts (Foster 1996, 35). At this scale, the Machars, or even the southern Machars, comprises a coherent territory. It has been suggested that Cruggleton Castle or Rispain camp might have been the local centre of secular power (e.g. Thomas 1992),

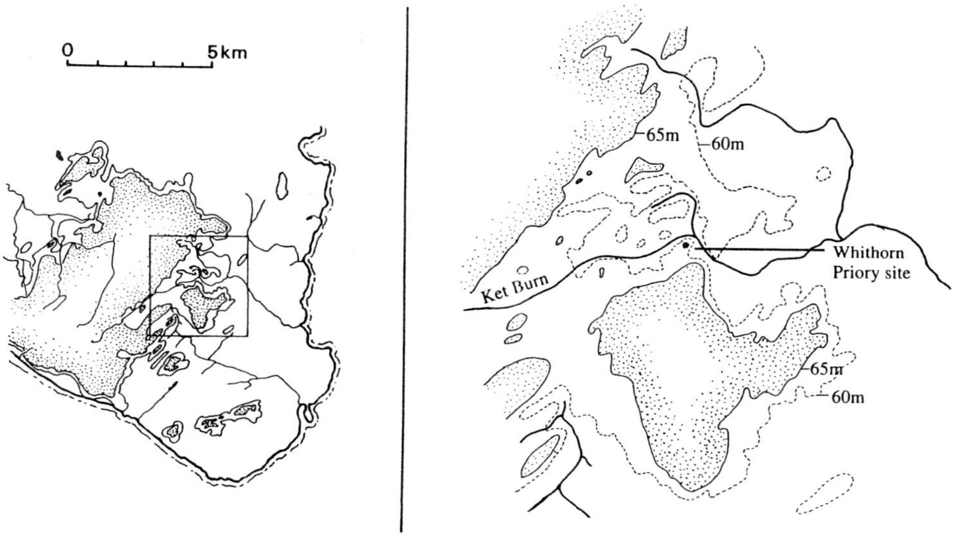

Fig. 2.4. Whithorn and the Isle.

but the fort at the Isle of Whithorn is a far more compelling candidate, and the Isle would have been an ideal marine base for a Dark Age ruler participating in trade, warfare and piracy (Fig. 2.4). The Isle was owned by the Priors of Whithorn in the fifteenth century, and wide-ranging imports from the excavations at Whithorn indicate a close linkage between the two places from the sixth century. In my model, a warlord ruling from the Isle of Whithorn would have made the original land grant to the religious settlers at Whithorn.

The Isle of Whithorn is now joined to the mainland by a broad causeway (Fig. 2.5). The modern village occupies both mainland and Isle, surrounding a large natural harbour currently used by fishing boats and pleasure craft, but formerly an important centre of transport and coastal trade. The Isle itself is divided into two parts by an isthmus flanked by narrow inlets facing south-west and north-east. The foundations of an old lifeboat station lie on the west side of the isthmus, the inlets giving two options for launching the boat in difficult conditions. The western part of the Isle forms one side of the harbour and contains a fourteenth-century chapel as well as an earlier curvilinear enclosure. The fort occupies the eastern half of the seaward part of the Isle, but has an annexe extending to the isthmus. The most obvious fortifications are triple ramparts suggesting a promontory enclosure, but areas of scree on the seaward side derive from dry-stone masonry, and show that the headland was almost completely surrounded with stone walling. The only gap in the defensive circuit is in a small area invisible from the neighbouring land and, I suspect, the fortifications were intended to look impressive from the land while remaining relatively invisible from the sea. The triple ramparts encompass large rock outcrops on both sides of the Isle, which help to emphasize the stepped appearance of the fortifications. Triple-ringed defences were the perquisite of royalty in early medieval Ireland, and may also denote a royal citadel at the Isle. The inner rampart encloses a level plateau, with traces of curvilinear (possibly oval or bottle-shaped) buildings. There are further ill-defined structures beyond it on the seaward side, including a rectangular foundation, possibly of later medieval date. The large annexe is featureless apart from broad cultivation ridges. It would have been suitable as a beach market or as a refuge for people and livestock in time of crisis. The opposed inlets would have provided advantages to warships similar to those enjoyed by the later lifeboat.

There are too many uncertainties in this thesis to draw firm conclusions, but there are grounds for a speculative interpretation of the earliest Christian community at Whithorn and how it came to be there. The *Latinus* stone is unequivocally Christian, is certainly literate, and may conceal a complex reference to the Temple of Solomon. It probably dates to the second quarter of the fifth century, and would thus have been broadly contemporary with the Pelagian diaspora, and the appointment of Palladius as bishop in Ireland. The *Latinus* stone may have been erected by a group of literate – possibly highly literate – Pelagians fleeing Britannia in the aftermath of St Germanus's mission. I suspect they gained the protection of a local potentate ruling a small territory from the Isle of Whithorn. The triple tiers of his citadel may identify him as a king, and I see him as a semi-civilized rogue with commercial and piratical control of a valuable sector of the Irish Sea. His motives for granting refuge to our hypothetical Pelagians are of course unknown. He may have been a Pelagian sympathizer; he may have wished to cock a snook at his neighbours in Britannia; or, more probably, he was paid (St Patrick was able to convert his British patrimony into wealth to fund his Irish adventures, and the *Life* of St Germanus records that the British Pelagians had flaunted their wealth). Patrick's adversary Coroticus provides a broadly contemporary model for this ruler, and it does not here matter whether he ruled in Ireland (Thompson 1985, 126–37; Dumville 1993), at Dumbarton, or elsewhere. Coroticus was a Briton, a Christian, and a bandit. He was either literate or had literate retainers, and was in contact with Picts and Scotti.

The site at Whithorn may have been deserted, or could have been a pagan shrine out of favour with our putative ruler. In the latter instance it might have had an established landholding which would have facilitated its transfer to the émigrés, and might have included agricultural land for their maintenance. The builders' debris shows the lengths that these people (or settlers of some other time) were prepared to go in furnishing their new home. The technology of making lime and working with it was unknown in Galloway, and dead or dying in Britannia. But we find it at Whithorn, where we also find the traditions of a 'shining' stone church. Mouldboard ploughs attested by plough-pebbles were also introduced (Hill 1997, 464–5), and the technological soph-

Fig. 2.5. The Isle fort and related features.

istication of the ploughs and lime mirrors the literary sophistication of the *Latinus* stone. The dating evidence is undeniably poor, but Pelagian émigrés versed in technological as well as literary skills could explain all the new arts brought to Whithorn in the early days of the settlement. Our Pelagian settlement may have left archaeological evidence. The early road might have led to an open settlement including Radford's *Candida Casa* and other buildings, or the ditch could have bounded an enclosed settlement, again with plastered buildings. I favour the latter suggestion. Traffic on the road had worn smooth the greywacke bedrock, suggesting long use, perhaps in the time of the putative pagan shrine. The later enclosure seems more appropriate to our early Christian 'refuge', and it provides a stratigraphic and organizational link with the settlement of the early sixth century.

It remains merely to accommodate the benign British bishop, Ninian. He might have been one of the fugitives, perhaps their spiritual leader, yet his hagiographers emphasized his regular training at Rome. He might, like Palladius, have been appointed to restore and sustain orthodoxy. He may, as Alan MacQuarrie maintains, pertain to a later phase of evangelization in the sixth century, or he may be a figment of scribal error, a wraith emerging from the more tangible Bishop Finian.

***

Rosemary Cramp's papers and lectures are characterized by the punctiliousness and generosity with which she acknowledges the contributions of others. I have tried to do the same here, bringing together the scintillating ideas of Charles Thomas with the clarity of Thomas Charles-Edwards' account of Palladius (1993), and adding ideas about the Isle of Whithorn that are shared with Ewan Campbell and Dave Pollock. I have not tried to conceal my soft spot for the Pelagians, and hope Rosemary will forgive these heretical leanings, for I have a soft spot for her too.

References

Blair, J. and Sharpe, R. (eds) 1992. *Pastoral Care before the Parish*, Leicester University Press

Brooke, D. 1999. *Saints and Goddesses: The interface with Celtic paganism* (Seventh Whithorn Lecture), Whithorn: Whithorn Trust

Campbell, E. 1999. *Saints and Sea-kings: The first Kingdom of the Scots*, Edinburgh

Charles-Edwards, T. M. 1992. The pastoral role of the church in early Irish laws, in Blair and Sharpe, 1992, 63–71

Charles-Edwards, T. M. 1993. Palladius, Prosper and Leo the Great: mission and primatial authority, in Dumville, 1993, 1–12

Craig, D. J. 1992. *The Distribution of Pre-Norman Sculpture in South-West Scotland: Provenance, ornament and regional groups*, unpublished Ph.D thesis, 4 vols, Durham University

Craig, D. J. 1997. The provenance of the early Christian inscriptions of Galloway, in Hill, 1997, 615–19

Dumville, D. N. 1993. *Saint Patrick AD 493–1993*, Woodbridge: Boydell Press

Esmonde Cleary, A. S. 1989. *The Ending of Roman Britain*, London: Batsford

Foster, S. 1996. *Picts, Gaels and Scots: Early historic Scotland*, London: Batsford

Green, M. 1986. *The Gods of the Celts*, Gloucester and New Jersey: Alan Sutton

Gregory, K. 1983. *The Second Cuckoo: A further selection of witty, amusing and memorable letters to The Times*, Boston: Allen & Unwin

Hill, P. H. 1997. *Whithorn and St Ninian: The excavation of a monastic town 1984–91*, Whithorn and Stroud: Whithorn Trust and Sutton Publishing

Levison, W. 1940. An eighth-century poem on St Ninian, *Antiquity*, 14, 280–91

MacQuarrie, A. 1987. The date of St Ninian's mission: a reappraisal, *Records of the Scottish Church History Society*, 23, 1–25

MacQuarrie, A. 1997. *The Saints of Scotland: Essays in Scottish church history 450–1093*, Edinburgh: John Donald

MacQueen, W. 1961. Miracula Nynie Episcopi, *Trans Dumfriesshire Galloway Natur Hist Antiq Soc*, 38, 21–57

MacQueen, W. 1999. Christian Celts – messages and images by Charles Thomas, *Trans Dumfriesshire Galloway Natur Hist Antiq Soc*, 73, 227–34

Pollock, D. C. 1995. *Whithorn 6: Interim report on the 1993 excavations at Whithorn Priory*, Whithorn: Whithorn Trust

Radford, C. A. R. 1950. Excavations at Whithorn, first season, 1949, *Trans Dumfriesshire Galloway Natur Hist Antiq Soc*, 3rd ser., 27, 85–126

Radford, C. A. R. 1957. Excavations at Whithorn (final report), *Trans Dumfriesshire Galloway Natur Hist Antiq Soc*, 34, 131–94

Thomas, A. C. 1992. *Whithorn's Christian Beginnings*, Whithorn: Whithorn Trust

Thomas, A. C. 1998. *Christian Celts – Messages and Images*, Stroud: Sutton Publishing

Thompson, E. A. 1985. *Who was Saint Patrick?* Woodbridge: Boydell Press

3

Space, Silence and Shortage on Lindisfarne
The Archaeology of Asceticism

Deirdre O'Sullivan

The late fourth and early fifth centuries saw the triumph of the discourse of monastic asceticism, promulgated forcefully by St Jerome, Augustine and John Cassian among others (Brown 1988; Marcus 1990). This was not, of course, the only possible outcome: recent scholarship has shed light on the moral debates of the fourth century, and it is clear that alternative and parallel conceptualizations of virtue, both pagan and Christian, were available. It has long been recognized that the practice of self-denial and celibacy found an important inspiration in Stoic philosophy (e.g. Chadwick 1967, 55–6), but it is clear that, in their collective assault on the perceived evil of human sexuality, Jerome *et al.* were actively contesting more positive contemporary views of the status and morality of marriage and procreation. For example, in her fascinating study of the concept of womanhood in Late Antiquity, K. Cooper has argued that, viewed from the perspective of an ethical Roman citizen, asceticism, especially if carried to immoderate lengths, was out of step with the contemporary idealization of marital concord. Christianity offered a 'competing moral language' of virginity which challenged the conventions of the Late Roman world (Cooper 1996, 3–4).

The reasons for the success of this new moral language are still hard to comprehend as the centuries distance us from the event. Early monastic writings may reflect a rhetorical rather than a substantive triumph of the ascetic ideal, and it can certainly be proposed that austerity was something admired by many, but practised by few. Even within ascetic practice, monks emerge from contemporary texts in very different guises. We may assume a world of difference between the unwashed illiterates of the Judean desert (Binns 1994) and the born-again virgins of five-star villa asceticism in Rome, who entertained Jerome as their personal spiritual adviser (Harlow 1997). However, amid the chaos and depravity of the collapsing Roman Empire in the west, asceticism came to occupy the moral high ground; the pinnacle of virtue was to be found in a life devoted to austerity, in which appetites of all kinds – gluttony, lust and luxury – were vigorously repressed. The human body was both literally and metaphorically a battleground for salvation.

From an archaeological perspective, there are clearly major areas of monastic ideology which are not readily accessible through surviving material culture. Salvation was ultimately a matter of individual success, not a team event, and the realities of personal spiritual struggle are even more invisible to the archaeologist than they are to the historian wrestling with formulaic *vitae sanctae*. However, as spiritual training grounds, monasteries provided the physical environment for this contest and these at least can be excavated, planned and reconstructed.

One of the problems with the archaeology of monasticism is the fact that, of necessity, we must deal with its physical materiality – buildings, monuments, texts, artefacts. For the monastic communities, however, their spiritual rather than their economic needs were (at least in theory) of supreme importance. Translated into rather simplistic physical terms, lifestyles were constructed around the ideal of 'doing without', rather than maximizing resources. Nonetheless, and in spite of the primacy given to an ascetic discourse in the texts, monasteries often developed as important economic institutions, major producers of 'culture', creating a fundamental tension between materiality and spirituality. The extent to which ascetic practice is manifest in material culture is one index of the strength of the monastic ideal, but study of the monastic landscape also offers interesting insight into the integrity of early Christian perspectives: I will explore both of these themes in this paper. The specific focus of my study is the monastery of Lindisfarne, the springboard for Northumbrian Christianity in the seventh century, and the subject of a long-term (though still partial) archaeological investigation, now nearing completion (O'Sullivan and Young 1995).

The founder of Lindisfarne, St Aidan, drew on the tradition of Columban monasticism, and recent work sheds light on his world view. A paper by O'Loughlain (1997) has explored perceptions of the sea in the writings of the Iona community, where it features not simply as a barrier or practical means of transport, but as an important element in their spiritual and ideological sense of place. The Columban texts show that the Iona monks were familiar with the contemporary geography of Isidore of Seville, and seem to reflect a shared understanding of the physical universe.

Isidore's model drew on earlier classical tradition, commonly known as a T-O map (Edson 1997, 44–5) in which Jerusalem is placed at the centre (Fig. 3.1), and the Islands of Britain are located in the Ocean which surrounds the three continents of Europe, Asia and Africa, at the limits of the known world. This liminality imparted a special spiritual character; in contrast to the Sea, that is the Mediterranean, the Ocean had high tides and rough seas, full of monsters and demons which could be compelled only by God's power. Such

Fig. 3.1. Diagram of a T/O map, a common geographical world view of the seventh century, showing the perceived relationship between continents.

creatures were perceived as necessary, natural and supernatural inhabitants of the monastic landscape – the distinction would indeed have had little contemporary meaning. These beasts were the Atlantic equivalent of the demons with which Anthony struggled in the desert, and are overtly encountered in Columba's spiritual battles and prophecies (i.e. *VC* III.8; Sharpe 1995, 211–12). While in one sense they may be real inhabitants of Atlantic waters, the analogy with desert demons is not simply a metaphorical borrowing: it reflects the way in which eastern monasticism was physically translated to the western seas. Columba and his successors and followers would have known that the turbulent waters which surrounded them placed them both physically and ideologically in the remotest of places, the watery desert of the Great Ocean. To separate the physical or natural and the spiritual in the landscape is to impose a post-Enlightenment, Cartesian perspective at odds with early monastic vision. The physical landscape was the spiritual landscape and God's purpose and design was everywhere apparent within it.

The representation of this landscape in early sources is of considerable interest. O'Reilly (1997) has drawn attention to the manner in which a didactic purpose was embodied in the use of place and space in Adamnan's narratives, with many levels of meaning. Her study shows that even some of the most apparently anecdotal aspects of Adamnan's writing were read through a biblical or patristic exigesis, validated by daily readings aloud from the scriptures. The text assumes knowledge of the tradition of *lectio divina,* and incidents in the saint's life are re-enactments of holy writ. The high place on Iona, the Hill of the Angels, where Columba met with heavenly guests, mirrors Moses receiving the Ark of the Covenant on Mount Sinai (Exodus 22), forming as vital an ingredient of the site as a church, a cemetery or a kitchen. When a drought threatens the food supply of the monastery (*VC* II.44; Sharpe 1995, 199–200), the fields become the focus of solemn processions, where the relics of the saint are transported to mimic the carrying of the Ark in the wilderness (Deuteronomy 31).

Thus, it is not simply Columba himself, but the embedded context of his life that provides evidence of divine intervention. The Iona landscape is a homology of Biblical terrain, a visible manifestation of God's purpose. This is not quite the same as the idea that the landscape can be read as a text, a notion popular with contemporary critical theorists; rather it is the lessons of The Text – i.e. the biblical texts, clarified by patristic authority, which are rendered manifest as visible phenomena in the landscape.

Elsewhere in Irish tradition a more-or-less contemporary parallel interest in 'explaining' the landscape can be identified, but this seems to represent a much simpler political strategy of appropriation. In a study that draws on theories of landscape and monumentality recently developed within British prehistoric studies, Aitchison (1994) has reviewed the place of royal sites in Irish early medieval cosmology. Monuments of an earlier era were claimed and explained by the aggrandizing Uí Neill kings in order to enhance their own prestige. These pagan sites also feature in Irish ecclesiastical writings, most notably in the well-known poem in the *Felire Oengusso* of *c.* 800 which contrasts the contemporary renown of the great churches of Armagh and Kildare with the desolation of Tara, Cruchain, Emain Macha and Dun Ailline. The later medieval *dindshenchas*, compiled in the eleventh century, demonstrate familiarity with the earthworks on the hill of Tara, for which various explanations are offered relating them to people and events in the Irish mythological tradition. This need to explain the visible landscape in the context of contemporary relations of power, utilizing antiquities for the purposes of legitimation, is a fairly widespread phenomenon, common to many times and places, the production of texts to explain the landscape forming part of a political strategy. Although there is some interesting resonance with the secular tradition, the exigesis proposed by O'Reilly is specifically Christian, and inconceivable without access to early monastic and patristic writings: it is the landscape itself that explains the text.

Early debates about the potential influence of the Eastern Mediterranean on the art of the West, or the interest in the physical geography of the Holy Land reflected in texts produced in both Iona and Northumbria, including Adamnan's own *De Locis Sanctis* (Meehan 1958), have sometimes failed to consider the specific significance of the broader framework of early monasticism. Whether or not insular monks had direct access to objects or texts from the Eastern Mediterranean, they took great interest in it (Parsons 1988, 5–11) and the world of the desert underpinned contemporary perceptions of what monasticism was all about.

The siting of the monastery was deliberate: as the quote from Bede cited below indicates, Lindisfarne was not simply Oswald's gift but Aidan's choice, and the popularity of small inshore or offshore islands as locations for eremitic communities has long been recognized (Cramp 1984a). The Lindisfarne landscape offers many echoes of Iona. Both are small islands within a short distance of neighbouring land, open and treeless, with comparable surface areas, tracts of arable and pasture, some stretches of wasteland and a small area of high ground. In the context of O'Loughlin and O'Reilly's work, I would suggest that these similarities are at least as much due to their relevance within a monastic discourse as to any simple, sentimental memorialization of Iona itself. Even though it was located within easy vantage of the centre of Northumbrian power at Bamburgh, Lindisfarne was still in the Great Ocean, with all its demonic and monstrous possibilities. The high place is the basalt ridge overlooking the village, the Heugh, and its continuation on the other side of the harbour, the Castle Rock. Functionally, this enabled the community to keep a close eye on the Northumbrian coast, but it is also a potential embodiment of Mount Nebo, overlooking the plains of Jordan (Deuteronomy 36) or, looking eastwards towards Bamburgh and Jerusalem, a place to contemplate the heavenly Jerusalem.

There is another sense in which Lindisfarne's physical location held unusual significance. Both Bede and Aethelwulf draw particular attention to its unique status as a tidal island, in terms which imply that this carried special meaning:

> On Aidan's arrival, the king appointed the island of Lindisfarne to be his see as he asked. As the tide ebbs and flows, this place is surrounded by sea twice a day like an island, and twice a day the sand dries and joins it to the mainland (Bede, *HE* III.3; Sherley-Price 1955, 142).

While for Aethelwulf, Eadfrith held sway

> ... where the waves are eager to curl over the shore with grey water, but rush to lay them bare as they go on their backward course, and the blue (depths) encircle a sacred land, and afford a ready journey, when they lay the shores bare (Aethelwulf, *de Abbatibus*, v; Campbell 1967, 10).

The mechanism of the tides seems to have been reasonably well understood in insular cosmology, and was discussed explicitly by Bede in *De Temporum Ratione* (Smyth 1996, 241–61). The ebb and flow of the sea was tangible evidence of the order of the world, a fundamental tenet of Christian faith. God had planned and created the tides as part of the workings of the universe; they were evidence of his regulation of the Ocean and only he could change the rules, as he did for the Israelites crossing the Red Sea (Exodus 14). The Lindisfarne monks would have been auspiciously reminded of this every time they thought to cross to the mainland.

Aethelwulf's verse represents Lindisfarne as a sacred place, and raises another interesting problem. To what extend did this sanctity adhere to the island itself, or simply to the monastic presence? Put more crudely, was the monastery perceived as being on the island, or identical with it? Again this is potentially another artificial, modern dichotomy. In a recent consideration of early monasteries in Palestine, Binns (1999) emphasizes the visible, physical difference between cenobitic and eremitic communities which has as much to do with topography as structure. In the account of the fifth-century founding of Mar Sabas provided by Cyril of Scythopolis, the gorge, the hillslopes and the natural caves at the Great Laura provide a ready-made setting for ascetic practice and spiritual journeys in both time and space. The scattered, unenclosed community was spread along a 1.5 km stretch of the Kidron Gorge.

The Iona texts likewise suggest that the monastery and the island shared the same sacred identity, but there was nonetheless a *vallum*, which implies an ideological need to divide the landscape into zones. Although it is often claimed that the monastic *vallum* defined the boundary between sacred and profane space (e.g. Aitchison 1994, 216–17), many sites have at least two concentric divisions (Swan 1985, 99) and the Irish texts indicate that these reflect different degrees of sanctity (Doherty 1985, 57–59). The Iona *vallum* had a fairly complex archaeological history, incorporating an earlier Late Iron Age earthwork (McCormick 1997, 49–51), and functioning parts of the monastery could be located outside of it (i.e. Relig Orain). It did not simply describe monastic space, but was a necessary part of it, a potential reference-point in ceremonial activities and an active element in the ideological landscape.

Aitchison's discussion of the ecclesiastical enclosures at Armagh (1994, 211–95) offers some useful insight into the role of such a boundary in praxis, although in the context of a general thesis which should be treated with caution. The hilltop of Armagh is surrounded by a series of three oval enclosures, variously preserved in street boundaries and property divisions, and recorded in early maps. Observing that 'the ecclesiastical boundaries which are fossilised within Armagh's street plan appear to define a circumambulatory way which spirals out from the central enclosure' (ibid., 267, fig. 59.4), he suggests that this was used on a regular basis for the procession of relics marking special occasions or the great feasts of the Church, such as Whitsun, on a regular basis (ibid., 266–7). Such processions validated the authority of the church within Armagh, and of St Patrick's claim to pre-eminence over other Irish saints. It is also proposed that in contemporary texts the topography of Armagh mirrored that of the heavenly Jerusalem, the ideal city, as depicted in Revelations (21), an idea that meshes well with O'Reilly's interpretation of the Iona texts, though from a completely different perspective. It is interesting to note that a schematic plan of Jerusalem is included in the Book of Armagh, the early ninth-century compilation of Patrician and other texts which set out Armagh's claim to supremacy (Alexander 1978, 76).

This theme is developed further by the suggestion that the topography of Armagh also acted as a microcosm of Irish political and ecclesiastical geography. The relative status of Patrick, Brigid and Columba was reflected in the location of their respective churches and divisions into trians or 'quarters', and wards which also mirror the physical division of Ireland into five provinces

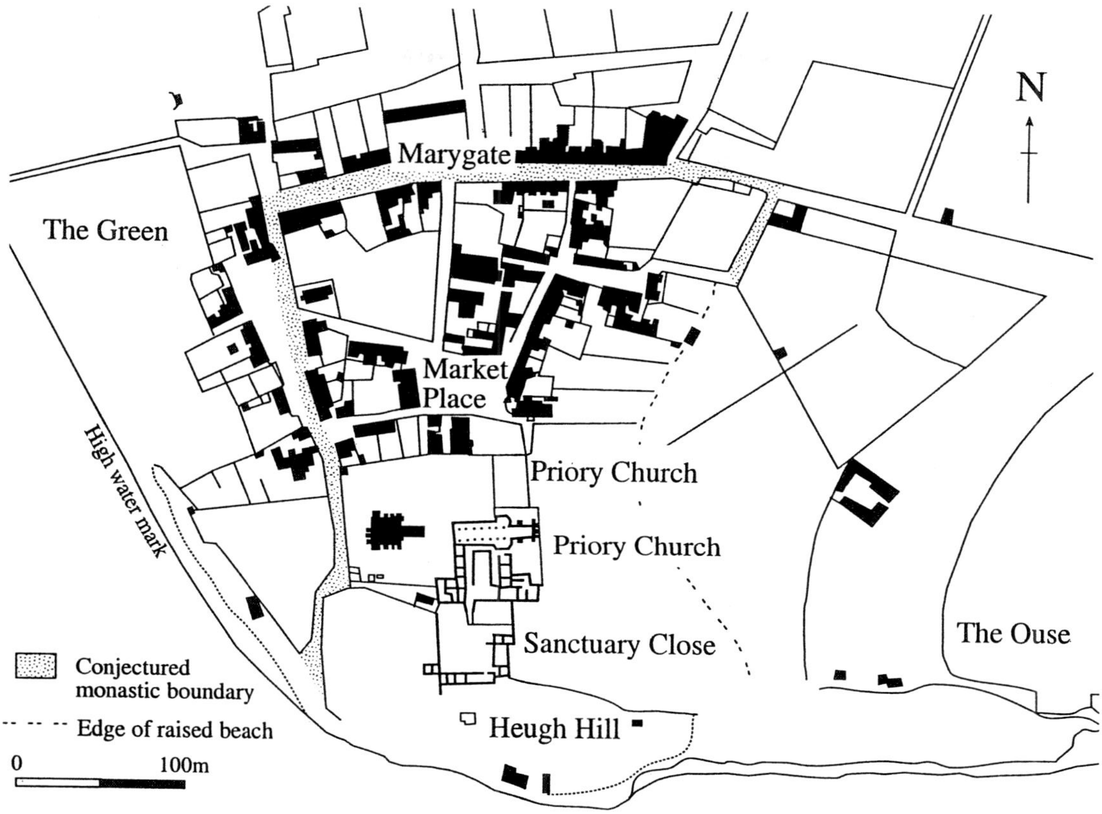

Fig. 3.2. Plan of Holy Island Village, showing the projected monastic boundary.

(Aitchison 1994, 244–55). Adopting a structuralist perspective, Aitchison (ibid., 255–65) further identifies a fundamental, binary opposition between, *inter alia,* Patrick and Brigid, north and south, male and female etc., reflected in the plan of the ecclesiastical city from its foundation. Neither the archaeological nor historical data justify such an integrated secular and religious cosmology at such an early date, although this is not to deny that some of these divisions and contrasts could have had important contemporary significance. Armagh may never have had great eremitic aspirations, and could well have developed in a different style although here, as elsewhere in Ireland, the surviving monuments are several centuries later than the foundation of the site and reflect a period when there was more overt engagement with secular patronage and politics (Herity 1995, 19–57).

The consideration of boundary processions highlights the need to withdraw from Cartesian spatial models in understanding early medieval use of space. The act of procession did not simply mark out the area of the monastery, in a concentric or linear formula; the boundary enabled the act. Indeed it can be proposed that the procession, the act itself, was what defined the boundary, and not the other way round.

I suggested some years ago that at least one monastic boundary, and possibly two, can be perceived in the street patterns of Holy Island Village (O'Sullivan 1989; O'Sullivan and Young 1995, 40–2) (Fig. 3.2), and it requires no great leap of the imagination to transform this into a processional way, though it must be made clear that actual historical evidence for this is lacking. The outer boundary could have been reached from the centre by heading north from the Market Place, passing along Marygate and through Fiddler's Green. The route then leads naturally to the west end of the Heugh, which is ascended by a well-worn path. The modern path running along the Heugh leads to a series of shallow foundations of small drystone buildings, discovered in field-survey, and a cross base. The buildings are of unknown date; one was excavated by Brian Hope Taylor in the 1960s but produced no significant finds. The little structures and the cross base could represent 'stations' where particular devotions were carried out on special feast days. Alternatively, at least one of them could have been the monastic watchtower. In his account of Cuthbert's death on Farne, Bede makes reference to the 'watchtower of the island of Lindisfarne' where one of the brethren waited for a signal from those attending the dying saint, that he had passed on. The monk then 'quickly ran to the church where the whole assembly of the brethren were gathered' (Bede, *VC* 40; Colgrave 1940, 287).

Little else has been recognized above ground of the monastery of Aidan and Cuthbert (O'Sullivan 1989). The present site of the eleventh- or twelfth-century Benedictine priory may reasonably be considered to mark the earlier resting place of St Cuthbert, and the thirteenth-century parish church conceals an earlier building with a high, narrow nave and irregular quoining at the angle of the chancel and the nave, which indicates an earlier stone church of potentially Anglo-Saxon type although of unknown date. It has been claimed by Blair (1991) that these churches are axially aligned, as in the case of the Jarrow churches, but there is actually a noticeable shift in east-west orientation. The founding churches built by Aidan and Finan were made of timber, although the second of these was later covered with lead (Bede, *HE* III.25; Sherley Price 1955, 182); these have disappeared under the later medieval ecclesiastical complex.

Other evidence for monastic activity is found in different parts of the village. Human bones uncovered in two discrete locations on the north side of the village suggest the existence of separate burial grounds. Less certainly at odds with the archaeology of the medieval village are an area of paving and a hearth under the new museum (O'Sullivan 1985), and a massive foundation under the midden excavated by the foreshore in 1986; both are likewise undated, but represent the earliest features to be found in the site stratigraphy (Beavitt, O'Sullivan and Young 1987, 13–16). Although it formed a personal retreat for Cuthbert and his successors (Bede, *VC* XVII, XLII; Colgrave 1940, 215, 293), the visible buildings on St Cuthbert's Island are of later medieval origin, although it is feasible that the low mound to the north-east of these, identified by virtually every writer on Lindisfarne as St Cuthbert's cell, is exactly that.

Structural evidence apart, and despite fairly extensive clearance in and around the priory as well as a number of excavations (O'Sullivan and Young 1995, 13–17), very little evidence of early monastic material culture has been found. The Anglo-Saxon sculpture in the museum was retrieved from within and around the priory at various dates in the nineteenth and early twentieth centuries (Stuart 1856–67; Cramp 1984), but apart from these, there is little else to consider. The Benedictine priory was cleared by the Ministry of Works in the early decades of the twentieth century (Peers 1925), and for what it is worth, the absence of evidence for the Anglo-Saxon monastery was explicitly noted, apart from a foundation in the north chancel aisle, which was recorded on a plan (although not published) by Peers; a brooch fragment and three coins were also found. Our own programme of field-walking has likewise drawn a blank, and the strenuous efforts in 1996 of a group of metal detectorists working in two fields on the island have likewise found nothing of Anglo-Saxon date.

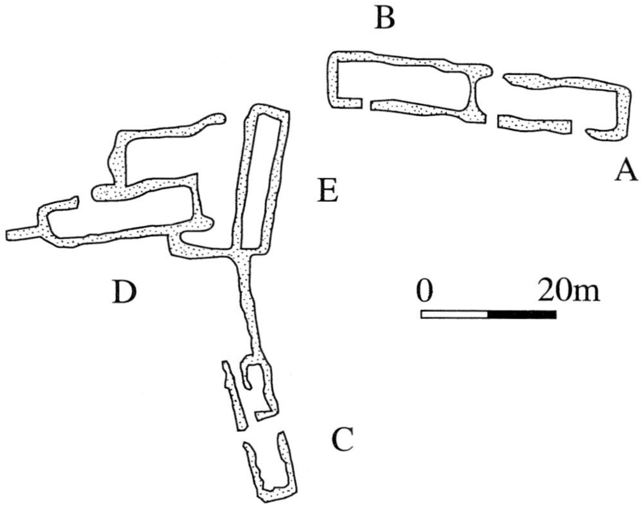

Fig. 3.3. Green Shiel, Lindisfarne: general plan of buildings.

In the light of this rather scattered and sparse picture, the results of the past 16 years of excavation at Green Shiel must now be considered (Figs. 3.3, 3.4, 3.5). The site, which has now been entirely excavated, consists of a complex of five linked buildings situated in the sand dunes close to the North Shore. Dating evidence at present is limited to artefacts, and indicates use in the seventh to ninth centuries (although it must be said that almost all of this evidence is represented by sixteen mid-ninth-century *stycas*). It seems reasonably clear that the buildings fell out of use in the ninth century and remained undisturbed for nearly a millennium. In the middle of the nineteenth century, workmen building a trackway between limekilns inland and the limestone outcropping on the north shore found the structures and used the walling for hardcore (Selby 1849).

Buildings A and B, at the east end of the site, were badly damaged in this process but the ground-plan, particularly the area of paving, suggests that the east ends of both were used as byres. Building C was divided into several compartments: originally this was also interpreted as a byre, but it now seems more likely that the compartments served some other function. Buildings D and E were extensively paved internally without obvious internal division; D contained the only constructed hearth although there was a burnt area at the west end of A. The buildings were very crude in construction, with no evidence for clay bonding or packing, and they show some similarity in plan. Coursing was irregular, and wall-lines far from straight. The stone for the buildings came from the immediate foreshore, where substantial limestone blocks could be acquired from the wave-cut platform, or large beach pebbles could be collected. The animal-bone assemblage has yet to be properly investigated, but consists mostly of cattle. There were a number of articulated skeletons underneath the rubble, some in pits under the floor of the buildings, and one most curious deposit, which consisted of a dump of juvenile and neonatal calves, under the floor of building E.

Apart from animal bone, to which I will return, there were very few finds, in spite of the fact that every excavated deposit was sieved through a 0.5 cm mesh. The commonest artefact is coinage – 17 coins found on site – and although bone is well-preserved, only two bone artefacts were recovered.

Until the final season, the site was interpreted as a 'normal' rural settlement, probably some kind of monastic 'proto-grange', but given the anomalies of the bone assemblage and the lack of evidence for routine domestic activities (especially the lack of evidence for heating) it seems likely to have been a more specialized production site, perhaps occupied only seasonally, which processed quantities of juvenile cattle remains, possibly for the production of calf skins for the monastic *scriptorium*, and an integral part of the monastery itself. The excavation therefore offers potentially the first substantial archaeological insight into an important aspect of early monastic life.

Fig. 3.4. Green Shiel, Lindisfarne: Building D, from the west. This was the only building to contain a hearth, visible on the left at the east end. Note the differing layout of paving in the east and west ends of the structure.

Looking in a positivist way at the totality of the physical evidence from Lindisfarne itself, it is clear that there is little which points to a luxurious lifestyle. There is a clear absence of monumentality: buildings were simple and temporary. Sculptural monuments were produced, but those from the early monastic period were unambitious. Iconographic representations are few and idiosyncratic: in Rosemary Cramp's words, 'no figural scene can definitely be assigned to a common Christian type' (1984, 21). The contrast with Flixborough (Loveluck, this volume) in terms of the lack of all types of material culture – dress-fittings, other types of personal possession – suggests that consumption of material goods was minimal. While we have virtually nothing on which to base a study of observance to attitudes to the body or rigorous dietary restrictions, elaborate dress is not evidenced by fittings nor food by the appropriate joints of meat.

Unfortunately, the obvious shortcomings of this cosy picture are all too evident. Where monastic diet is concerned, for example, no deposits which reflect the consumption of fish, birds and mammals for food have been securely located, although it will be interesting to see what is revealed by an overall study of the fish- and bird-bones from Green Shiel. Ervynck (1997, 74) has considered critically the evidence for meat avoidance in faunal assemblages from monastic sites in Flanders, and concludes that we still await the discovery of a refuse context 'that indicates the obedience to the rule of abstinence form the meat of quadrupeds'. Meat bones were found in many areas of the monasteries which he studied, and in all periods, although he emphasizes that much of the material in his review has been unsatisfactorily sampled, or is poorly stratified or poorly dated. Only one site, the eleventh- to eighteenth-century Benedictine house of Ename, offered a group of sieved contexts which could be clearly identified as food waste and dated within reasonably limited periods. Here, although it was clear that mammal bones were a definite element in the diet, the prevalence and variety of fish was also striking. A comparison with material from contemporary non-monastic sites indicates that fish formed a much more significant part of the diet at Ename, and also that the monastery had access to a wide range of both fresh- and salt-water species (Van Neer and Ervynck 1996).

Benedict's Rule is quite clear about restrictions in the monastic diet (*Rule* 39; Doyle 1995, 200), but other texts reveal greater flexibility. At Tallaght in the ninth century, the Rule indicates that meat abstinence was no longer essential, though it could form a personal act of piety. Meat consumption was, however, restricted to wild deer or wild pig (Gwynn and Purton 1911, 159; Kelly 1998, 344). There is, as yet, surprisingly little archaeological material from insular monastic sites which can be used to investigate this question; where excavation has taken place, contexts are often disturbed, or span long or uncertain periods, and collection without sieving has necessarily biased the sample towards bones of larger mammals. Interestingly, Iona has produced quite a high percentage of wild game, including red deer and seal. As a marine

Fig. 3.5. Green Shiel, Lindisfarne: Building C, from the north. This structure was divided into walled compartments.

mammal, the latter may have been considered as honorary 'fish'. Cuthbert was provided with miraculous dolphin flesh (*delphini*) on a midwinter visit to Pictland (ASC II.4; Colgrave 1940, 83) and the analogy drawn by the narrator with the marriage feast of Cana may indicate a necessary metamorphosis. One of the 'Canons of Adamnan', a text surviving in a ninth-century manuscript but probably not correctly attributed, implies that beached marine mammals were acceptable food (Bieler 1963, 9, 177). However the regulation is among those dealing with acceptable forms of death for animals intended for human consumption, and it is not clear that this relates specifically to a monastic lifestyle. Adamnan (*VC* I.41; Sharpe 1995, 143) reveals that the community had proprietary rights over seals on a nearby island, though these may have been exploited for their skins and blubber. Fish included large cod, which had been caught in deep water (McCormick 1997, 56–60). At Jarrow, some contexts containing food refuse associated with the early monastic phase indicated an avoidance of red meat (R. Cramp, pers. comm.). This is an area of considerable potential interest in future monastic studies.

In a material sense, the most notable products of the Northumbrian monasteries were the manuscripts, and it is here that economic surplus and spiritual purpose meet. The Rule of Benedict (Doyle 1989) strongly suggests that, after prayer, the practice of writing was the most important activity of the devout monk within the western monastic tradition. In the sections which deal with the prohibition of private property, writing equipment seems to have offered the most common temptation:

> Let no one presume to give or receive anything without the Abbot's leave, or to have anything as his own – anything whatever, whether book or tablets or pen or whatever it may be – since it is not permitted to have even their bodies or wills at their own disposal ... (*Rule* 33; Doyle 1989, 198).
>
> ... the Abbot should provide all the necessary articles: cowl, tunic, stockings, shoes, girdle, knife, pen, needle, handkerchief, tablets; that all pretext of need may be taken away (*Rule* 55; Doyle 1989, 206).

All choir monks would have been literate or would have been required to become so: it was clearly an issue on being accepted into the novitiate:

> Let him write this petition (to be accepted into the community) with his own hand: or if he is illiterate let another write it at his request ... (*Rule* 58; Doyle 1989, 208).

Books formed an important focus of the *opus dei* in both communal prayer and private devotion. The most important works were learned by rote (every week the entire rota of 150 psalms was worked through; *Rule* 18; Doyle 1989, 193) but exemplars of these would have been essential. The key texts required for liturgical services, the psalter and the gospels constituted the absolute minimum, but Benedict's Rule clearly implies that other sections of the Bible, and patristic commentaries, were also available. Works to be read at Vigils included specifically the Old and New Testaments, as well as 'explanations of them which have been made by well known and orthodox Catholic Fathers' (*Rule* 9; ibid., 190). The Heptateuch and Kings were deemed unsuitable for reading after dinner (*Rule* 42; ibid., 201).

Apart from regular services, a substantial part of the monastic day was devoted to reading, either communally – 'The meals of the brethren should not be without reading' (*Rule* 38; ibid., 199) – or in private, although this depended on available daylight. Sundays were largely given over to reading (*Rule* 48; ibid., 204) and more intensive study was required as a preparation for Easter:

> On the days of Lent, from morning until the end of the third hour let them apply themselves to their reading, and from then until the end of the tenth hour let them do the work assigned to them. And in these days of Lent they shall each receive a book from the library, which they shall read straight through from the beginning. These books are to be given out at the beginning of Lent.
>
> But certainly one or two of the seniors should be deputed to go about the monastery at the hours when the brethren are occupied in reading, and see that there be no lazy brother who spends his time in idleness or gossip and does not apply himself to the reading ... (*Rule* 48; Doyle 1989, 203).

Even allowing for a fairly restricted literary diet, Benedict's Rule, which was followed at Lindisfarne in the eighth century along with that of Cuthbert (*AVC* 3.II: Colgrave 1940, 97), indicates that monasteries would have needed at least as many texts as monks. The range of manuscripts which survive from the early Middle Ages in Britain reflects in some degree the types of text which appear to have been in most demand (Gneuss 1981) but it is impossible to know what scale of loss is attributable to the passage of time, assisted by the more deliberate efforts of Vikings, Normans, and Protestant reformers. A recent estimate gives a minimum number of nine scribes operating on Lindisfarne in the mid eighth century, based on a study of surviving hands linked to the Lindisfarne *scriptorium* (Brown 1989, 162).

The scale of output overall is unknowable, but we do have some information about the status of the scribe himself. Whatever its quality, insular art in other media tells us nothing of individual metalworkers, sculptors architects or embroiderers; the names surviving on such objects seem to reflect patronage rather than personal skill. But we know the names of a number of scribes in insular monasteries, from both historical texts and colophons, short commemorative passages which record the name of those involved in the preparation of individual manuscripts. The most famous is Columba himself, transcribing a copy of the Psalms on the day of his death (*VC* III.23; Sharpe 1995, 228); his successor Baithene, who was left to complete this work, had previously made a copy of the same text (ibid. and *VC* I.23; Sharpe 1995,

129–30). Other documented scribes include Eadfrith, bishop of Lindisfarne; Ultan, the famous scribe of *De Abbatibus*, usually considered an inmate of one of the monasteries of the Lindisfarne community (Campbell 1967, 18–19; Howlett 1975, 121–4); Dorbbene, Abbot of Iona in the early eighth century and the scribe of the earliest surviving manuscript of Adamnan's life; Ferdomnach, principal scribe of the Book of Armagh, and sufficiently important to have his death recorded in the Annals of Ulster in 845 (Alexander 1978, 77); Mac Reagol, scribe of the ninth-century gospels which bear his name; Cuthbercht, one of the scribes of the Cuthbercht Gospels, probably a Northumbrian but working on the Continent; and Wigbald, who contributed to the Barberini Gospels in what is potentially a Lindisfarne hand. This use of colophons may represent a particularly Irish style, passed on to the Lindisfarne community as Brown has indicated (1989, 156) but it is surely also a reflection of the status of the scribe and his product.

Any attempt to view early book production in purely material terms is misconceived. There can be little doubt that the reproduction of the word of God stood at the pinnacle of insular monastic achievement and the preparation of a sacred text was not something casually undertaken. The high quality of script on the Springmount tablets indicates that scribes were carefully trained in the use of more temporary media before they attempted a calfskin text (Webster and Backhouse 1991, 80–1). Brown has suggested that the preparation of an elaborate manuscript may have been seen as an act of personal devotion, an individual's *opus dei*. In more materialistic terms, this could be seen as a significant career move: she postulates the concept of the 'hero-scribe' (ibid.,154–6). The status of scribes is also demonstrated iconographically: the full-page representation of the evangelists as scribes begins with the Lindisfarne Gospels (although clearly earlier models were used) and was later widely adopted (Brown 1989, 157). Although the images are highly conventionalized and stylized, the accoutrements are clearly those of real scribes, equipped with pens, knives and inkwells (O'Neill 1997, 73–5).

The figure of Columba is particularly significant in this respect, partly because of the historical standing of Adamnan's *Life*, but also because of his personal significance as both a real historical figure and a didactic role-model. In a recent study, O'Neill (1990) makes use of both Adamnan and the later Irish *Lives* of Columban saints to investigate scribal practice. Adamnan's work is clearly the best guide to these matters in the early period and he makes a number of references to Columba's scribal activities. Works were carefully checked: Columba miraculously knows that the psalter text which Baithene has copied has but a single spelling mistake in it (*VC* 1.23; Sharpe 1995 129–30). Columba was the copier of several texts which were treasured by the Iona monks, which again demonstrates that it was considered entirely appropriate that such work should be carried out by the most senior and respected figure in the community. Although scribes may have 'worked hard' in our contemporary sense, it is surely completely inappropriate to consider scribal effort as a routine chore in an early medieval book production line.

The study of early monasteries in Northumbria, to which Rosemary Cramp has devoted such fruitful energy, is still an exciting and developing field. In this paper I have tried to identify two areas where new approaches offer fresh insight into the depth and complexity of the 'designer-simple' monastic ideal. In general terms, three principal issues have emerged from this somewhat fractured investigation into the material evidence for ascetic practice on Lindisfarne.

First, in grappling with the meanings contained in early monastic landscapes Lindisfarne is clearly important if we are to address medieval ideas of space and place. Ideology was embedded in the monastery and its surroundings, and the material record suggests that at Lindisfarne and elsewhere, certain types of display and certain types of activity were avoided, zoned or otherwise restricted, in order to keep the community in touch with its priorities. The importance of spiritual struggle and the observation of Divine Order in the world around them were key concerns. In spite of an obvious minimalism and the practical limitations imposed by situation, the monastic perspective was impressively global – more strongly rooted in the desert sands of Jordan than in the sandhills of the little island.

Secondly, economic determinism is not an adequate approach to the archaeology of monasticism; it may not be appropriate at any level. Although the physical remains available for study may be every bit as sparse as any found on a prehistoric settlement in the Cheviots, the 'materiality' which we study has little in common with the kind of materialist archaeology which centralizes the maximizing of resources in appropriate ecological niches. If we are to understand early monastic production we must at least consider some of the priorities of the monastic communities themselves. Obviously such groups occupied ecological niches, and made use of resources unavailable in the eastern Egyptian desert (such as Hebrideian seal pups), but we ignore the impact of monastic economic practice at our peril.

Thirdly, it is possible to see some dimensions of what one might call a monastic 'identity' which, like other types of identity, was essentially performative, i.e. constructed through a series of actions. Indeed the practice of asceticism is by definition performative: sanctity was claimed and observed on the basis of a series of appropriate types of behaviour. At the highest level, these mirrored those of figures of the Old and New Testaments, reflected in hagiography in the performance of miracles, a clear indication that the actor was an agent of divine purpose; but it can also be seen in the mundane – but still very tangible – realization of ritual in the monastic day, including the production of texts. The writing of scripture was a sacred act: one wonders what Aidan, Cuthbert or indeed Eadfrith himself would have thought to hear the Lindisfarne Gospels described as a 'luxury'. This is surely a fundamental misunderstanding. It is only ignorance that permits such works to be crudely objectified as 'art objects'. In the rhetoric of the seventh and eighth centuries, they exemplified monastic discipline, a discipline that revealed an equally sacred purpose and place in the changing tides, a beached whale, or the near-perfection of Baithene's Psalter script.

References

Aitchison, N. B. 1994. *Armagh and the Royal Centres in Early Medieval Ireland: Monuments, cosmology and the past*, Woodbridge: Boydell & Brewer / Cruithne Press

Alexander, J. J. G. 1978. *Insular Manuscripts, 6th to the 9th Century* (Survey of Manuscripts illuminated in the British Isles 1), London: Harvey Miller

Beavitt, P., O'Sullivan, D. and Young, R. 1987. Fieldwork on Lindisfarne, Northumberland 1980–88, *Northern Archaeology*, 8, 1–23

Bieler, L. 1963. *The Irish Penitentials. Scriptores Latini Hibernae*, V, Dublin: Institute for Advanced Studies

Binns, J. 1994. *Ascetics and Ambassadors of Christ. The monasteries of Palestine, 314–631*, Oxford: Clarendon Press

Binns, J. 1999. The concept of sacred space in the monasteries of Byzantine Palestine, in T. Insoll (ed), *Studies in Archaeology and World Religion. Proceedings of the Cambridge Conference* (Brit Archaeol Rep, Int Ser, 755), 26–31, Oxford: BAR

Blair, J. 1991. The early churches at Lindisfarne, *Archaeologia Aeliana*, 5th ser., 19, 47–54

Brown, M. 1989. The Lindisfarne Scriptorium from the late seventh to the early ninth century, in G. Bonner, D. Rollason and C. Stancliffe (eds), *St Cuthbert, His Cult and His Community to AD 1200*, 151–163, Woodbridge: Boydell Press

Brown, P. 1988. *The Body and Society: Men, women and sexual renunciation in early Christianity*, New York: Columbia University Press

Campbell, A. (ed and trans) 1967. *De Abbatibus*, Oxford: Oxford University Press

Chadwick, H. 1967. *The Early Church* (1st edn), Harmondsworth: Penguin Books

Colgrave, B. (ed and trans) 1940. *Two Lives of St Cuthbert*, Cambridge: Cambridge University Press

Cooper, K. 1996. *The Virgin and the Bride. Idealized womanhood in Late Antiquity*, Cambridge, Ma. and London: Harvard University Press

Cramp, R. J. 1984(a). *Corpus of Anglo-Saxon Stone Sculpture, 1, County Durham and Northumberland*, Oxford: British Academy / Oxford University Press

Cramp, R. J. 1984(b). *The Hermitage and the Offshore Island* (National Maritime Museum Occasional Paper No. 4), London: National Maritime Museum

Doherty, C. 1985. The monastic town in early medieval Ireland, in H. B. Clarke and A. Simms (eds), *The Comparative History of Urban Origins in Non-Roman Europe: Ireland, Wales, Denmark, Germany, Poland and Russia from the ninth to the thirteenth centuries* (Brit Archaeol Rep, Int Ser, 255), 45–75, Oxford: BAR

Doyle, L. J. 1989. Saint Benedict: rules for monasteries, in P. J. Geary (ed), *Readings in Medieval History*, 180–215, Peterborough, Ontario: Broadview Press

Edson, E. 1997. *Mapping Time and Space: How medieval mapmakers viewed their world*, London: British Library

Ervynck, A. 1997. Following the rule? Fish and meat consumption in monastic communities in Flanders, in G. De Boe and F. Verhaeghe (eds), *Environment and Subsistence in Medieval Europe* (Papers of the 'Medieval Europe Brugge 1997' Conference, Vol. 9), 67–81, Zellik

Gneuss, H. 1981. A preliminary list of manuscripts written or owned in England up to 1100, *Anglo-Saxon England*, 9, 1–60

Gwynn, E. J. and Purton, W. J. 1911. The monastery of Tallaght, *Proc Royal Irish Acad*, 29 C, 115–80

Harlow, M. 1997. Male into Female won't go: gender and early Christian asceticism, in J. Moore and E. Scott (eds), *Invisible People and Processes. Writing Gender and Childhood into European Archaeology*, 169–77, Leicester: Leicester University Press

Herity, M. 1995. *Studies in the Layout, Building and Art in Stone of Early Irish Monasteries*, London: Pindar Press

Howlett, D. 1975. The provenance, date and structure of *De Abbatibus*, *Archaeologia Aeliana*, 5th ser., 3, 121–30

Kelly, F. 1998. *Early Irish Farming: a study based mainly on the law-texts of the 7th and 8th centuries AD* (Early Irish Law Series IV), Dublin: Institute for Advanced Studies

Marcus, R. A. 1990. *The End of Ancient Christianity*, Cambridge: Cambridge University Press

McCormick, F. 1997. Iona: the archaeology of the early monastery, in C. Bourke (ed), *Studies in the Cult of St Columba*, 45–68, Dublin: Four Courts Press

Meehan, D. (ed) 1958. *Adamnan's De Locis Sanctis. Scriptores Latini Hiberniae*, III, Dublin: Institute for Advanced Studies

O'Loughlin, T. 1997. Living in the Ocean, in C. Bourke (ed), *Studies in the Cult of St Columba*, 11–23, Dublin: Four Courts Press

O'Neill, T. 1997. Columba the Scribe, in C. Bourke (ed), *Studies in the Cult of St Columba*, 69–79, Dublin: Four Courts Press

O'Reilly, J. 1997. Reading the scriptures in the life of Columba, in C. Bourke (ed), *Studies in the Cult of St Columba*, 80–106, Dublin: Four Courts Press

O'Sullivan, D. 1985. An excavation in Holy Island Village, 1977, *Archaeologia Aeliana*, 5th ser., 13, 25–116

O'Sullivan, D. 1989. The plan of the Early Christian monastery on Lindisfarne: a fresh look at the evidence, in G. Bonner, D. Rollason and C. Stancliffe (eds), *St Cuthbert, His Cult and His Community to AD 1200*, 125–42, Woodbridge: Boydell Press

O'Sullivan, D. and Young, R. 1995. *Lindisfarne: Holy Island*, London: Batsford / English Heritage

Parsons, D. 1988. *Books and Buildings: Architectural description before and after Bede*, Jarrow: Jarrow Parochial Council

Peers, C. R. 1925. The inscribed and sculptured stones of Lindisfarne, *Archaeologia*, 74, 255–70

Selby, J. S. D. 1849. On the foundations of ancient buildings, and coins of the Saxon kingdom of Northumbria, recently discovered at Holy Island, *History of the Berwickshire Naturalists Club*, 11, 159–63

Sharpe, R. (trans) 1995. *Adomnan of Iona, Life of Columba*, Harmondsworth: Penguin Books

Sherley Price, L. (ed and trans) 1955. *Bede, A History of the English Church and People*, Harmondsworth: Penguin Books

Smyth, M. 1996. *Understanding the Universe in Seventh Century Ireland*, Woodbridge: Boydell Press

Stuart, J. (ed) 1856–67. *Sculptured Stones of Scotland*, 2 vols, Aberdeen: Spalding Club

Swan, L. 1985. Monastic proto-towns in early medieval Ireland: the evidence of aerial photography, plan analysis and survey, in H. B. Clarke and A. Simms (eds), *The*

Comparative History of Urban Origins in Non-Roman Europe: Ireland, Wales, Denmark, Germany, Poland and Russia from the ninth to the thirteenth centuries (Brit Archaeol Rep, Int Ser, 255), 77–102, Oxford: BAR

Van Neer, W. and Ervynck, A. 1996. Food rules and status: patterns of fish consumption in a monastic community, *Archaeofauna*, 5, 155–66

Webster, L. and Backhouse, J. (eds) 1991. *The Making of England. Anglo-Saxon art and culture 600–900*, London: British Museum Press

4
Monuments in a Landscape
The Early Medieval Sculpture of St David's

Nancy Edwards

Rosemary Cramp's research has centred upon the archaeology of the early medieval church, especially stone sculpture. Though her work has focused primarily on Anglo-Saxon England, and particularly on Northumbria, she has always maintained an enthusiastic interest in the early medieval archaeology of Celtic Britain and Ireland. During my student years in Durham she nurtured my interest in the carved stone crosses of early medieval Ireland and taught me many of the skills I have since employed in research on the early Christian archaeology of Wales, particularly the stone sculpture. This paper is offered as a token of gratitude to Rosemary for her inspiration and help.

Introduction

My subject is St David's, the most important ecclesiastical site in early medieval Wales. It was located within a religious landscape of lesser sites: chapels, cemeteries and holy wells. My intention here is to examine the large group of early medieval carved stone monuments from St David's and its environs. The earliest are located outside St David's, while those of the ninth century onwards are mainly from within the Cathedral Close. By studying the forms of these monuments, their ornament and inscriptions, it is possible to shed light upon the changing contacts between St David's and elsewhere, especially Ireland (including the Hiberno-Norse community) as well as likely influences emanating from Anglo-Saxon England and the Mediterranean.

St David's is located, as Asser, King Alfred's biographer, describes, in 'the remote, westernmost parts of Wales' (*Alfred*, ch 79). Yet it was the most important ecclesiastical foundation in early medieval Wales: a monastery with an early ascetic tradition (*Life of David*, chs 2, 21–32) and clear evidence of learning, the seat of a bishop, and by the eleventh century an established place of pilgrimage (*Ann. Camb.*, 1079, *recte* 1081).

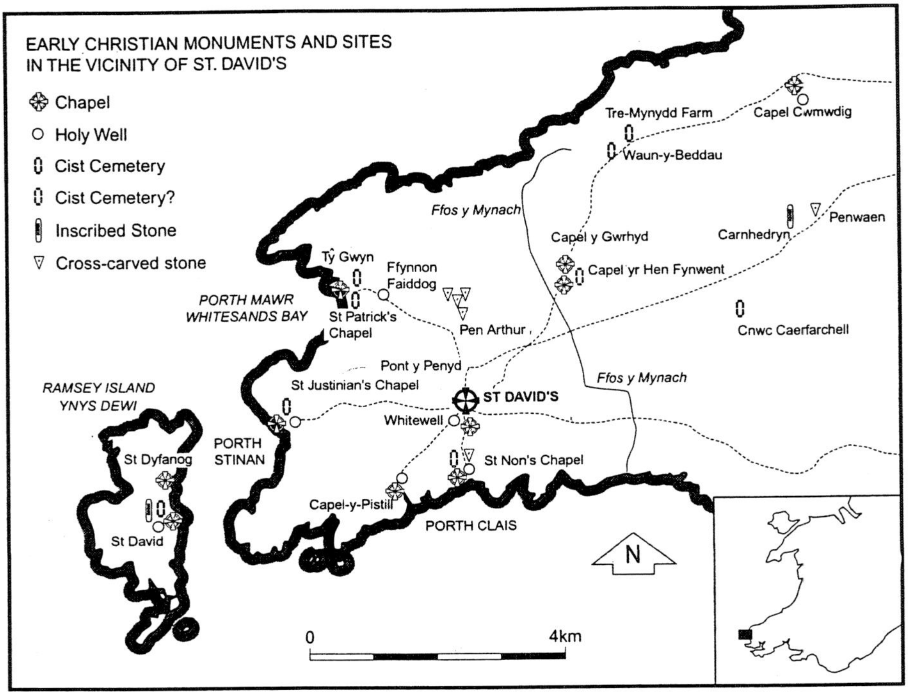

Fig. 4.1. The early medieval religious landscape of St David's and its environs (based on James 1993).

The significance of the site and the spread of the cult of its patron saint may be charted in the sparse documentary record both in Wales and elsewhere. Latin annals (Hughes 1980, 68–74) were compiled at St David's from the late eighth century onwards. Early entries were drawn partly from an Irish prototype and the inclusion of St David in the Martyrologies of Tallaght and of Oengus the Culdee *c.* 830 (*Mart. Tall.*, 20; Oengus, 80, 86; Ó Riain 1990) indicate the spread of his cult to Ireland. Likewise his appearance in the *Life* of St Paul de Léon by Wrmonoc in 887 (*Vie de Saint Paul*, 422) suggests his influence in Brittany. Alfred's invitation in 885 to Asser to join his intellectual circle (*Alfred*, 51–6, chs 79–80) testifies to St David's as a place of learning and the cult of the saint became known in Wessex around the same time (Harris 1940, 8–9). In Wales itself, evidence for the importance of the cult is most clearly seen in the vernacular poem *Armes Prydain* ('The Prophecy of Britain') *c.* 930, where David is portrayed as the patron saint of the Welsh in their struggle against the Anglo-Saxons (*Armes Prydain*), and the late eleventh century *Vita Davidis* (Life of David) by Rhygyfarch (d. 1099), the son of Bishop Sulien.

St David's is one of the largest parishes in Dyfed encompassing the *cantref* of Pebidiog, later known as Dewisland – the 'Land of David'. Geographically it is a peninsula with Ramsey Island (*Ynys Dewi*) at its south-western tip (Fig. 4.1). Consequently sea contact was formerly of great importance, not only around and across the Irish Sea – Ireland is only 80km away – but also along both shores of the Bristol Channel and beyond. The stunning beauty of the rocky, coastal scenery contrasts with the windswept moor and scrubland of the interior, much of which has now been tamed for grazing. Although hagiographical tradition suggests that the monastery may have originated nearby (*Life of David*, ch 14),[1] it was at the present site of St David's, in the small, steep-sided, sheltered valley of the River Alun, that it flourished. Its early medieval Welsh name, *Mynyw* (Latin: *Menevia*), is topographical, meaning a 'thicket' or 'brake', and the Irish called it *Cille Muine*. These were gradually replaced by St David's (Welsh: *Tŷ Ddewi*) in the twelfth century (Charles 1992, 283–4). Today the site is dominated by the late twelfth-century cathedral built by Bishop Peter de Leia which replaced the Romanesque building of Bernard, the first Norman bishop, consecrated in 1131, by the close wall, which was in existence before 1326, and by the bishop's palace built by Bishop Henry Gower (1328–47) (Evans 1991). There has been very little archaeological excavation on the site, but these later developments are likely to have destroyed most of the remains of the early medieval foundation, the buildings of which would almost certainly have been constructed of wood.[2] At any rate the only archaeological evidence for the pre-Norman period which has so far been identified is the stone sculpture, most of which has come to light built into the later fabric.

It would be a mistake, however, to view the early medieval monastery at St David's in isolation because, as Heather James (1993) has shown, the surrounding hinterland is dotted with smaller sites – chapels, cemeteries and wells – many of which, by the end of the eleventh century (*Life of David*), had been incorporated into a ritual landscape connected with the cult of the saint. On several of these sites there are also examples of early medieval sculpture (Fig. 4.1).

My intention here is to re-examine this large and diverse group of early medieval sculpture from St David's and its environs. Although many pieces are now fragmentary and the close dating of nearly all is fraught with difficulty, they nevertheless shed an interesting light on the monastery of St David's and its environs, and illuminate the different contacts between 'Dewisland' and the outside world in the early Middle Ages.

The early Latin-inscribed stone from Carnhedryn Farm

There are no early inscribed stones or other early sculpture from St David's itself. Indeed, the only definite early inscribed stone from the whole parish was found in 1895, acting as a gate-post on reclaimed moorland at Carnhedryn Farm (SM 799 279), probably not far from where it had once served as a grave-marker (Rhys 1896, 104–5; Macalister 1945, no 448; Nash-Williams 1950, no 370).[3] This rough, unshaped, approximately quadrangular, dolerite pillar (Fig.

4.2) is carved with a Latin inscription, lightly punched using a thin line, in two lines reading vertically downwards. In the past there was some doubt as to whether the first letter was a P or an R, but it is quite clearly an R with the diagonal stroke veering towards the horizontal, a characteristically Insular feature. The first word should therefore be read as RINACI, a personal name in the genitive case. There has also been considerable discussion of the second word NOMENA and its meaning. *Nomena* is a variant of *nomina* showing the influence of living Vulgar Latin in Merovingian Gaul, whereby 'i' is frequently written as 'e' (Jackson 1953, 191). It is therefore in the neuter plural. There are a number of early Christian funerary inscriptions, particularly in fourth-century North Africa, which include the name of the deceased, often a saint or martyr, in the genitive, preceded by *nomen* or *nomina*. It has been suggested (Vendryes 1955) with reference to these inscriptions that *nomen* (literally 'name') takes on the meaning of 'person', with the subsidiary meanings of 'mortal remains' and 'relics' when it is used in the plural. *Rinaci nomena* may therefore be translated as 'The remains (or relics) of Rinacus'. The use of *nomena* in this inscription is undoubtedly Christian and suggests external contacts, quite possibly with North Africa, or alternatively with the Mediterranean via Gaul. The only other version of the formula found in Wales is on an inscribed stone from Llandanwg (Gwynedd) where it appears as *nomine* (Macalister 1945, no 414; Nash-Williams 1950, no 279; Thomas, C. 1994, 204–5). The parallel connection has also been noted (Rhys 1896, 107; Vendryes 1955) between *nomen* and the Old Irish *anm* 'name' found on some of the later ogam stones in Ireland. The *Rinaci* stone is difficult to date. The exclusive use of Roman capitals could suggest the late fifth century, but the first half of the sixth seems equally possible. This period spans other contacts with the Mediterranean archaeologically evidenced by the imported pottery termed A and B ware (Campbell 1996, 85–8).

The early monastery founded by St David in the sixth century, and called *Cille Muine* by the Irish, had an early ascetic tradition. This might also fit into an Irish and Mediterranean milieu, having more in common with the early ascetic monasteries with *cell* names in Ireland – to be expected in view of the Irish settlement of Dyfed at the end of the Roman period – and the ascetic monasticism of the eastern Mediterranean and North Africa than with the more temperate monastic villa estates of Gaul which may also be identifiable in south-east Wales at Llandough (Thomas, C. 1995; Owen-John 1988; Thomas, A. and Holbrook, N. 1994).

The cross-incised pillar from St Non's Chapel

A different and slightly later tradition is represented by a rough, tapering, quadrangular dolerite pillar some 1.15 m tall, one face of which is deeply incised with a simple linear Latin cross with a ring (Nash-Williams 1950, no 372) (Fig. 4.3). It was first noted in the mid nineteenth century built into St

Fig. 4.2 (on the left). Latin-inscribed stone, Carnhedryn Farm.
Fig. 4.3 (on the right). Cross-incised stone, St Non's Chapel.

Non's Chapel (SM 7507 2434) (Jones, W. B. and Freeman, E. A. 1856, 227), a ruinous quadrangular building of uncertain date with an adjacent holy well which overlooks the rocky coast near Porth Clais at the mouth of the River Alun (James 1993, 108; Evans 1991, 53–5). It is clearly a religious site of early origin. There was already a church there in the late eleventh century, mentioned in Rhygyfarch's *Life of St David* (ch 6) as the place where Non gave birth to the saint, and probable long-cist graves were uncovered there at the beginning of the nineteenth century (Fenton 1903, 63). The cross-carved stone might have functioned as a grave-marker, possibly originally associated with one of these graves. Alternatively, because of its size, it could have marked the cemetery, either standing as a focus amongst the graves, or, in the manner of the pillar at Reask, Co. Kerry, on the edge of the burial ground (Fanning 1981, 86, fig 6). There is a very similar pillar incised with a Latin cross with a ring (Nash-Williams 1950, no 395) from the nearby parish of St Elvis, where it may also originally have been associated with a long-cist cemetery (Laws and Owen 1908, 37.6; Charles 1992, 330), and another from St Kennox Farm near Llawhaden (Nash-Williams 1950, no 342; Charles 1992, ii, 422–3). Such cross-incised stones are notoriously difficult to date because of their simplicity, but there is a degree of consensus, supported to some extent by recent excavated examples from Whithorn, Galloway (Craig 1997, 433), that they begin in the late sixth or early seventh century (Thomas, C. 1971, 112–25) and reflect Christian contacts around and across the Irish Sea. The St Non's example, when compared with other, more complex cross-carved monuments from the vicinity (see below), would seem to fit best into a late sixth-, seventh- or eighth-century horizon.

The inscribed stone from Ramsey Island

Not all the early sculpture associated with St David's demonstrates Irish Sea contacts. One of the most interesting pieces is a small fragment of local mudstone (height 255 mm max.) from Ramsey Island (Fig. 4.4) which was found in 1967 in the garden of the Farmhouse (SM 7059 2373) (Okasha 1970). This is also the site of a long-cist cemetery (Fenton 1903, 69; Laws and Owen 1908, 44.8; RCAHMW 1925, no 1003), 'headstones' from which may still have been visible in 1963 (Okasha 1970, 68). It is very probably the site of St David's Chapel mentioned by George Owen (1892, 112; see also James 1993, fig 14.1). Unfortunately the slab is broken on all four sides and the surface of the stone is rather uneven. At the top are the fragmentary remains of one vertical, deeply and sharply incised line and to the right three narrower, more lightly incised diagonal lines. Each terminates in a drilled hole; that at the bottom of the vertical line is more clearly marked than the other three. Elisabeth Okasha (1970, 68) suggested that these lines and holes could be part of a sundial. This seems very likely but difficult to prove due to the fragmentary nature of the remains. Although the lines are not enclosed in a characteristic half-circular frame and the spaces between them are rather uneven, they do appear to radiate. The number and position of the extant lines do not resemble those on either of the two definite Welsh sundials from Clynnog and Tywyn (Gwynedd) (Nash-Williams 1950, no 85; Thomas, W. G. 1989), which are comparable with those in Ireland. On the other hand, they are quite similar to Anglo-Saxon sundials, notably the probable ninth-century example, Bishopstone 1, Sussex, where the frame is less marked than usual, the lines are spaced in a similar way to those visible on the Ramsey Island fragment, and the terminals of the

Fig. 4.4. Fragmentary inscribed stone with sundial(?), Ramsey Island.

lines are likewise indicated by drill-holes; however, the vertical line and those at 45° have crossed ends with drill-holes at their terminals (Tweddle, Biddle and Kjølbye-Biddle 1995, 124–5, figs. 6–7).

Towards the bottom of the Ramsey Island fragment is a horizontal one-line inscription, lightly incised, which most probably reads S[AT]VRNBIV. The second letter, which is obscured by a vertical fault in the stone, is most likely to be an A, though no horizontal crossbar is visible. The third letter is most probably a T. The left vertical appears to continue to the bottom of the fragment and could be the result of subsequent damage. *Satvrnbiv* is an Old Welsh name and it would be very tempting to link it with *Saturnbiu Hail* ('the Generous'), the bishop (?) of St David's (*Miniu*) who died in 831 (*Welsh Annals*, 48, 89; *Ann. Camb.*, 13; Leland, VII, 140; Okasha 1970, 69). The lettering of the inscription (see below) is not inconsistent with such a date, and therefore a link is possible, but the identification certainly cannot be proved since there is no accompanying title or epithet. A Saturnbiu, possibly the same man, is also mentioned twice in the marginalia (5, 8) of the St Chad Gospels which were added during the ninth century when the manuscript was in Llandeilo Fawr, Carmarthenshire (*Llan Dâv*, xlvi, xlvii; Jenkins and Owen 1983, 52–3, 56–7).

The inscription is incised in Insular display letters with a mixture of full, half and split serifs, a feature unique amongst the early medieval inscriptions of Wales. Such letters are characteristic of Insular manuscripts, for example the Lindisfarne Gospels, the St Chad's Gospels and the Book of Kells (Alexander 1978, nos 9, 21, 52) but they are also occasionally found on metalwork, notably the Ardagh Chalice (Higgitt 1994, 126). The letters in manuscripts and on metalwork may in fact have been influenced by epigraphic forms. There are quite a number of examples on Northumbrian sculpture: these include some of the round-headed grave-markers of mid seventh- to mid eighth-century date from such sites as Hartlepool, Lindisfarne and Monkwearmouth (Cramp 1984, e.g. figs. 600, 1119, 1122, 1129), as well as some other sculpture, for example the Ruthwell Cross (Okasha 1971, no 105; Cassidy 1992, pls 11–32) datable to the first half of the eighth century, the eighth-century crosshead Carlisle 1 (Bailey and Cramp 1988, illus. 96), the late seventh- to early ninth-century stele(?) York Minster 20 (Lang 1991, illus. 80) and two eighth- or ninth-century fragments from Thornhill and Whitby (Okasha 1971, nos 116, 133–4). However, Anglo-Saxon examples outside Northumbria are rare (Okasha 1971, nos 18, 120–1). Likewise there are only occasional examples from Celtic areas: two probable eighth-century inscriptions, Lethnot and Tarbat, from Scotland (Higgitt 1982; Macalister 1945, no 509; 1949, no 924B), two from Toureen Peakaun in Ireland (Lionard 1961, fig. 3), and one of late seventh- or eighth-century date from Lanrivoaré, Brittany (Davies *et al.* 2000, Finistère 2, 113–20).

If the letters are examined in more detail, it may be noted that the S is a rectangular form of the capital with a central vertical and short, straight horizontals branching off to left and right before the ends (Higgitt 1994, 230–1, S4). This form is paralleled on Carlisle 1, the Ardagh Chalice (reversed) and in Insular manuscripts including the St Chad's Gospels (p 221) and the Book of Kells (fol 15v). The A has no known parallels but the T may be a more complex form of those in the Lindisfarne Gospels fol 3r (end of l. 4) and St Chad's Gospels p 5 (two examples) but with the addition of a loop to the right and a horizontal at the base of the ascender to the left as well as the right. There are two types of V: the first is a Roman capital form (Higgitt 1994, 232 U/V3) which may be compared with that in the Lindisfarne Gospels (fol 29) and one on Whitby DCCXXXIII; the second, also a capital but with intersecting diagonals (Higgitt 1994, 232, U/V4), is also found on Whitby DCCXXXIII (Okasha 1971, no 134) and in manuscripts including the St Chad's Gospels (pp 143, 221). The B is a rectangular version of the half uncial letter with a very short protruding vertical stroke with a loop on the right which finds parallels in the Lindisfarne Gospels (Higgitt 1994, 225, B2). The I, R and N (Higgitt 1994, 227–30, I, N1, R1) are common forms. In general Insular display capitals seem to have been used on sculpture, in manuscripts and occasionally on metalwork, perhaps as early as the second half of the seventh century and continued until the early ninth century, though the only approximate fixed point in the chronology is the Lindisfarne Gospels (late seventh to early eighth century, *c.* 698?) (Alexander 1978, no 9). The forms of the letters on the Ramsey Island inscription seem to suggest an eighth- or possibly early ninth-century date.

To the left of the S are three very lightly scratched straight lines which may be identified as a second and smaller S. This is certainly secondary and might have been added to explain the unusual form of the display letter S in the primary inscription. Above the inscription is a very lightly scratched, rather uneven, linear cross. It has the appearance of a graffito and contrasts with the relative clarity of the rest of the carving. It too is likely to be secondary.

If the fragment functioned as a sundial, as seems likely, the inscription most probably accompanied it. Therefore S[AT]VRNBIV is most likely to be the name of the patron, though the name of the sculptor is also possible. This may be compared with the personal name, EADRI[C], on Bishopstone 1. The presence of a sundial would suggest a monastic foundation, most probably a hermitage which would have functioned as an offshoot of the monastery at St David's.[4] Both the form of the sundial and the use of Insular display letters suggest contacts with Anglo-Saxon England, though the presence of the St Chad Gospels in Llandeilo Fawr demonstrates that the models for the display letters would have been readily available in south-west Wales if not in the *scriptorium* at St David's itself.

Sculpture associated with St David's

Probably the earliest piece of sculpture associated with the monastery at St David's was found shortly before 1879, during restoration of the Cathedral (Allen 1896, 293; Nash-Williams 1950, no 377) (Fig. 4.5). It is the top-left corner of a large, rectangular sandstone slab (height 685 mm) which may be reconstructed to measure approximately 680 mm wide and, judging by the proportions of the cross-head, perhaps as much as 1.8 m tall. It was presumably designed to stand upright. The form of the cross-head with its ring, rounded armpits, and elongated top cross-arm (Allen and Anderson 1903, ii, 52, no 102A), is a common form in both Ireland and Scotland. The surviving interspace within the ring is more deeply sunken (the punch-marks may still be clearly seen) than the rest of the background around the crosshead. The cross-head is surrounded by narrow, perimeter roll mouldings. Punch-marks are also visible on the surface of the cross-head which is carved in medium relief with rather poorly planned, irregular interlace knotwork, based largely on an Adcock Encircled C pattern (Cramp 1984, xxxvii) using a strand with a median groove. At the end of the left cross-arm the strands terminate in two confronted dragonesque beasts shown in profile. The upper has the remains of a pointed ear, almond-shaped eye, curled upper jaw and teeth(?). Between the two beasts a third strand terminates in a human head, shown face-on with fragmentary facial features. Confronted dragonesque or serpentine beasts with a human head or figure set between them or dragonesque beasts grasping human heads in their jaws are a feature of late eighth- and early ninth-century Insular metalwork. A good parallel is provided by the crest of an Irish bell(?) shrine of probable early ninth-century date from Killua Castle, which has an *orans* figure flanked by confronted serpentine beasts with spiralled jaws (Youngs 1989, no 137). There are also examples on Insular sculpture, notably the ninth-century Ardchattan slab, Argyll, where the interlace on the top cross-arm terminates in a central human figure holding a book with dragonesque beasts on either side (RCAHMS 1975, 110–11, fig. 99; Edwards 1990, 39–40, 53–5).

In the top-left corner is an angel shown in profile facing right with hair, a very large outlined, almond-shaped eye, pointed nose, traces of a mouth, pointed chin, a small upper body and three wings, each divided horizontally into two by a relief band and terminating at the base in a spiral which together form a triskele. Macalister (1931) suggested the three wings were representative of six, thereby identifying it as a seraphim. It may be closely compared with the similarly stylized angels on the Irish eighth-century crucifixion plaque from St John's, Rinnagan, near Athlone, Co. Westmeath (Youngs 1989, no 133). Angels are also found in identical positions on the Class 2 Pictish cross-slabs Eassie and Glamis 1 (Allen and Anderson 1903, iii, figs 231A, 233A), where they have four wings with spiral terminals.

Overall this monument has parallels with Insular metalwork and sculpture in both Ireland and Scotland and is most likely to reflect contacts with Ireland during the ninth century. Although cross-slabs are found elsewhere in Wales (Nash-Williams 1950, pls LIV-LV), comparisons are not close.

Secondly, there is a fragmentary local sandstone cross-head (Nash-Williams 1950, no 378) (Fig. 4.6) which was first noted in the garden of the Chancellor's House at the north end of the Cathedral Close in the mid nineteenth century (Westwood 1876–9, 129; Allen 1905, 89). It is possible that this find-spot could reflect the original location of the cross which might have stood at the edge of the monastic enclosure. It consists of two opposing horizontal(?) cross-arms of a cross with a ring and rounded armpits with a small roll in the centre, expanded arms and the remains of cabled roll-mouldings on the angles. The ring was positioned near the ends of the cross-arms but only the stubs remain. The cross-head is carved in medium rounded relief on both broad faces which are decorated in a similar way. In the centre of the cross-head is a roundel carved with a rosette surrounded by a roll-moulding. The cross-arms are decorated with a four-strand plait with bifurcations, using a strand with a median groove; it continues as a single strand around the roundel. At the end of the complete surviving cross-arm are two slightly curved, parallel, vertical roll-mouldings.

Originally this fragment would have been part of a large and impressive freestanding cross. The original diameter of the cross-head may be recon-

Fig. 4.5 (above). Fragmentary cross-slab, St David's Cathedral.
Fig. 4.6 (below). Fragmentary cross-head, St David's Cathedral Close.

structed as approximately 930 mm; it could therefore have been in the region of 3 m tall. The two parallel roll-mouldings on the ends of the cross-arms on both broad faces are positioned directly above and below the stubs of the ring. This suggests that the mouldings were there to give the impression of a continuous ring passing over the cross-arms. The presence of rolls in the armpits is a characteristic of some Irish crosses of ninth- and early tenth-century date (Harbison 1992, ii, figs 343, 345, 472, 496). The interlace is simple but the use of bifurcated strands may be a late feature indicative of Viking influence found elsewhere at St David's (see below) and also on a cross-slab at Nevern (Nash-Williams 1950, no 359). The cable-mouldings and possibly the rosette may indicate the influence of metalwork. The original form of the monument is impossible to reconstruct, but it could have been similar to the badly damaged cross at Coychurch, Glamorgan (Nash-Williams 1950, no 194; RCAHMW 1976, no 934). A tenth- or early eleventh-century date seems likely.

Even less can be said about the fragmentary lower part of a sizable shaft (height 790 mm), which was probably once part of another large cross. It is interesting to note that it is carved from Ordovician dolerite from Carn Meini located at least 40km to the east in the Preseli hills. It has subsequently been cut down, hollowed out and reshaped, probably for use as a holy water stoop (Nash-Williams 1950, no 379). It has the remains of a six-line horizontal inscription in incised minuscules but only a few letters can now be read. Macalister's reconstruction (1949, no 1040), which included the name of David, is certainly untenable.

The grave-marker (Nash-Williams 1950, no 382; Macalister 1949, no 1039) commemorating Hedd and Isaac, the sons of Bishop Abraham (1078–80), who was killed in a Viking raid on St David's (*Brut*, 30–1), is of particular significance, not only because it is datable to the late eleventh or early twelfth century, but also because it has a number of features which appear on other grave-markers from St David's and its environs (see below), making it possible to identify a group of sculpture which seems to span a century or more before the Norman takeover under Bishop Bernard in 1115. This time-span included the period when Sulien, the famous scholar from Llanbadarn Fawr, Ceredigion, was bishop (1073–78; 1080–85) and when his son Rhygyfarch wrote the Life of St David.[5]

The grave-marker was found in 1891 during Cathedral restoration (Dean of St David's 1892; Westwood 1892). It is an incomplete slab of local sandstone (height 685 mm) with a rounded head (Fig. 4.7). It is carved on both broad faces and was therefore designed to be free-standing. Face A is decorated with a cross with a double ring and stem (now fragmentary). A medium relief Latin cross with slightly expanded arms and a slightly lower relief, flat perimeter moulding defined by a finely incised line springs from the outer ring, which is undecorated. At the bottom the outer ring meets the stem which contracts as it goes down. The stem has a double perimeter roll-moulding which bifurcates on the left to form a triangular shape with incised lines inside. Below

Fig. 4.7. Cross-carved grave-marker commemorating Hedd and Isaac, Face A, St David's Cathedral.

is a roughly triangular sunken area with punched tool-marks clearly visible and a raised, rounded pellet with a flat top in the centre. Within the outer ring is an equal-arm cross with a ring and slightly expanded cross-arms carved in high relief. The interspaces are deeply sunken and tooled. The centre of the cross-head is carved with a closed-circuit interlace pattern of four Adcock Simple E elements using a strand with a finely incised median groove. The cross-arms are also carved with pairs of Simple E elements separated by glides using a similar strand. Those at the ends of the cross-arms are distorted and the interlace strands flow into frets composed of 'Z' elements, which are placed clockwise and anti-clockwise in alternate quadrants.

This cross form is unusual and difficult to parallel, though the triangular areas beneath the ring are possibly reminiscent of very stylized foliage which might suggest that Romanesque influences were already reaching south-west Wales. However, the frets and interlace are more conservative and are also characteristic of other pieces associated with the St David's area (see below).

In contrast, on Face C (recently removed from wall) there is an incomplete, plain, outline Latin cross carved in relief with expanded cross-arms, triangular armpits and a slightly elongated top cross-arm. The shaft expands towards the base (Westwood 1892, 78–9).

In addition, on Face A there are finely incised horizontal monograms in each interspace of the upper cross which read 'alpha' (top left) and 'omega' (top right), and 'Jesus' (bottom left) and 'Christus' (bottom right). The inscriptions are in a mixture of Greek and Latin letters, some majuscules, some minuscules, some with serifs. The alpha has a handle-bar with a horizontal bar across the top and a suspension mark above; the outer strokes of the omega meet in the centre and the central stroke is extended upwards terminating in a short horizontal bar with a swung suspension mark above.

The use of alpha and omega and the abbreviated sacred monograms in the interspaces around the cross is also found on two smaller grave-markers carved from local waterworn boulders found within the Cathedral Close (Nash-Williams 1950, no 380; Craster 1957).[6] The larger is 560 mm in height and carved on both broad faces. Face A (Fig. 4.8) has a quite deeply punched, double-outline Latin cross with similar alpha, omega and the sacred monogram abbreviations in their alternative form (with Greek sigma), all with swung suspension marks, in the interspaces. Face C has a deeply and broadly punched linear Latin cross. There is a further example from Pen-Arthur Farm outside St David's (see below). The type also spread beyond St David's to other sites in Pembrokeshire at Walton West, St Edrens and possibly St Ishmaels (Kay 1958; Nash-Williams 1950, nos 392–3; RCAHMW 1925, no 1051, iii).[7] Nash-Williams (1950, 208–9) suggested, convincingly, that the cross with the alpha and omega and sacred monograms was intended to symbolize the crucifixion and their use at St David's probably reflects Irish influence (Bischoff 1990, 154). The sacred monograms are found on sculpture perhaps as early as the mid eighth century on Tullylease 1, Co. Cork (Henderson and Okasha 1992) but there are closer parallels with later graveslabs which also

Fig. 4.8. Cross-carved grave-marker with inscriptions, Face A, St David's Cathedral Close.

include an alpha and omega from Church Island, Lough Currain, Co. Kerry, Dunleer and Kells, Co. Meath and two from Glendalough, Co. Wicklow (Macalister 1949, nos 578, 585, 887–8, 917). One of those from Glendalough, now destroyed, commemorated Corpre Mac Cathail, an anchorite who died in 1013.

The inscription in the top-left corner of the slab commemorating the sons of Bishop Abraham is of great importance. It is poorly placed and planned, appearing almost as an afterthought, and is framed by a horizontal line above and an irregular vertical line to the right. It is a horizontal Latin inscription in five lines and reads:

+PONTIFICIS
ABRAHAM·
FILII·HIC·HED
7ISAC·QUIES
CUNT·

+Pontificis Abraham ·filii ·hic ·Hed 7(=et) Isac ·quiescunt·

It may be translated 'Here rest Hed [Hedd] and Isac [Isaac] the sons of Bishop Abraham'. The inscription has an initial cross and is in uneven letters with a mixture of majuscule and minuscule forms. The flat, attenuated D (l. 3) is a typical late eleventh-century type (pers. comm. Helen McKee). Some of the words are interpunctuated with single points set above the line. The formula, *hic quiescit (-unt)*, is very long-lived but it was reintroduced into Britain after the Norman Conquest and its use at St David's is likely to be the result of such contacts (Nash-Williams 1950, 212). Hed is a Welsh name (modern Welsh, Hedd) while the other two are Biblical. Bishop Abraham is here termed *pontifex*[8] rather than the more usual *episcopus*. It has been suggested (Nash-Williams 1938, 54–6) that the grave-marker should be be dated to 1078–80, the years of his episcopate. However this is not necessarily so, since Abraham's sons may well have outlived him; instead, 1078 provides a *terminus post quem*. Overall, despite the poorly placed inscription, the grave-marker is a well-executed monument using Insular ornament, but there are also details which suggest the beginnings of Romanesque influence.

Another incomplete, upright grave-marker found during Cathedral restoration is now built into the altar of the Chapel of the Holy Trinity with a further plain, cross-carved grave-marker beside it (Nash-Williams 1950, nos 383, 381) (Fig. 4.9). The former consists of a carefully smoothed piece of local Caerbwdy sandstone which would originally have had a rounded top. On the upper half of the face is an equal-arm cross with a ring carved in low, flat relief with a slightly recessed, narrower outer ring beyond the ends of the cross-arms. The interspaces within the ring are slightly recessed and traces of punched tooling are still visible. The cross has a circular centre with a small compass-point in the middle to aid construction. The cross-arms are slightly expanded with triangular terminals.

The cross is decorated with finely but roughly incised interlace. In the centre of the cross is a circle of irregular ring-knots (Cramp 1984, xlv, fig 27, iv). A strand from one of these extends upwards to form a small, asymmetrically placed cross in the centre. The terminals of the three cross-arms each bifurcate to form adorsed curlicues, the centres of which have been cut away. The ring-knots extend on to the lower cross-arm where they terminate in a series of rough interlace strands. The cross-arm terminal is plain but the edge is delineated by an incised line to form a flat perimeter moulding. The top cross-arm is incised with misunderstood interlace and the right cross-arm with a crude plait. The left cross-arm is roughly divided into horizontal bands. The topmost is decorated with zig-zags; the middle with rough interlace including a double ring-knot (Adcock Simple F); the lowest is cabled. Strands from all three interlace in the cross-arm terminal, the lowest part of which is lightly incised with cross-hatching. Similarly the upper part of the outer recessed ring is very lightly scratched with cross-hatching, as is the lower left arc of the inner ring. The outer part of the lower half of the outer recessed ring is incised with a thin band of 'Z' element frets. Below the cross is a series of finely incised compass-drawn arcs and circles, some overlapping.

In addition there is a lightly incised Latin inscription in the four interspaces of the cross-head, immediately inside the inner ring. It reads clockwise from the bottom left: MATHEVS (written right to left and reversed apart from the H) / MARCVS / LVC[AS] / [I]OHANNES ('Matthew / Mark / Luke / John'), the names of the four Evangelists. Nash-Williams (1950, 211) suggested that the inscription was in Romanesque-style capitals but it also includes Insular majuscule forms such as handle-bar A and minuscule H. Some letters have serifs and some have inset panels.

The form of the cross with its double ring may be closely compared with the adjacent grave-marker (Fig. 4.9). However, the elegantly carved relief and counter-relief of the cross contrast sharply with the less accomplished, lightly incised inscription and ornament which appears incomplete. It may therefore be suggested that these were additions, either to a plain cross-slab, or one that had been roughed out but not completed. The layout of the ornament and some of the patterns used – for example the frets – are found on other grave-markers from the vicinity of St David's (see below) as well as on the grave-slab commemorating the sons of Abraham. However, the sculptor seems to have little understanding of the construction of interlace patterns: the style of carving gives the impression of a motif-piece rather than a competently executed, finished product. The interlace includes plait-work and ring-knots which recall Hiberno-Norse interlace, for example the ring-knots on a wooden knife-handle from Dublin (Lang 1988, 56, fig 66), though I have been unable to find any close parallels. The ornament on this monument is probably of a similar date to no 382 but the apparent use of Hiberno-Norse-influenced interlace adds another decorative ingredient. This is not surprising since the annals record three Viking raids on St David's in this period (*Brut* 1073, 1080,

1091) and the presence of Viking place-names in the area suggest settlement (Davies 1982, 116–20, figs 25, 45). The region is likely to have been the subject of increased Hiberno-Norse activity from the late tenth century onwards as trade-links developed between Dublin and south-west Britain (Wallace 1988, 156).

Fig. 4.9. Two cross-carved grave-markers, St David's Cathedral.

The monuments from Pen-Arthur Farm

Four carved stone monuments (Nash-Williams 1950, nos 373–6) came to light in the nineteenth century to the north of Pen-Arthur Farm, either built into field walls or re-used as gate-posts (Tegid 1847, 373; Jones, W. B. and Freeman, E. A. 1856, 234; Westwood 1876–9, 128). It was originally reported that they were found on a nearby moor but a different location, 'around a well famous for its healing powers' (Anon 1864, 352), has generally been accepted. This was subsequently identified as Ffynnon Pen-Arthur (SM 7508 2656) to the east of the farmhouse (Jones, F. 1954, 17; James, H. 1993, 109). However, recent research by Peter Marks has shown that the association with Ffynnon Pen-Arthur is incorrect. Instead nos 373 and 374 were found near Ffynnon Parc-y-Berth (SM 7490 2680) two fields north of the farmhouse. Marks has argued persuasively that in fact they did originally came from nearby moorland to the west (SM 747 269) where a partially buried stone with an inscription and a ring-cross, known as 'Arthur's Stone' – almost certainly no 376 – was described and illustrated by an anonymous late sixteenth-century writer and reproduced by Browne Willis (1717, 64–5; Atkins 1946). A small parcel of land at this location known as 'Arthur Stone' was still in the possession of the Bishop of St David's in the late nineteenth century (Pembrokeshire Record Office DB/13/96). It is likely therefore that this parcel of land had been retained by the Bishop because it was on the site of an ancient graveyard located between St Patrick's Chapel and cemetery at Whitesands Bay and St David's itself (Fig. 4.1). The grave-markers were cleared during the first half of the nineteenth century when the land was improved.

The first monument is a rough, unshaped quadrangular pillar of local gabbro lightly punched with an outline Latin cross with a linear Latin cross inside, both with bifid terminals (Nash-Williams 1950, no 373) (Fig. 4.10). A variety of cross-carved stones, the majority of which probably functioned as upright grave-markers, are characteristic of North Pembrokeshire, with a local concentration of outline crosses at Llanwnda and in the Gwaun Valley (Lewis 1976, 183, figs 2–3). The closest comparisons may be made with two monuments from Llanllawer and one from Llanychaer (Nash-Williams 1950, nos 323–4, 337). The simplicity of many of the designs makes such cross-carved stones extremely difficult to date. They could span several centuries, though it seems more likely that the majority were produced over a much shorter space of time, perhaps the ninth to eleventh centuries. The North Pembrokeshire distribution suggests continuing contacts across the Irish Sea.

The other three monuments (Nash-Williams 1950, nos 374–6) are all rough, unshaped blocks of local gabbro and dolerite carved with cruciform motifs set in roundels decorated with a fret pattern border of 'Z' elements carved in low relief. In the centre of no 374 (Fig. 4.11) is a well-executed, closed-circuit interlace pattern of four Simple E elements using a strand with a median groove; the pattern forms an incised equal-arm cross in the middle. The pattern in the centre of no 375 (Fig. 4.12) is a complex cross motif of diagonal frets

4.10

4.11

4.12

4.13

Four carved stones from Pen-Arthur Farm. Fig. 4.10. Cross-carved pillar. Fig. 4.11. Stone with interlace roundel. Fig. 4.12. Stone with fret-carved roundel. Fig. 4.13. Cross-carved grave-marker commemorating Gurmarc, Face A.

adapted to a circular shape. A drilled hole is visible in the middle of the roundel and was used with ruler and compasses in the construction of the ornament. The fret pattern is remarkably sophisticated since it contains several different types of equal-arm cross symbol within the pattern. First, there is an outline cross with right-angle bars across the arms; second, there is a diagonal cross with triangular cross-arms; third, there is a linear cross with a ring round the outside; and lastly, there is a smaller outline cross with triangular terminals. The equal-arm cross on Face A of no. 376 (Fig. 4.13) has a double ring, small rounded armpits and triangular recessed areas in the interspaces within the ring. Above the cross are incised an alpha and omega, as well as the sacred monograms and below GURMARC in minuscules, the name of the man commemorated. The form of the 'a' in Gurmarc is of Welsh reformed minuscule type which was current during the ninth and tenth centuries (pers. comm. Helen McKee). On Face C is a smaller outline cross with a ring. The use of the ring with Z-shaped frets on all three monuments, the interlace roundel on no 374 and the alpha and omega and sacred monogram inscriptions on no 376 all indicate parallels with St David's no 382 (Fig. 4.7) but there are no signs of Romanesque influence. A tenth-century date seems likely.

Conclusion

In all there are eighteen extant pieces of early medieval carved stone from the parish of St David's, both from the monastery itself and from cemeteries in the vicinity.[9] Other cross-carved stones appear to have marked the pilgrim route from the east.[10] The St David's monuments are a diverse group which together span the late fifth or sixth century up to the late eleventh or early twelfth century. As might be expected, contacts are strongest across the Irish Sea and are evident throughout; in addition, the advent of Hiberno-Norse influences has been suggested at the end of the period. However, there is also evidence for direct or indirect contacts with the Mediterranean or Gaul in the late fifth or sixth centuries and with Anglo-Saxon England in the eighth or early ninth century, though, interestingly, not in the late ninth century when Asser was at the court of King Alfred. Romanesque influences were probably reaching St David's by about 1100.

The earliest monuments from Carnhedryn Farm and St Non's come from outside St David's. The remainder have a close association with the monastery itself or with the probable hermitage on Ramsey Island (*Ynys Dewi*). Although the earliest surviving sculpture from St David's begins around the ninth century (Fig. 4.5), the majority of the monuments from the Cathedral Close and Pen-Arthur Farm are centred on the century or more before the installation in 1115 of the first Norman bishop, Bernard, and their influence can also be detected on some monuments elsewhere in Pembrokeshire at this time. This seems to signal the increasing prestige of St David's in the eleventh century as a place of pilgrimage and burial, set within the wider religious landscape indicated in Rhygyfarch's *Life* of the saint.

Acknowledgements

This study stems from research for a larger project to compile a new corpus of early medieval inscribed stones and stone sculpture for Wales. This project is funded by the University of Wales Board of Celtic Studies, the University of Wales Collaboration Fund, the British Academy, the Royal Commisssion on Ancient and Historic Monuments Wales and the Cambrian Archaeological Association with the assistance of the National Museums and Galleries of Wales. I would like to thank Heather Jackson for the geological identifications, Peter Marks for giving me access to his unpublished research, Dr Helen McKee for her comments on the palaeography, Dr Huw Pryce for his help with documentary references and Professor Patrick Sims-Williams for help with the Ramsey Island inscription. I am also grateful to the Very Revd J. Wyn Evans, Dean of St David's, for access to the stones in the care of the Cathedral and Dr Mark Redknap of the National Museums and Galleries of Wales for access to the Ramsey Island fragment. All photographs are Crown copyright: RCAHMW except Fig. 4.3 which is reproduced by permission of the NMGW. Figure 4.1 is by L. A. Dutton.

Notes

1. The *Life* of St David (chs 49–53) also indicates an association of the saint with Ceredigion. See also the Idnert inscribed stone (Thomas, C. 1996).
2. The site would undoubtedly benefit from a closer examination of the topography and a programme of geophysical survey which might reveal earlier features. I am grateful to Heather James for discussing this with me.
3. The stone was not found on Carnhedryn Uchaf Farm as first reported (RCAHMW 1925, no 941). It is now located in Llanhowel Church (SM 7998 2801).
4. The grouping of a major monastery with a nearby island hermitage where monks could retire for prayer and contemplation is found elsewhere in Wales, for example Penmon and Ynys Seiriol (Anglesey) and Penally and Caldey Island (Pembrokeshire). The same arrangement is found in Ireland, for example Roscrea and Mona Incha (Co. Tipperary) and in England, for example Lindisfarne and the Inner Farne.
5. For more on the intellectual and artistic achievements of the family of Sulien, see Lloyd 1941; Lapidge 1972–4; Edwards 1995.
6. A third grave-marker carved from a similar waterworn boulder is decorated on both broad faces with a lightly punched Latin cross with a ring, but there are no inscriptions (unpublished).
7. Caerbwdy sandstone, which is local to St David's, is also used for two monuments from St Edrens and the grave-marker from St Ishmaels. St Ishmaels was one of the seven bishop houses of Dyfed indicating another link with St David's (Charles-Edwards 1971, 251).

8. The same term for bishop is also found in Ieuan ap Sulien's poem *Carmen Iohannis de uita et familia Sulgeni* (1085 x 91), line 135, *Pontifex Dauid cathedram qui rexit amoenam* (Sulien 'ruled the beautiful bishopric of Bishop David') (Lapidge 1972–4, 86). Similarly, *Pontifex* is used in early twelfth-century Glamorgan in the Book of Llandaf (*Llan Dâv*, eg. 85, 108, 109, 111).
9. In addition to the monuments discussed there is a possible inscribed stone (now lost) which was found *c.* 1865 at Cnwc, Trewellwell Farm, Caerfarchell (Laws and Owen 1908, 35.8; RCAHMW 1925, no 978). It has also been suggested that there are two monuments from St Patrick's Chapel, Whitesands Bay. The first is now lost and the drawing is too vague to aid identification (RCAHMW 1925, no 963). The carving on the second, a small fragment found covering a cist grave during excavations in 1969 and identified as a cross-carved stone (Hague 1970), consists of a series of rough scratches and the existence of a cross-symbol is uncertain.
10. For example, the lost stone from Pen-Waen Cottage, St David's (SM 8049 2820) (Nash-Williams 1950, no 371), the stone known as *Mesur-y-Dorth*, Llanrhian (SM 8384 3065) (Nash-Williams 1950, no 325) and the newly discovered stone from *Park Maen Dewi* ('The Field of David's Stone'), Penwaun, Fishguard South (SM 9839 3737) are all located on or close to the line of the modern A487, the road from St David's to Fishguard.

References

Unpublished documentary sources

Pembrokeshire Record Office, Haverfordwest, DB/13/96: Record of sale of Arthur Stone, 1862

Published documentary sources

Alfred *Alfred the Great. Asser's Life of King Alfred and other contemporary sources*, M. Lapidge and S. Keynes (trans), Harmondsworth: Penguin Books, 1993

Ann. Camb. *Annales Cambriae*, J. W. ab Ithel (ed), Rolls Series, Longman, Green, Longman and Roberts, 1860

Armes Prydein *Armes Prydein*, I. Williams (ed) and R. Bromwich (trans), Dublin: Dublin Institute for Advanced Studies, 1982

Brut *Brut y Tywysogyon or The Chronicle of the Princes, Red Book of Hergest Version*, T. Jones (ed and trans), Cardiff: University of Wales Press, 1955

Leland *Itinerary of John Leland*, T. Hearne (ed), 9 vols, 2nd edn, Oxford: J. Fletcher and J. Pote, 1744

Llan Dâv *The Text of the Book of Llan Dâv*, J. G. Evans and J. Rhys (eds), 1893, reprinted Aberystwyth: National Library of Wales, 1979

Life of David *Rhygyfarch's Life of St David*, J. W. James (ed and trans), Cardiff: University of Wales Press, 1967

Mart. Tall. *The Martyrology of Tallaght*, R. I. Best and H. J. Lawlor (eds), Henry Bradshaw Society, 1931

Oengus *The Martyrology of Oengus the Culdee*, W. Stokes (ed), Henry Bradshaw Society, 1905

Vie de Saint Paul *Vie de Saint Paul de Léon*, C. Cuissard (ed), *Revue Celtique* 5, 413–59, 1881–3

Welsh Annals *Nennius, British History and The Welsh Annals*, J. Morris (ed and trans), London and Chichester: Phillimore, 1980

Secondary sources

Anon 1864. Haverfordwest meeting – 1864, *Archaeol Cambrensis*, 3rd ser., 10, 337–66

Alexander, J. J. G. 1978. *Insular Manuscripts 6th to the 9th Century*, London: Harvey Miller

Allen, J. R. 1896. Catalogue of the early Christian monuments in Pembrokeshire, *Archaeol Cambrensis*, 5th ser., 13, 290–306

Allen, J. R. 1905. Head of the cross at St David's, Pembrokeshire, *Archaeol Cambrensis*, 6th ser., 5, 89–90

Allen, J. R. and Anderson, J. 1903. *The Early Christian Monuments of Scotland*, 3 pts, reprinted 1993, Balgavies: Pinkfoot Press

Atkins, I. 1946. The authorship of the XVIth century description of St David's printed in Browne Willis's Survey (1717), *National Lib Wales J*, 4 (3–4), 115–22

Bailey, R. N. and Cramp, R. 1988. *Corpus of Anglo-Saxon Stone Sculpture, 2, Cumberland, Westmorland and Lancashire North-of-the-Sands*, Oxford: British Academy / Oxford University Press

Bischoff, B. 1990. *Latin Paleography, Antiquity and the Middle Ages*, D. Ó Cróinín and D. Ganz (trans), Cambridge: Cambridge University Press

Campbell, E. 1996. The archaeological evidence for external contacts: imports, trade and economy in Celtic Britain AD 400–800, in K. R. Dark (ed), *External Contacts and the Economy of Late Roman Britain and Post-Roman Britain*, 83–96, Woodbridge: Boydell Press

Cassidy, B. (ed) 1992. *The Ruthwell Cross*, Princeton: Princeton University Press

Charles, B. G. 1992. *The Place-names of Pembrokeshire*, 2 vols, Aberystwyth: National Library of Wales

Charles-Edwards, T. M. 1971. The seven bishop houses of Dyfed, *Bull Board Celtic Stud*, 24 (3), 247–62

Craig, D. 1997. The sculptured stones, in P. Hill, *Whithorn and St Ninian: The excavation of a monastic town 1984–91*, 433–41, Whithorn and Stroud: Whithorn Trust and Sutton Publishing

Cramp, R. 1984. *Corpus of Anglo-Saxon Stone Sculpture, 1, County Durham and Northumberland*, Oxford: British Academy / Oxford University Press

Craster, O. E. 1957. Early Christian stone found at the Bishop's Palace, St David's, *Archaeol Cambrensis*, 106, 118

Davies, W. 1982. *Wales in the Early Middle Ages*, Leicester: Leicester University Press

Davies, W. *et al* 2000. *The Inscriptions of Early Medieval Brittany*, Aberystwyth: Celtic Studies Publications

Dean of St David's 1892. Discovery of an inscribed stone at St David's, *Archaeol Cambrensis*, 5th ser., 9, 78

Edwards, N. 1990. Some crosses of County Kilkenny, in W. Nolan and K. Whelan (eds), *Kilkenny: history and society*, 33–61, Dublin: Geography Publications

Edwards, N. 1995. 11th-century Welsh illuminated manuscripts: the nature of the Irish connection, in C. Bourke (ed), *From the Isles of the North*, 147–55, Belfast: HMSO

Evans, J. W. 1991. *St David's Bishop's Palace*, Cardiff: Cadw: Welsh Historic Monuments

Fanning, T. 1981. Excavation of an early Christian cemetery and settlement at Reask, County Kerry, *Proc Royal Irish Acad*, 81C, 67–172

Fenton, R. 1903. *A Historical Tour through Wales*, Brecknock: Davies & Co.

Hague, D. 1970. Whitesands Bay, *Archaeol Wales*, 10 (no. 47), 27–8

Harbison, P. 1992. *The High Crosses of Ireland*, 3 vols, Bonn: Rudolf Habelt

Harris, S. M. 1940. *Saint David and the Liturgy*, Cardiff: University of Wales Press
Henderson, I. and Okasha, E. 1992. The early Christian inscribed and carved stones at Tullylease, Co. Cork, *Cambridge Medieval Celtic Stud*, 24, 1–36
Higgitt, J. 1982. The Pictish Latin inscription at Tarbat in Ross-shire, *Proc Soc Antiq Scot*, 112, 300–21
Higgitt, J. 1994. The display script of the Book of Kells and the tradition of Insular decorative capitals, in F. O'Mahony (ed), *The Book of Kells*, 209–33, Aldershot: Scolar Press
Hughes, K. 1980. *Celtic Britain in the Early Middle Ages*, Woodbridge: Boydell Press / Rowman & Littlefield
Jackson, K. 1953. *Language and History in Early Britain*, Edinburgh: Edinburgh University Press
James, H. 1993. The cult of St David in the Middle Ages, in M. Carver (ed), *In Search of Cult: Archaeological investigations in honour of Philip Rahtz*, 105–12, Woodbridge: Boydell & Brewer
Jenkins, D. and Owen, M. E. 1983. The Welsh marginalia in the Lichfield Gospels. Part I, *Cambridge Medieval Celtic Stud*, 5, 37–66
Jones, F. 1954. *The Holy Wells of Wales*, Cardiff: University of Wales Press
Jones, W. B. and Freeman, E. A. 1856. *The History and Antiquities of St David's*, London: Parker, Smith & Petheram / Tenby: Mason
Kay, R. E. 1958. An early Christian monument from Walton West (Pembs.), *Archaeol Cambrensis*, 107, 122–3
Lang, J. 1988. *Viking-Age Decorated Wood* (Medieval Dublin Excavations 1962–81, Ser. B, 1), Dublin: Royal Irish Academy
Lang, J. 1991. *Corpus of Anglo-Saxon Stone Sculpture*, 3, *York and East Yorkshire*, Oxford: British Academy / Oxford University Press
Lapidge, M. 1973–4. The Welsh-Latin poetry of Sulien's family, *Studia Celtica*, 8–9, 68–106
Laws, E. and Owen, H. (eds) 1908. *An Archaeological Survey of Pembrokeshire 1896–1907*, Tenby: John Leach
Lewis, J. M. 1976. A survey of early Christian monuments west of the Taf, in G. C. Boon and J. M. Lewis (eds), *Welsh Antiquity*, 177–92, Cardiff: National Museum of Wales
Lionard, P. 1961. Early Irish grave-slabs, *Proc Royal Irish Acad*, 61C, 95–169
Lloyd, J. E. 1941. Bishop Sulien and his family, *National Lib Wales J*, 2 (1), 1–6
Macalister, R. A. S. 1931. A slab in St David's Cathedral, *Archaeol Cambrensis*, 86, 353–4
Macalister, R. A. S. 1945, 1949. *Corpus Inscriptionum Insularum Celticarum*, 2 vols, Dublin: Stationery Office
Nash-Williams, V. E. 1938. Some dated monuments of the 'Dark Ages' in Wales, *Archaeol Cambrensis*, 93, 31–56
Nash-Williams, V. E. 1950. *The Early Christian Monuments of Wales*, Cardiff: University of Wales Press
Okasha, E. 1970. A new inscription from Ramsey Island, *Archaeol Cambrensis*, 119, 68–70
Okasha, E. 1971. *Hand-list of Anglo-Saxon Non-Runic Inscriptions*, Cambridge: Cambridge University Press
Ó Riain, P. 1990. The Tallaght Martyrologies, redated, *Cambridge Medieval Celtic Stud*, 20, 21–38

Owen, G. 1892. *The Description of Pembrokeshire*, H. Owen (ed), parts 1–2, London: Honourable Society of Cymmrodorion
Owen-John, H. 1988. Llandough: the rescue excavation of a multi-period site near Cardiff, South Glamorgan, in D. M. Robinson (ed), *Biglis, Caldicot and Llandough: three late Iron Age and Romano-British sites in south-east Wales. Excavations 1977–79* (Brit Archaeol Rep, Brit Ser, 188), 123–77, Oxford: BAR
RCAHMS 1975. *An Inventory of the Historical Monuments in the County of Argyll*, Vol. 2, *Lorn*, Edinburgh: HMSO
RCAHMW 1925. *An Inventory of the Historical Monuments in the County of Pembrokeshire*, London: HMSO
RCAHMW 1976. *An Inventory of the Historical Monuments in the County of Glamorgan*, Vol. 1, part 3, *The Early Christian Period*, Cardiff: HMSO
Rhys, J. 1896. Epigraphic notes, *Archaeol Cambrensis*, 5th ser., 13, 98–128
Tegid [Jones, J. O.] 1847. Cromlechs etc. in Pembrokeshire, *Archaeol Cambrensis*, 2, 373–4
Thomas, A. and Hollbrook, N. 1994. *Excavations at Great House Farm, Llandough, Cardiff, South Glamorgan* (Cotswold Archaeological Trust Report 94213), unpublished
Thomas, C. 1971. *The Early Christian Archaeology of North Britain*, Oxford: Oxford University Press
Thomas, C. 1994. *And Shall these Mute Stones Speak? Post-Roman inscriptions in Western Britain*, Cardiff: University of Wales Press
Thomas, C. 1995. Cellular meanings, monastic beginnings, *Emania*, 13, 51–67
Thomas, C. 1996. The Llanddewi-Brefi 'Idnert' stone, *Peritia*, 10, 136–83
Thomas, W. G. 1989. An early sundial from the Towyn area, *Archaeol Cambrensis*, 138, 111–13
Tweddle, D., Biddle, M. and Kjølbye-Biddle, B. 1995. *Corpus of Anglo-Saxon Stone Sculpture, 4, South-East England*, Oxford: British Academy / Oxford University Press
Vendryes, J. 1955. Sur en emploi du mot AINM 'nom', *Études Celtiques*, 7, 139–46
Wallace, P. F. 1988. Archaeology and the emergence of Dublin as the principal town of Ireland, in J. Bradley (ed), *Settlement and Society in Medieval Ireland*, 123–60, Kilkenny: Boethius Press
Westwood, J. O. 1876–9. *Lapidarium Walliae: The early inscribed and sculptured stones of Wales*, Oxford: Oxford University Press, reprinted 1993, Macclesfield: Redesmere Press
Westwood, J. O. 1892. Inscribed stone at St David's, *Archaeol Cambrensis*, 5th ser., 9, 78–80
Willis, B. 1717. *A Survey of the Cathedral Church of St David's*, London: R. Gosling
Youngs, S. (ed) 1989. *'The Work of Angels', Masterpieces of Celtic metalwork, 6th-9th centuries AD*, London: British Museum Publications

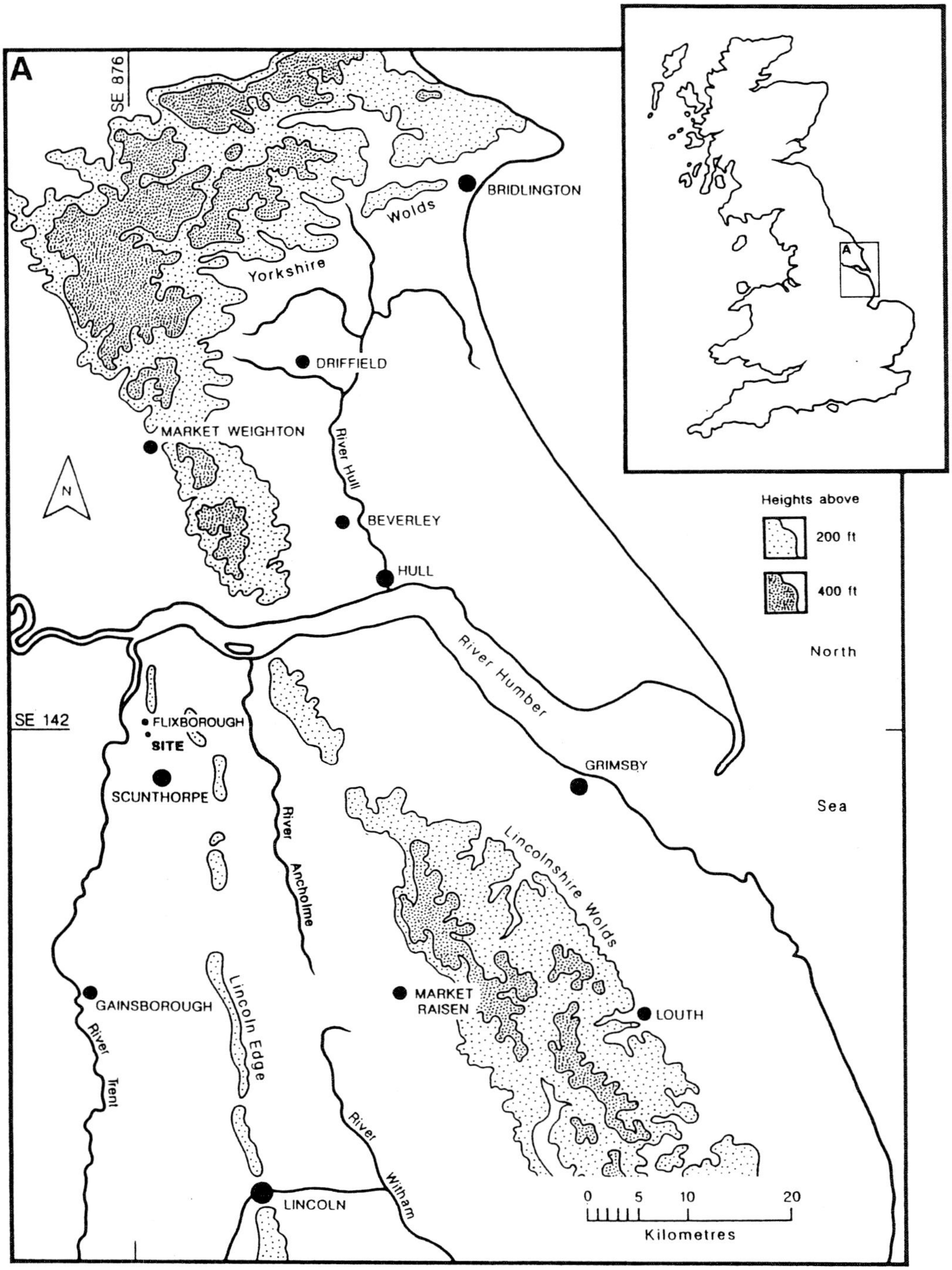

Fig. 5.1. Location of Flixborough and the Humber estuary region, in northern England.

5
Wealth, Waste and Conspicuous Consumption
Flixborough and its importance for Middle and Late Saxon rural settlement studies

Chris Loveluck

Between 1989 and 1991, excavations within the parish of Flixborough, north Lincolnshire, uncovered the remains of an exceptionally wealthy Anglo-Saxon settlement, situated 8 km south of the Humber estuary and overlooking the floodplain of the River Trent (Fig. 5.1). Post-excavation analysis, interim results of which are presented here, has demonstrated that the excavated part of the settlement was occupied, or used for settlement-related activity, throughout the Middle and Late Saxon periods. In a vertical stratigraphic sequence unprecedented on an Anglo-Saxon rural settlement, nine main phases have been identified, dating from the early seventh to the early eleventh century, with a subsequent phase of medieval activity. The remains of approximately 40 buildings and other structures have been uncovered and vast quantities of artefacts and faunal remains have been retrieved. The evidence provides an exceptionally detailed picture of many aspects of daily life on a high-status settlement during the Middle and Late Saxon periods, while its detailed analysis reveals the changing character of occupation during this time.

The quality of the evidence contained within the settlement sequence proves to be important for both the examination of site-specific issues and for the investigation of wider research themes. The remains provide an exceptional opportunity for reconstructing the changing character of the settlement's economy and its relationships with its surrounding landscape. Within a broader context, the analysis of the Flixborough remains is enabling a re-assessment of the problems of defining the status and character of Middle and Late Saxon rural settlements from their archaeological remains. In addition, continuing analysis is shedding light on the changing relationships between rural and urban settlements, and on the effect of patterns of artefact supply and discard on the archaeological visibility and recognition of settlements through the Middle and Late Saxon periods.

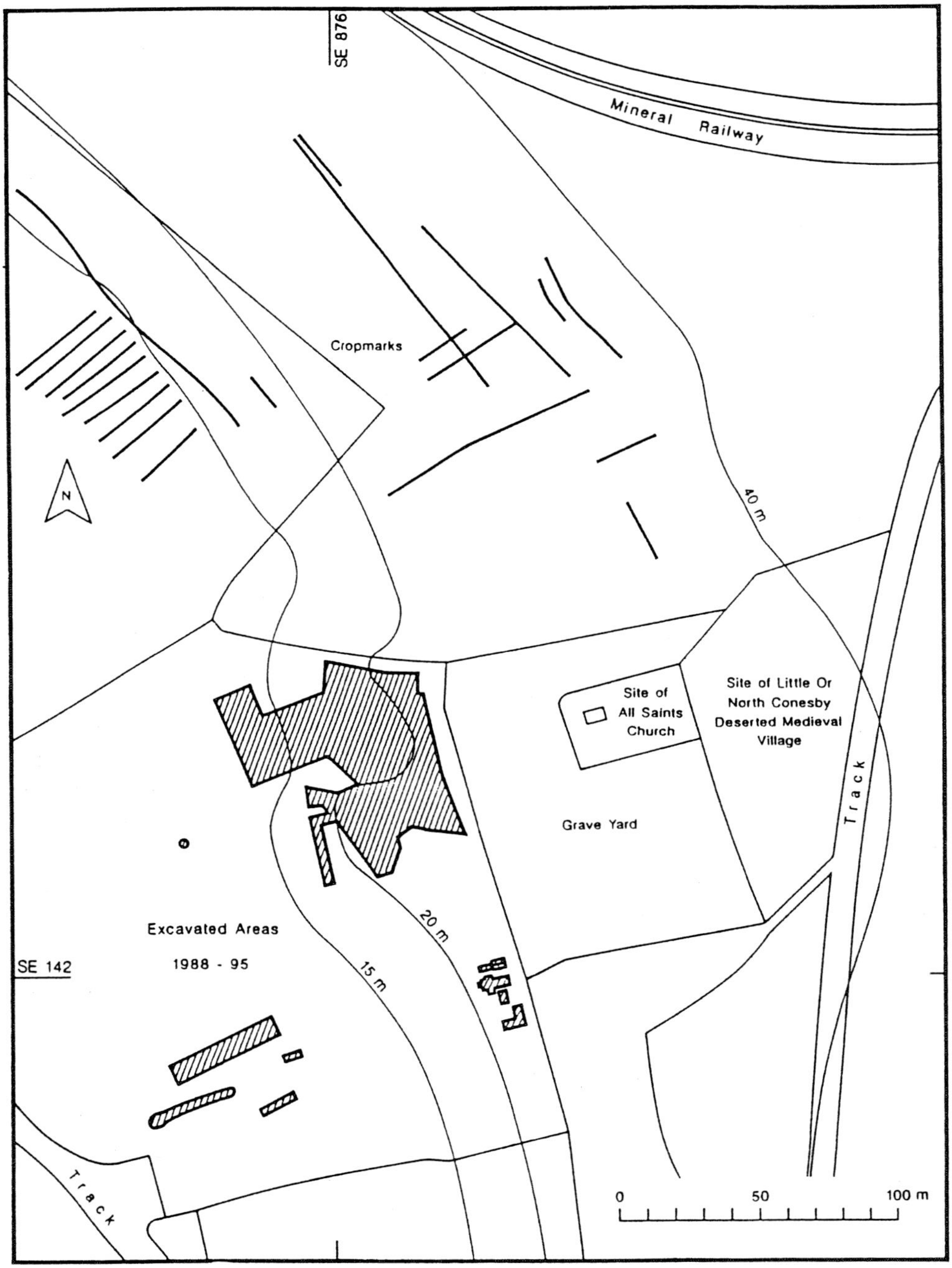

Fig. 5.2. Location of the Flixborough excavation and the evaluation trenches (hatched), in relation to surrounding topography and settlement evidence.

The Anglo-Saxon settlement at Flixborough was situated on a belt of wind-blown sand which had built up against the liassic limestone and ironstone escarpment of the Lincolnshire Edge, immediately to the east of the excavations (Gaunt forthcoming a). Until the seventeenth and eighteenth centuries, this belt of sand was located at the interface between two environmental zones, comprising the wetlands of the lower floodplain and delta areas of the River Trent, situated to the west and north, and the well-drained soils of the escarpment to the east (Gaunt 1976, 15; Gaunt forthcoming a; Lillie and Parkes 1998, 51–2). Descriptive impressions of this landscape, with its meres, marshes, sand-belts of pasture and arable land, together with occasional woodland, can be gleaned from the Domesday survey of 1086 (Foster and Longley 1924; Darby 1987,103–8). They can also be visualized more fully from John Leland's account of his journey of 1544, from Gainsborough through to the Isle of Axholme (Chandler 1993, 294–7).

The excavated part of the settlement was located upon and adjacent to a spur on the sand-belt, with a shallow valley extending into the central part of the site. Derrick Riley first identified settlement remains in this area in 1933, following the recovery of pottery and loom-weights. The type of pottery recovered was not identified as Middle Saxon in date until Addyman's excavation of similar wares at Maxey, in Northamptonshire (Addyman *et al.* 1965, 20–73); at the time, Riley concluded that the settlement was Romano-British in date (unpublished notebook, Humber Sites and Monuments Record, Hull). At a similar date, Dudley also referred to his recovery of Anglo-Saxon remains from nearby Conesby, although the geographical relationship of these finds to the excavated settlement is unclear (Dudley 1931, 44).

Prior to the quarrying of sand on the site, the settlement was confirmed as dating from the Anglo-Saxon period during an archaeological evaluation by Kevin Leahy of Scunthorpe Museum, in 1988. This evaluation uncovered the remains of 11 east-west aligned inhumation graves, without grave-goods. Some of the burials were interred in coffins or chests, with iron fittings identical to those from Anglo-Saxon cemeteries dating from the period between the seventh and ninth centuries (cf. Mortimer 1905, 254–7; Ottaway 1997, 99–100; Nicholson 1997b, 412–5). The foundations of possible buildings were also partially uncovered during this exercise, as a consequence of which English Heritage funded the Humberside Archaeology Unit (now Humber Field Archaeology) to conduct further evaluations, which resulted in a two-year programme of excavations, from 1989 to 1991 (Fig. 5.2).

Between 1991 and 1995 further geophysical, magnetic susceptibility and surface-collection surveys were undertaken, and additional evaluation trenches were excavated. They demonstrated that Middle and Late Saxon archaeological evidence, as well as scatters of Romano-British and medieval artefacts, extended both to the north and south on the sand-belt, and also eastward towards the limestone escarpment. The remains from the Flixborough excavations, therefore, represent only a sample of the multi-period settlement activity in the vicinity (Loveluck forthcoming a; Payne forthcoming).

Fig. 5.3. View of the excavations looking to the south-west, showing refuse dumps and superimposed buildings in the depression, in the centre of the excavated area.

The Anglo-Saxon occupation sequence

The Anglo-Saxon settlement evidence was sealed by wind-blown sand, up to 2 m deep in places. Below this sand inundation lay ten phases of settlement activity dating from at least the early seventh century until the mid fourteenth century. The overall stratigraphic sequence can be summarized as a series of structural phases, often associated with large refuse deposits cast into a shallow valley that ran into the centre of the excavated area. Several of the main structural phases were separated by demolition and levelling dumps, and it is this superimposition that has resulted in the exceptional Anglo-Saxon occupation sequence (Fig. 5.3). The majority of the 15,000 artefacts and 250,000 animal bones recovered were found within these deposits. The high wood-ash content of many of the dumps, their rapid build-up and the constant accretion of sand within them formed a micro-environment which was chemically neutral, the alkalinity of the wood-ash and sand accretion preventing acid leaching (Canti 1992, 18; Canti forthcoming) and so ensuring excellent preservation conditions.

The earliest period of activity, ascribed to the seventh century, is represented by the remains of four superimposed buildings on two building plots, with an additional structure – building 11 – constructed in the shallow depression at some time in the second half of the seventh century. Where it is possible to estimate, the buildings range from 9 to 11 m in length, and 5 to 6.5m in width. The later of these building phases (1b) is shown in Fig. 5.4. The earlier buildings, in the south of the site, had post-hole foundations, although ghosts of posts or planks were absent. The partial plan of building 11 possessed elements of a continuous foundation trench for earth-fast posts or

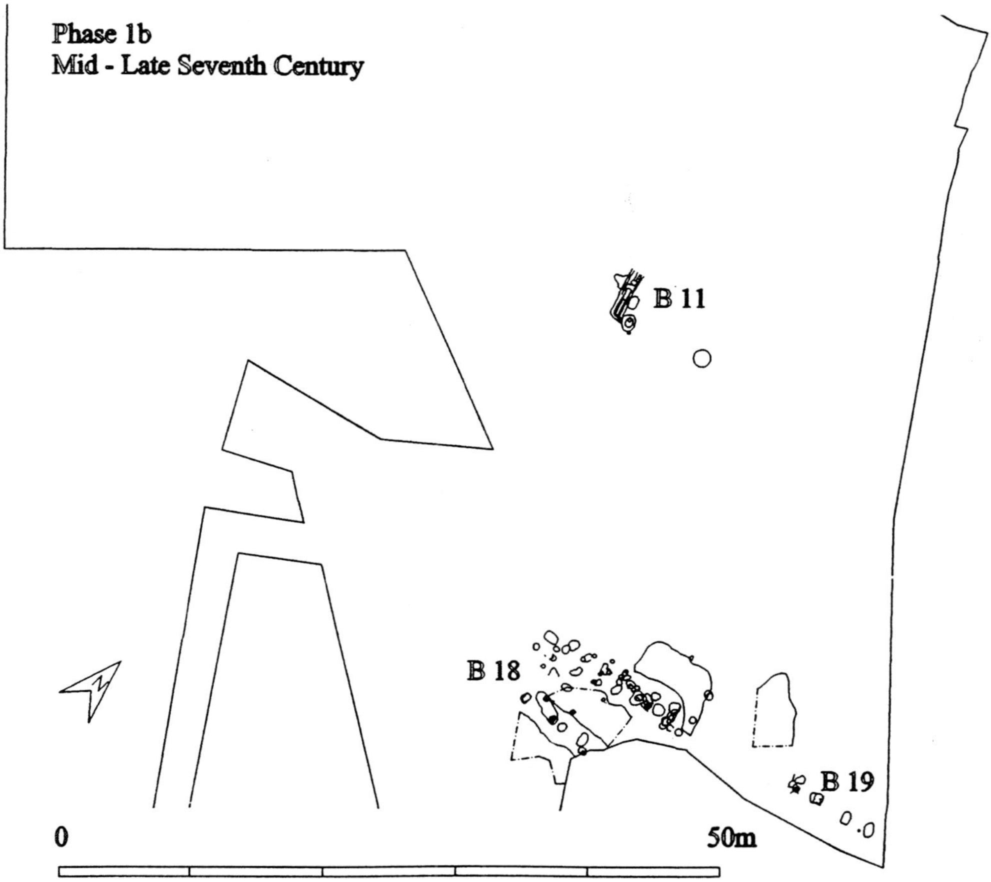

Fig. 5.4. Plan of the excavated buildings, floor and external yard deposits, mid to late seventh century.

planks. The fills of the post-holes from the southern buildings contained predominantly mid to late fourth-century pottery, early Saxon local wares, and early Saxon Charnwood ware from Leicestershire (Young forthcoming; Williams and Vince 1998, 219–20). The location of the earliest buildings in the south-eastern part of the excavated area suggests that they represent the periphery of an early Anglo-Saxon settlement focus. The recovery of sixth-century small-long brooches, annular brooches, and a mid sixth-century great square-headed brooch (Hines forthcoming), as residual finds in Middle Saxon phases, also hints at the presence of an early Saxon settlement – and possibly a cemetery – nearby.

Between the late seventh and mid eighth centuries, the whole of the excavated area was inhabited, with buildings located to the north and south of the shallow depression in the centre of the site. The new buildings were

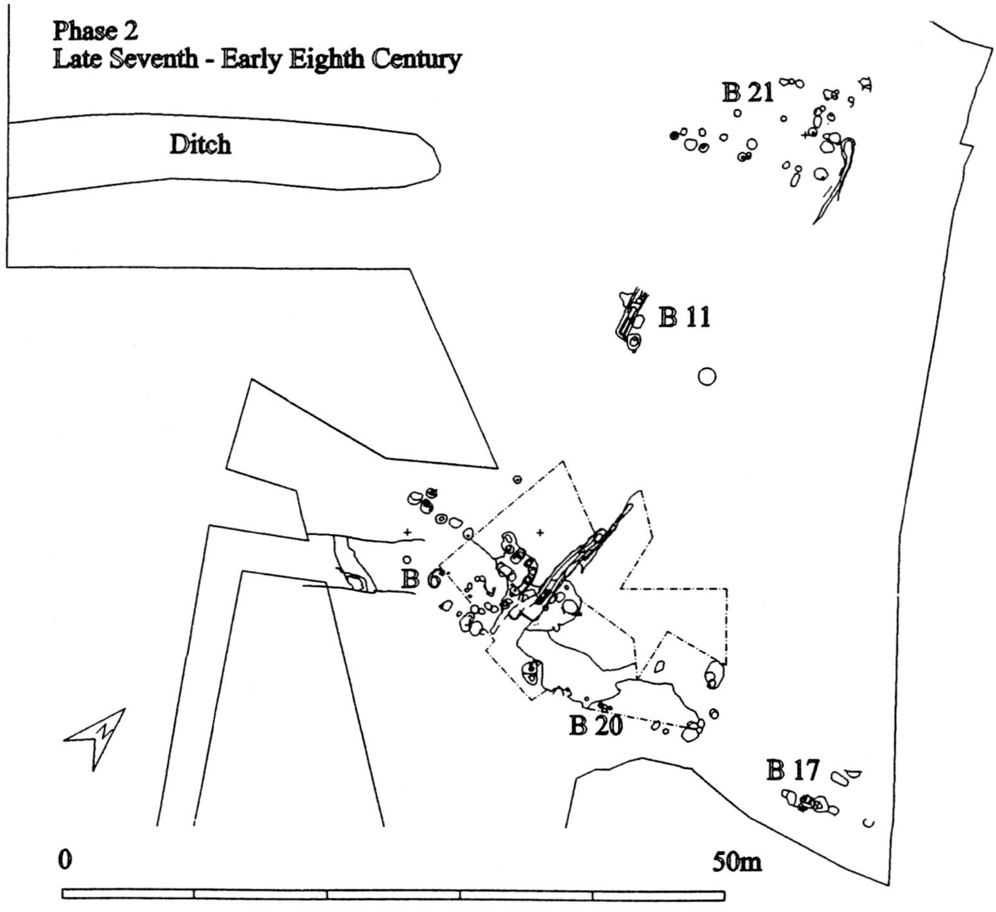

Fig. 5.5. Settlement features from the late seventh to early eighth century, including buildings, key occupation-related deposits, and the linear ditch.

constructed on a different alignment from those of phase 1b, the majority of them on new building-plots, aligned on a more east-west axis (Fig. 5.5). The building dimensions were similar to those of the preceding period. This phase also coincided with the first occurrence of Maxey-type ware at Flixborough, the appearance of which is dated to the late seventh century (Young forthcoming). At some time within this period, a large boundary ditch was dug, running approximately on an east-west alignment, from the shallow valley down the slope towards the Trent floodplain.

Two buildings and their associated archaeological features are particularly noteworthy from the late seventh to early eighth century, namely buildings 6 and 21. Each of these structures had post-hole foundations and stone-lined 'soakaways' which ran from the central post along one of the short-walls. Both seem to have drained water from their roofs into the depression, once building 11 had been demolished. Rubbish was dumped immediately outside the buildings.

In the course of the early to mid eighth century, building 20 was replaced by an exceptional structure, constructed on what appears to be a gravel foundation for a sill-beam and timber superstructure. This building (1a) was internally divided, with a fired-clay hearth at its eastern end. It can be seen under excavation in Fig. 5.6. Building 1a also contained the graves of four

Fig. 5.6. Building 1 under excavation looking west, showing its two phases. The earliest phase (1a) comprised a two-cell building constructed on a gravel foundation, with a fired clay hearth in its eastern half (foreground). The central fired clay hearth (background), and the large opposing post-holes are from its subsequent rebuilding (1b).

individuals, buried along its long walls on an east-west alignment. Two additional burials were placed outside the building to the south and south-east. Examination of the skeletal remains has shown that all but one of the burials were juveniles between the ages of 3 and 12 years old. The exception to this is the skeleton of a woman, aged between 20 and 30 years, who had been buried in close association with the skeleton of a perinatal infant (Mays forthcoming; Fig. 5.7).

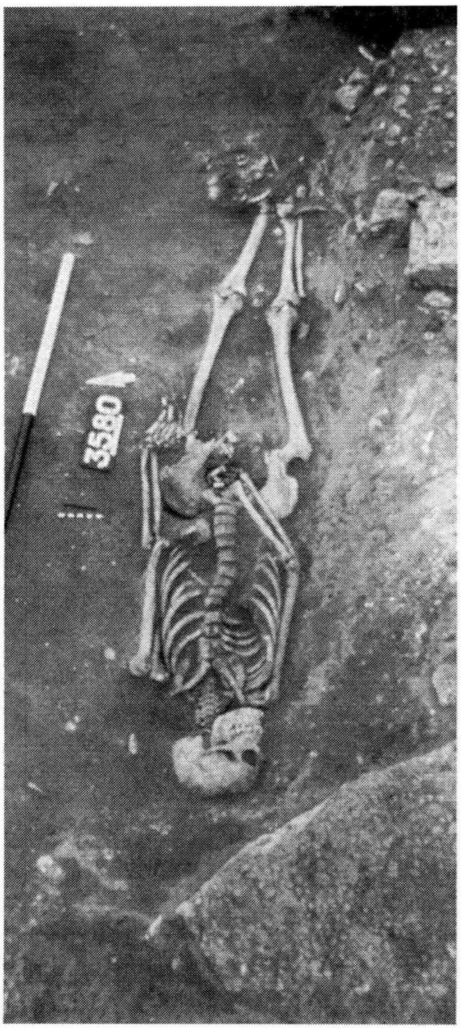

Fig. 5.7. The grave of the woman buried in building 1a with a perinatal foetus at her feet.

A range of ailments is evident from traces on the skeletal remains, particularly in relation to the adult female. These include indications of a calcified lymph node which could have occurred as a result of tuberculosis (Mays forthcoming). The skeletons of the children nearly all showed evidence of iron deficiency (*Cribra orbitalia)* around the orbits of their skulls. This condition is most likely to have resulted from parasite infection in the intestines of the children, preventing the uptake of iron from food, or from a response to other forms of chronic infection (Mays forthcoming; Stuart-Macadam 1989, 212–13). The graves from building 1a also showed a marked contrast to those from the cemetery discovered in 1988, in that the burials from the latter were all adult men and women, between the ages of 17 and 60. Nevertheless, the apparent lack of children in the 1988 cemetery could be the result of a more hostile burial environment (Mays forthcoming).

The next broad period of similarity in layout and land-use occurred between the mid eighth and mid ninth century. During this time, there were two phases of buildings on either side of the shallow depression, in the majority of cases superimposed on the same building-plots. The buildings themselves were earth-fast constructions, predominantly within continuous trench foundations, although buildings with post-hole foundations also existed. They ranged from 9 to 13.5 m in length, and 5.5 to 7.5 m in width. Several also contained internal fired-clay hearths. Within the valley itself there were also two phases of buildings, although they were not directly superimposed, and their construction was separated by a period of refuse dumping. Indeed the cyclical use of the depression for construction and dumping is an important feature of this period, since the dumps contained large quantities of artefacts and animal bones. Fig. 5.8 shows the appearance of the settlement during the mid ninth century, with the dumps gradually filling up the depression forming the termination of the shallow valley. The ditch was also completely filled-in with domestic and craft-working debris at this time.

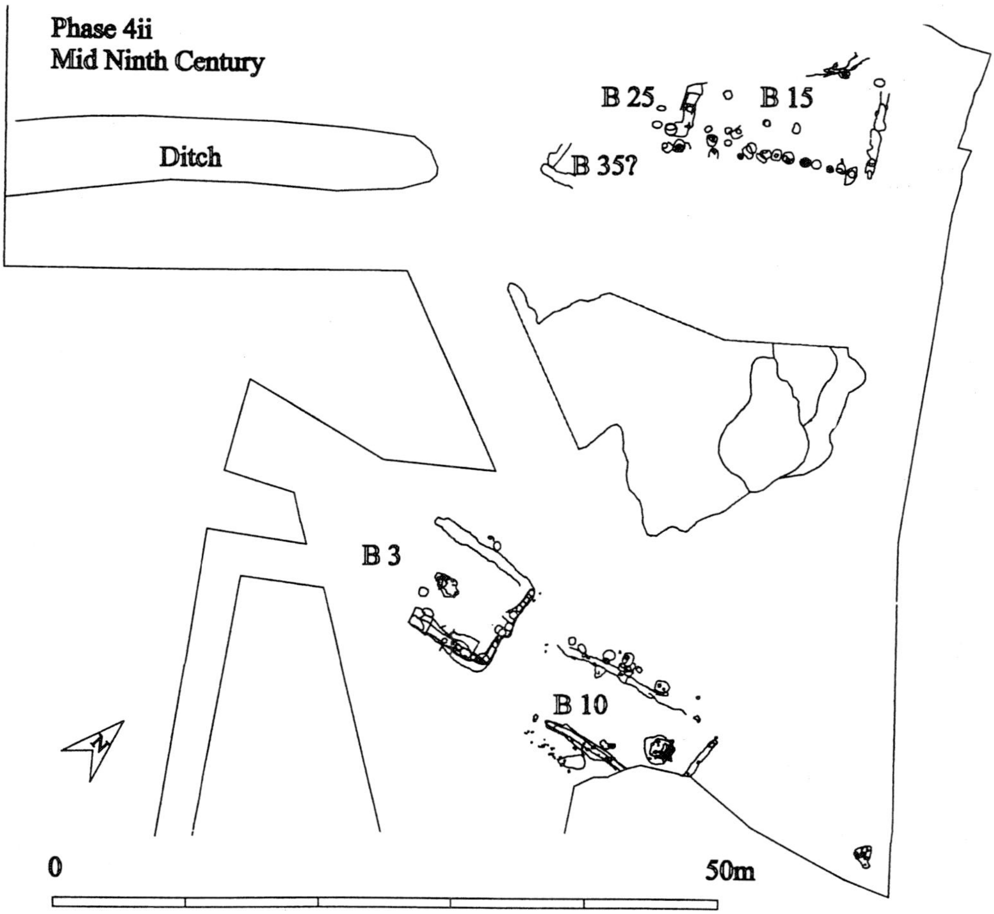

Fig. 5.8. The excavated settlement, during the mid ninth century, with buildings situated either side of a central refuse dumping area. The ditch was also completely filled with refuse at this time.

The pattern of the settlement that existed between approximately 750 and 850 changed radically between the mid to late ninth century. The building-plots and the organized layout of the previous period were abandoned; in their place, smaller buildings with post-hole foundations were constructed – some with fired-clay hearths – in the southern part of the excavated area (Fig. 5.9). The vast majority of buildings were less than 10 m in length, and less than 6 m in width. The former depression, in the centre of the site was again used as a refuse dumping zone, whilst several buildings were constructed cutting the line of the former ditch. On the basis of parallels with similar structures in middle to late Saxon phases of other settlements such as Wicken Bonhunt and West Heslerton, it is possible that the latter buildings were granaries or haylofts (Wade 1980, 97–8; Powlesland pers. comm.). To the north of the refuse dumping area was a zone of domed, fired-clay ovens. These ovens were linked

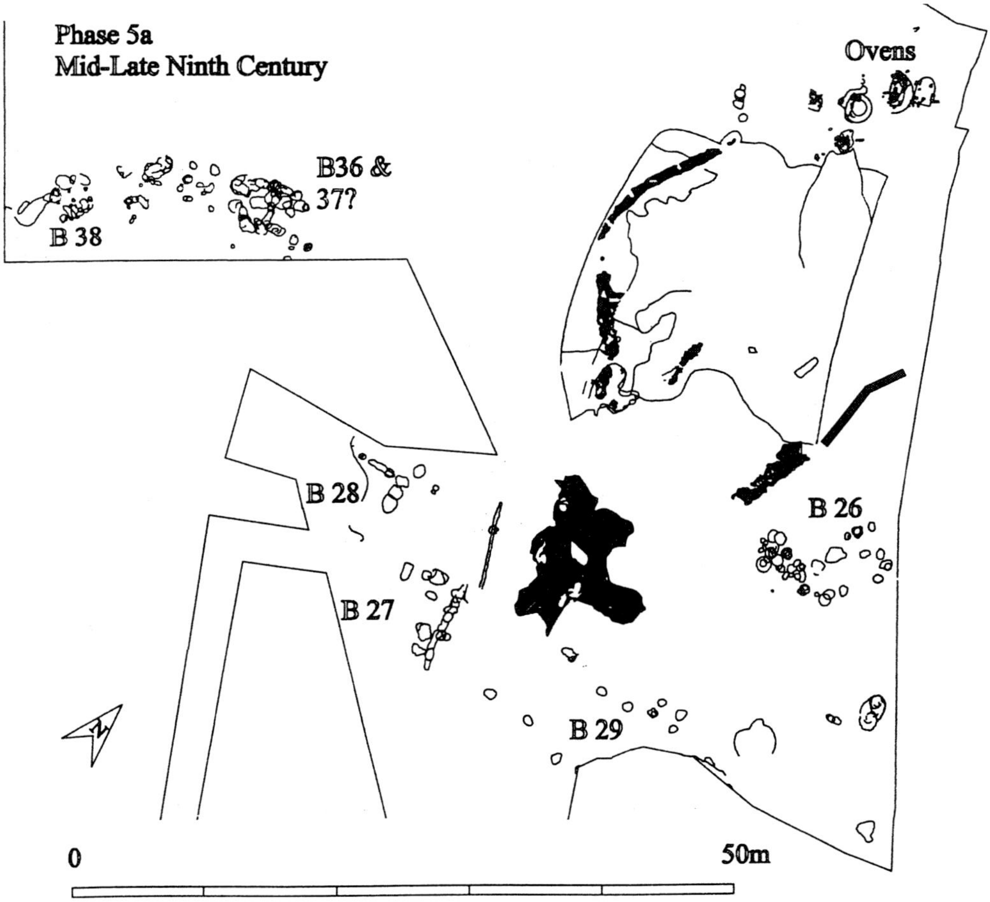

Fig. 5.9. Occupation features during the mid to late ninth century, with a southern zone of small buildings, a central refuse dumping area, and a line of fired clay ovens to the north, linked to the buildings by gravel paths.

with the buildings to the south by gravel paths which crossed the central refuse dumps. The presence of the paths and the varying characteristics of the dumps themselves suggest that the central part of the site acted as an open midden for an extended period, and that the dumps were not deposited in one episode of levelling. Between the late ninth and early tenth century, some of the small buildings were replaced whilst others were constructed over the central midden, cutting through the former gravel paths. The southern sector of the site was then used as a refuse dumping zone.

At some point between the early and mid tenth century, the small buildings, possible granaries and ovens were completely demolished, to be replaced by the largest buildings seen within the occupation sequence, all of which had continuous trench foundations (Fig. 5.10). None of the new buildings was positioned to respect earlier building plots. The largest structure,

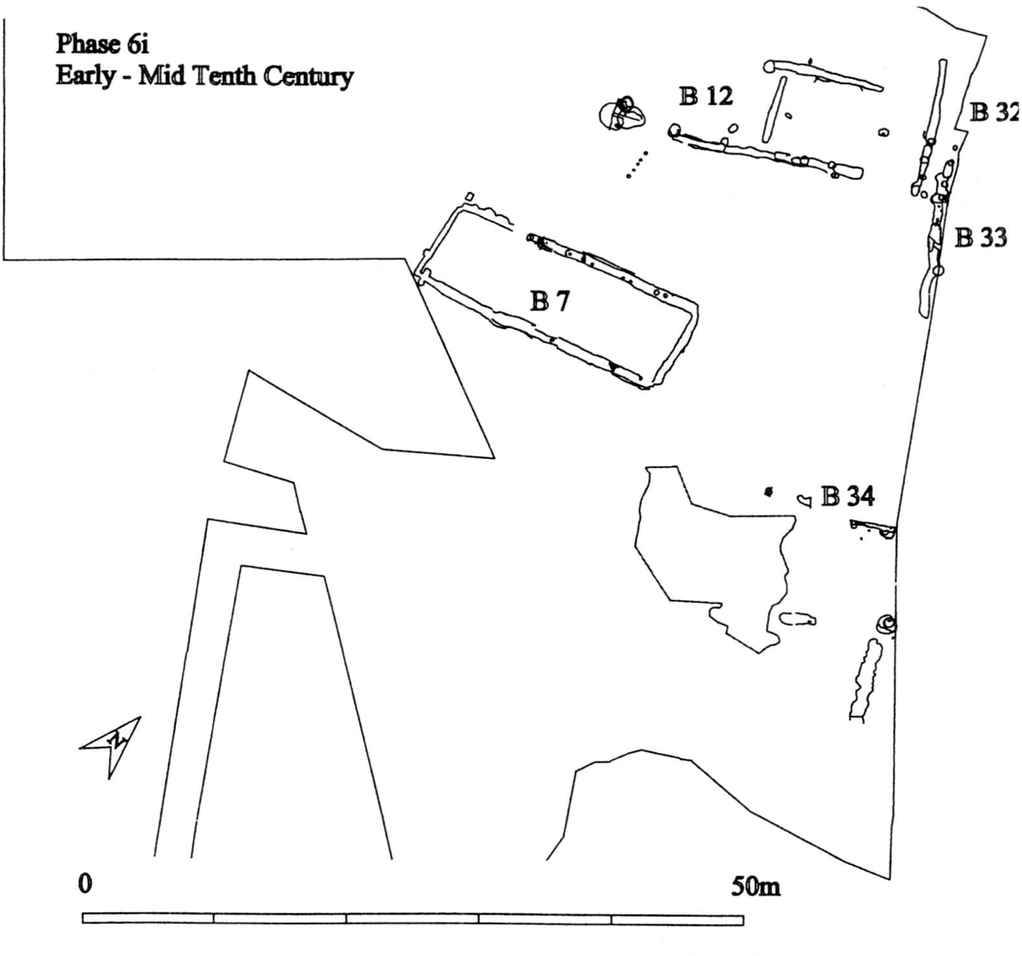

Fig. 5.10. Plan of settlement features belonging to the early to mid tenth century, including the largest building in the occupation sequence.

building 7 – almost 20 m by 6.5 m in size and possibly with more than one storey – cut across the central part of the site, while building 16 cut through the demolished ovens. The other buildings of this phase are noteworthy for the fact that all continued under the eastern edge of the excavations. The latest buildings (32 and 33) also had different alignments, having been placed on a north-south axis, rather than approximately east-west.

During the mid tenth century, building 7 was demolished to be covered by a dump comprised of a vast quantity of animal bones and a small range of tenth-century pottery types. This dump may have accumulated during the time that building 33 was in use. The impression given by the evidence, therefore, is that during the tenth century the habitation area was shifting eastwards, towards the limestone escarpment. Between the mid tenth and early eleventh century, the whole of the excavated area was then used as a refuse dumping zone.

This migration eastward would place the late tenth- to eleventh-century settlement in the vicinity of All Saints' Church, documented from the thirteenth century (Roffe pers. comm), and the deserted medieval settlement of North Conesby. All Saints' Church was also known as North Conesby Church and as Flixborough Old Church (Coppack 1986, 51). Like Flixborough, North Conesby was mentioned in the Domesday survey, and Foster and Longley noted that a moated enclosure to the east of the church was buried under ironstone mining debris in the early 1920s (Foster and Longley 1924, liii and 149). The place-name Conesby, deriving from Old Danish *Kunungrsby*, King's farm or settlement (Cameron 1998, 33; Cameron forthcoming), may have been associated with the excavated Anglo-Saxon settlement from the tenth century, if not slightly earlier, the gradual eastward shift of the settlement accounting for its eventual linkage with the deserted medieval site.

An explanation for the settlement shift could relate to the church. During the mid to late tenth century, the first stone churches were built on other nearby settlements in north Lincolnshire, such as Burnham, thought to have been linked to aristocratic proprietors and estate centres (Coppack 1986, 47–50). It is possible that a late Saxon stone precursor also exists below All Saints' Church, as was the case at Burnham. Interestingly, however, the Domesday survey makes no mention of churches at Flixborough, North Conesby or Burnham (Foster and Longley 1924, 148–51). The construction of a new stone church on the stable foundation of the limestone-ironstone escarpment, rather than on windblown sand, could provide one reason for the eastward shift of the main settlement during the second half of the tenth century. Subsequent, peripheral settlement features such as an oven, pits and a drainage ditch, in use between the twelfth and fourteenth centuries, also support the idea that the focus of the medieval settlement lay to the east of the excavated area.

Depositional patterns of artefacts and faunal remains, and some aspects of site taphonomy

Our understanding and interpretation of the Anglo-Saxon settlement is of necessity viewed through the filter of site taphonomy and patterns in the discard of artefacts and faunal remains. Our ability to examine the economy and character of the settlement is therefore reliant upon an understanding of the refuse disposal strategies used during the occupation sequence; survival factors relating to particular types of evidence, for example, artefact fragmentation and animal bone taphonomy (Ervynck 1999, 129–33); and the presence of intact occupation surfaces, within or in association with structures.

Varied organization of refuse disposal in different occupation phases also has an impact on our ability to associate specific activities with particular parts of the excavated area. Added to these factors, the reworking of earlier refuse material has resulted in a high degree of residuality of eighth- and ninth-century artefacts. Consideration of all the above archaeological factors is fundamental to the interpretation of the archaeological evidence from the Anglo-Saxon settlement at what should correctly be referred to as North Conesby, in Flixborough parish.

The potential for reconstructing profiles of artefact and faunal remains varies within the five defined periods in the occupation sequence. For example, floor deposits and two external yard deposits were found in association with only one of the buildings in phase 1b, dated to the mid to late seventh century (Fig. 5.4), but the floor was kept relatively clean, and very few finds were recovered from the yards. As a result, the majority of the finds from the seventh-century phases were found in post-hole fills, and in comparison with other periods, the number of finds is small. This limits the extent to which trends from the seventh century can be viewed as comparable to those from the eighth, ninth and tenth centuries.

In other periods, there were distinct changes in the organization of larger-scale refuse dumping and this again has an effect on the extent to which conclusions can be drawn on aspects of life in the settlement through the Middle and Late Saxon periods. For example, between the late seventh and early eighth century, refuse was dumped immediately outside the buildings, in the fills of post-holes, and occasionally in pits (Fig. 5.5). In contrast, from approximately 750 to 850, refuse was collected and dumped in the central part of the site. Artefact residuality and fragmentation studies suggest that during this period both heavily reworked and undisturbed refuse deposits were dumped in this area (Fig. 5.8). A similar pattern of refuse disposal also existed in the mid tenth century, following the demolition of building 7. When dumping is focused within one particular settlement zone, it is difficult to identify the origins of refuse material, and the main challenge lies in distinguishing the extent to which finds relate to activities undertaken within the settlement as a whole, or merely in the excavated area.

Fortunately, certain types of artefact – mainly adjoining fragments of individual pottery vessels found in more than one deposit – provide hints as to the derivation of the material in the massive dumps. The sheer quantity of finds in the refuse deposits at certain periods also suggests use of the depression as a communal dumping zone for the settlement as a whole. Proof that material was being transported from unexcavated parts of the settlement is provided by residual Romano-British pottery (Didsbury forthcoming; Loveluck forthcoming b).

Between the seventh and mid eighth century, adjoining sherds of a small number of late fourth-century vessels were reworked and deposited in a series of post-holes and dumps, probably reflecting disturbance of underlying or nearby Late Roman remains. Earlier Roman pottery, dating from before the fourth century, was completely absent. Then from the mid to late eighth century onwards, early second-century pottery, such as Samian ware, was deposited in the major dumps, and fourth-century pottery was extremely scarce. This sudden appearance of early Roman pottery suggests that material from a different part of the Anglo-Saxon settlement, which had disturbed early Roman deposits, was being dumped in the excavated area.

As a consequence of the depositional circumstances of the Flixborough finds, it is possible to produce profiles of the deposition of artefacts and faunal remains relating to four of the five structural-periods defined above. From the quantity of finds and the character of the deposits resulting from organized refuse disposal in the central depression, it can be suggested that the finds profiles are representative of the settlement as a whole between the mid eighth and the early eleventh centuries. Quantities of finds prior to the late seventh century are too small to act as a basis for wider conclusions. Similarly, the practice of dumping refuse outside houses between the late seventh and early eighth centuries makes it difficult to be sure that the finds are representative of the settlement as a whole during that period.

Changing lifestyles at Flixborough during the Middle and Late Saxon periods

The following section presents some provisional results of the analysis of the archaeological evidence from Flixborough, dealing with the four periods defined within the occupation sequence, dating between the late seventh and the early eleventh centuries.

Late seventh to mid eighth century

As already stated, the finds from this period of occupation may relate to activities within the excavated part of the site only (Fig. 5.5). Nevertheless, the finds allow for some interpretation of the character of the agricultural economy, the exploitation of the surrounding landscape, and aspects of the craft-working activities undertaken. Imported luxury commodities also hint at the trade and exchange links between at least some element of the settlement's population and the wider world.

The evidence – provided primarily by the animal bones, but also by rare, charred cereal remains, more abundant molluscs and also artefacts – indicates that the settlement was supported by a mixed agricultural economy. The animal husbandry component comprised the rearing of sheep, cattle and pigs – with sheep predominating slightly – and a much smaller number of horses (Dobney *et al.* forthcoming). Significant quantities of domesticated geese and chickens were also recovered. One of the most interesting features amongst the main domesticated livestock species relates to the size of the cattle. Bio-metrical measurement of the bones indicates a significant proportion of very large cattle for the period: in fact they are some of the largest recorded from Anglo-Saxon England.

The arable component is represented by charred grains of cereals and pulses, although their numbers are very small due to adverse survival conditions for botanical remains (Hall forthcoming). Cultivation and processing of arable and leguminous crops was also indicated by the recovery of iron tools throughout the overall occupation sequence, such as a plough-share, iron spade-sheath, and bill-hook (Ottaway forthcoming; Fig. 5.11). Fragments of lava querns for making flour were also imported from Mayen, Germany (Parkhouse 1997, 97).

In addition to the evidence for arable and pastoral regimes, provisional findings from vertebrate, plant and mollusc remains also demonstrate the exploitation of the surrounding ecological habitats. A range of foodstuffs and raw materials was derived from the wetlands of the Trent floodplain, and from the river itself. Various species of waterfowl and waders were exploited, including cranes, ducks and wild geese (Dobney and Loveluck 1998, 162; Dobney *et al.* forthcoming). Numerous fish bones and fish-hooks reflect the catching, trapping or netting of riverine, estuarine and some marine fish species (Barratt forthcoming). Molluscs and charred plant-stem fragments also indicate the exploitation of both freshwater fen and saltmarsh environments (Rackham 1986, 377–82; Carrot forthcoming; Hall forthcoming). The molluscs and stem fragments may have been transported to the settlement on reeds for thatching, or on other vegetable matter. This faunal and floral evidence for the nature of the palaeo-environment in the vicinity of the settlement concurs with that obtained from recent pollen analysis of bore-hole sediments from the wetlands adjacent to Flixborough. These show the existence of raised mires during the post-Roman period, and the emergence of alder-dominated fen on their margins from approximately 1000; to the east of the settlement a more open agricultural landscape is indicated (Lillie and Parkes 1998, 51–2).

More surprisingly, the population also exploited a significant number of cetaceans – dolphins, porpoises and/or pilot whales (Dobney and Loveluck 1998, 162; Dobney *et al.* forthcoming). The cetaceans could represent beached specimens, or they could have been caught intentionally or accidentally as a

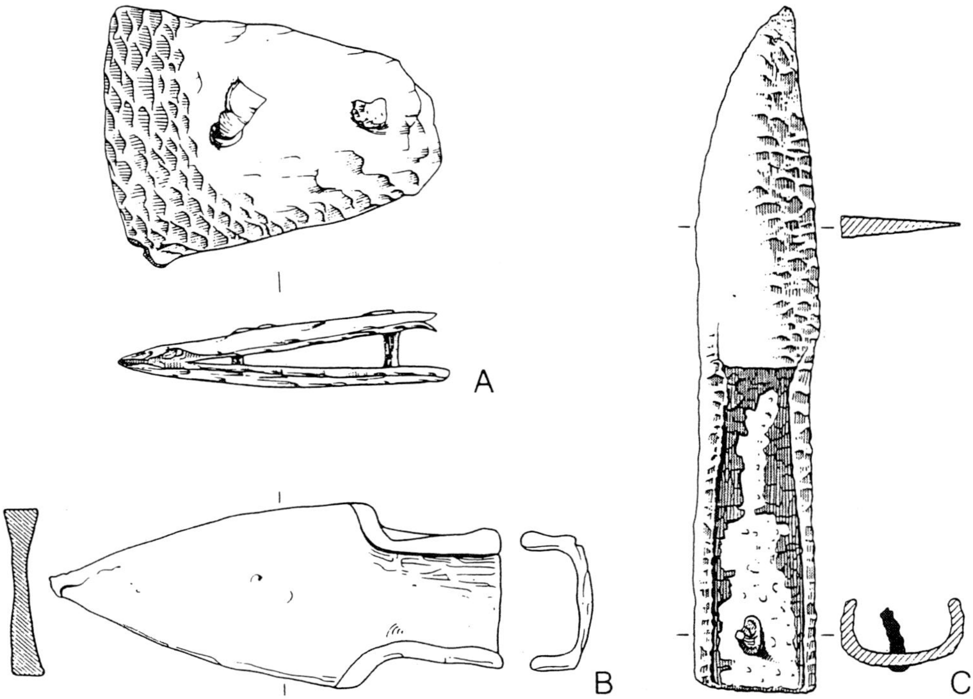

Fig. 5.11. Agricultural tools from Flixborough: a) hoe blade (1:3); b) plough-share (1:5); c) bill-hook (1:3).

result of various fishing strategies. Present-day sightings of dolphins and porpoises occasionally swimming up the River Trent from the Humber, suggest that the inhabitants of Flixborough need not have procured them from estuarine or marine waters (Buck 1997, 100.3). In addition to the evidence for exploitation of the wetlands themselves, there are indications of the exploitation of wetland edge, woodland and more open habitats, reflected by the presence of roe deer and hares.

Between the late seventh and mid eighth centuries, evidence for craft-working and specialist raw material production is more limited than for subsequent periods. This is probably due to the fact that the deposited material relates more to activities undertaken in the vicinity of the excavated area. Small-scale textile manufacture is indicated by the recovery of heckle teeth, a spindle-whorl, a pin-beater, shears and a small number of loom-weights. The presence of small quantities of smelting and smithing slag, hammer-scale, and a crucible fragment with copper and zinc residues, also reflects some iron-working and non-ferrous metalworking (Starley forthcoming; Mortimer forthcoming; Wastling forthcoming). In addition, an axe-head and punches indicate wood-working and metalworking.

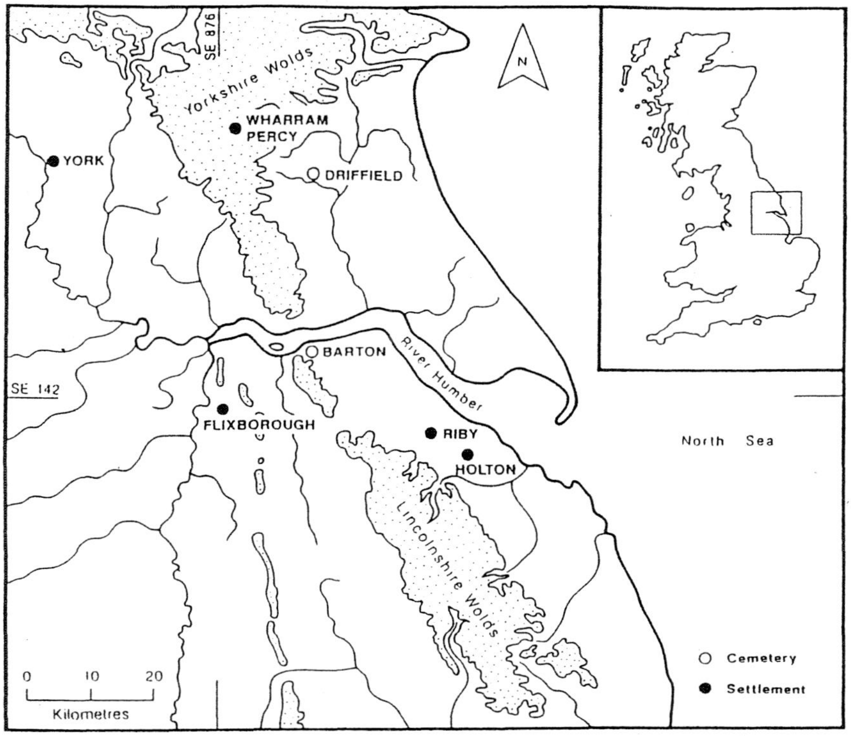

Fig. 5.12. Sites with imported Continental pottery dating from the seventh to ninth centuries, in the hinterland of the Humber estuary.

Set alongside this general paucity of craft-working evidence, the imported commodities from this period suggest a population integrated within both regional and long-distance trade and exchange networks. Fragments of imported glass vessels – some with reticella decoration – were found in post-hole fills and in occupation deposits within the majority of the buildings. They are probably derived ultimately from the Rhineland or the Low Countries. Identical parallels for the reticella-decorated bowl fragments have been found in eighth- to ninth-century contexts at Dorestad in the Netherlands, Ribe in Denmark, and Valsgärde in Sweden (Stiegemann and Wemhoff 1999, 171–3; Jensen 1991, 15; Steuer 1999, 411–3; Evison forthcoming). Similarly, sherds of wheel-thrown pottery made in the same areas were also recovered, for example, Walberberg ware and grey-burnished wares (Hodges 1981, 184; Mainman 1993, 569–76; Vince forthcoming). Finds of 'primary' and – 'intermediate' series *sceatta* coinage – Series D runic and Series E 'porcupines' also reflect links with Frisia, the Rhine estuary and the Low Countries (Archibald forthcoming). Indeed, the majority of the *sceattas* from the period between 700 and 750 were imported ultimately from the Continent. Bearing in mind the unusual proportion of very large cattle from Flixborough, it is possible that these were also being imported from areas of continental Europe with demonstrably larger breeds, such as Flanders (Dobney forthcoming; Ervynck pers. comm.).

The character and derivation of the imported commodities at Flixborough are representative of what can be called the 'Humber zone' between the end of the seventh and the ninth century (Loveluck 1998, 157–9 and 1998a, 44–5). Fig. 5.12 shows other sites around the Humber estuary which have yielded finds of Continental pottery, dating to this period. From approximately 700 to 800 in particular, the estuary appears to have acted as a trading interface and thoroughfare with the area of the continental North Sea coast stretching from the mouth of the Rhine to Ribe (Bendixen 1981, 64–7; Bencard and Bender Jørgensen 1990, 144–7; Steuer 1999, 411–13). Settlements on both sides of the Humber were in receipt of commodities from the Rhineland, the Low Countries, and possibly northern France and western Denmark.

Flixborough appears to be extraordinary in terms of the quantity of imports present at what by the eighth century can be termed a 'rural' settlement. Yet, it is difficult to determine why it is extraordinary. Its exceptional appearance could be partly a result of the circumstances of deposit formation and survival conditions. Alternatively, the number of imported luxuries present at the site could form an accurate indicator of a high-status element in the settlement's population (see below).

Mid eighth to mid ninth century

During the mid eighth century, all the structures were rebuilt, the majority upon the building-plots established in the early eighth century. At some time, between the late eighth and early ninth century, building 13 in the shallow depression was demolished and the whole of the central part of the site was used as a refuse dumping area, possibly for the settlement as a whole. There are observable differences in terms of the character of the finds within the period from the late seventh and mid eighth centuries, which could relate to a more representative sample of the settlement's refuse or alternatively to a change in the character of the settlement (see below).

Provisional findings from the analysis of the faunal remains suggest major changes to the animal husbandry component of the agricultural economy within the period from approximately 750 to 850. These changes can be observed primarily in two major dumping episodes in the centre of the site, separated by a phase of building between the early to the mid ninth century. In the first extended phase of dumping during the late eighth century, cattle bones reached a peak in comparison with sheep and pigs – the relative numbers of the latter declining sharply as a proportion of the main domesticated livestock species (Dobney *et al.* forthcoming). The majority of the cattle were adults or sub-adults when killed, with very few juveniles. Such a pattern has previously been viewed as indicative of settlements provisioned from non-local livestock, possibly from linked estate holdings (Crabtree 1990,

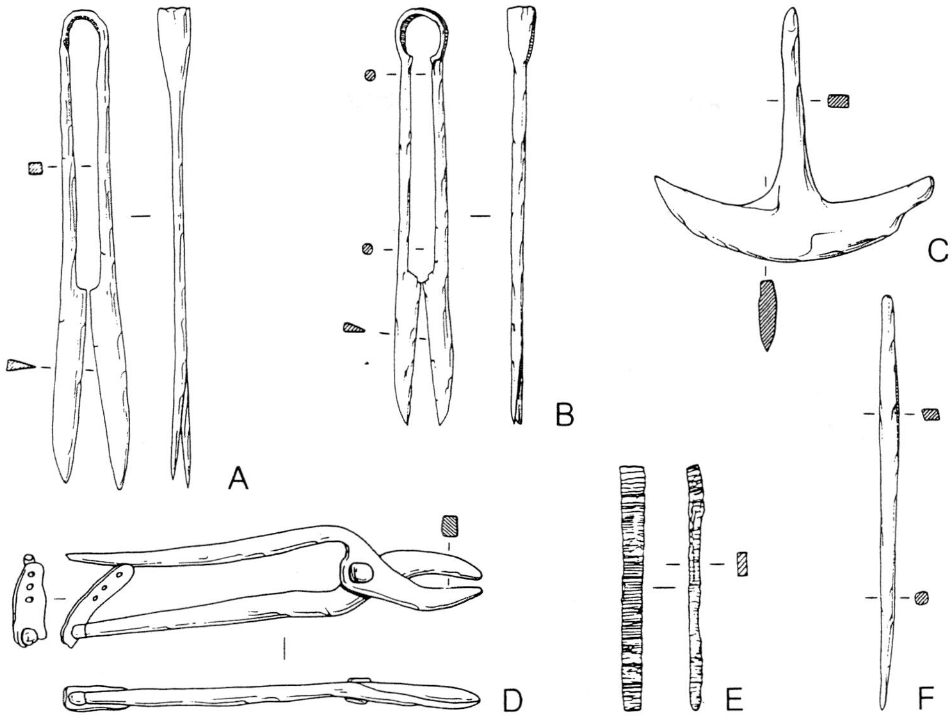

Fig. 5.13. Range of craft-working tools from Flixborough: a) and b) shears for textile production (1:3); c) lunette knife for leatherworking (1:3); d) hand-vice/pincers (1:3), e) file (1:2) and f) punch (1:3) for metalworking.

75; Hooke 1998, 50). At the same time, the evidence for wild species shows continued exploitation of the Trent wetlands, with wild geese, cranes and waders increasing slightly, with cetaceans also present. Further remains of roe deer and hares also reflect continued access to animals from woodland and more open landscapes.

Between the early and mid ninth century, however, cattle bones constituted only 10 percent of animal bones deposited, while at the same time almost 60 percent of bones from amongst the three main domesticated species were from sheep. During the same period, exploitation of wildfowl from the wetlands also appears to have fallen significantly across a range of species, especially with regard to cranes and geese, while quantities of roe deer and hares remained consistent, and wild boar and pine martens also made a limited appearance (Dobney *et al.* forthcoming).

The late eighth-century refuse deposits provide a more comprehensive view of the craft-working infrastructure of the settlement. Greater quantities of textile manufacturing debris, iron-working and non-ferrous metalworking evidence were all present amongst a wide range of domestic finds. In addition

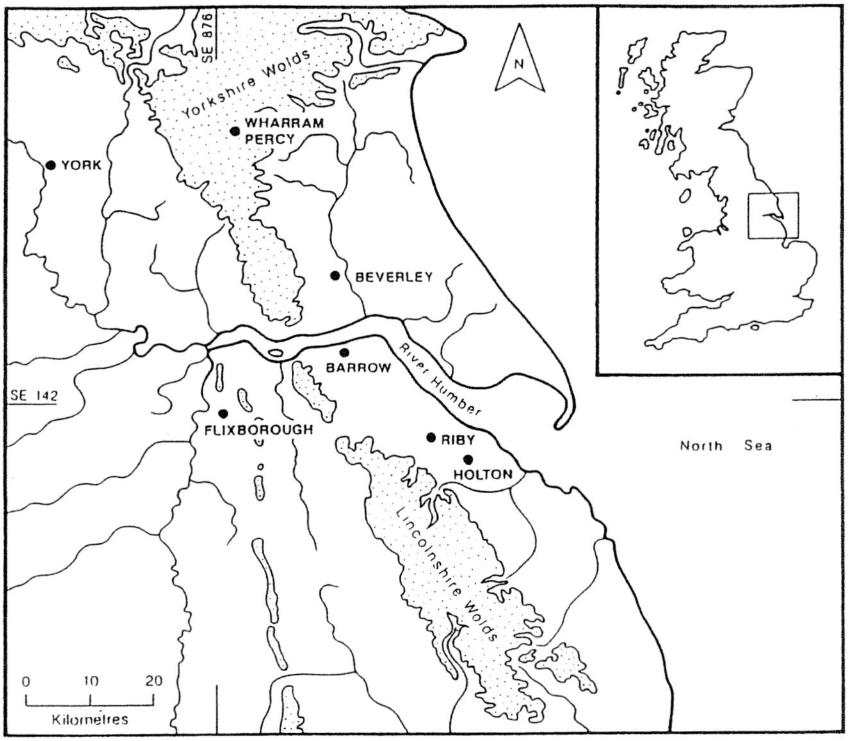

Fig. 5.14. Distribution of sites with Ipswich ware in the hinterland of the Humber estuary.

to crucible fragments with copper and zinc residues, lead melt also indicates the working of the latter metal. A larger collection of tools than from previous periods relates to wood-working, leather-working and metal-working (Ottaway forthcoming; Fig. 5.13).

Even though the evidence from the late eighth-century dumps indicates a settlement with inhabitants involved in a broad range of activities, the tools, industrial and manufacturing debris, deposited predominantly in the middle of the ninth century, suggest a significant increase in the scale of specialist commodity production between approximately 800 and 850. This is reflected across a broad range of crafts: tools relating to non-ferrous metalworking include a hand vice (Pinder pers. comm.), punches, crucibles, mould fragments, scrap metal and lead melt, whilst slag, hammer-scale and partly finished objects reflect iron-smithing. Adzes, rasps, draw-knives and wedges for wood-working were also recovered from the ditch fills and the dumps, together with a collection of slickers and awls for leatherworking.

Nevertheless, the evidence for these craft activities pales into insignificance beside the quantity of textile-manufacturing debris, comprising over 200 loom-weights, together with implements associated with the various stages of textile manufacture. There was also distinct zonation in the deposition of textile-working debris, in that heckle teeth were all found in the ditch fills, whilst weaving-related artefacts were all in the dumps in the centre of the site (Fig. 5.8). This may well reflect the spatial organization of different stages and types of textile manufacture. It is also noteworthy that the size of loom-weight used became significantly smaller during the first half of the ninth century, perhaps reflecting the production of a finer-quality cloth, possibly for export (Walton Rogers forthcoming b). The potential link between the overwhelming dominance of sheep amongst the domesticated livestock and textile manufacturing equipment amongst the craft-working evidence is of primary importance. The age at death data may indicate whether the predominance of sheep does indeed relate to the provision of wool for cloth manufacture (Dobney pers. comm.).

Prior to the early ninth century, patterns of integration within regional and longer-distance exchange networks were identical to those of the early eighth century. That is to say, Continental pottery, Frisian *sceattas*, glass vessels and Eifel lava querns reflect international links while Maxey-type wares reflect either regionally traded pottery or a regional tradition in pottery production (Young pers. comm.). Changes occurred, however, in the late eighth or early ninth century. From this time Ipswich ware, made at the proto-urban settlement or *Wic* of the same name in Suffolk, started to be deposited (Blinkhorn forthcoming). This date for the appearance of this type of pottery is also mirrored at Lurk Lane in Beverley, East Yorkshire (Watkins 1991, 62), and as with imported Continental pottery, the distribution of Ipswich ware on Middle Saxon settlements straddles the Humber Estuary (Fig. 5.14). Ipswich ware was also recovered from eighth- and ninth-century contexts at Fishergate, York, with only four out of a total of 36 sherds having been deposited prior to the late eighth or ninth century (Mainman 1993, 566). Consequently, a broad pattern is emerging of the arrival of Ipswich ware in significant quantities at York and around the Humber estuary, from the later eighth and early ninth centuries.

The distribution patterns of Continental imports and Ipswich ware may well reflect the use of the same sea-borne communication routes from the Continent, up the eastern coast of England to the Humber estuary (Loveluck 1994, 312; 1998, 158). Commodity movement along the east coast is also reflected by the presence of West Saxon silver pennies from the mid ninth century. This is a recurrent pattern for the second half of the ninth century, with West Saxon pennies also coming from Fishergate, from Cottam, East Yorkshire, and from Lindisfarne, Northumberland (Kemp 1996, 83; Richards 1997, 237; O'Sullivan pers. comm.).

It is perhaps significant that it was also from the end of the eighth or from the early ninth century that styli and window glass were first deposited at Flixborough. Indeed, the majority of stratified styli and window glass fragments were recovered from contexts dating from the period between approximately 800 and 850 (see below). The refuse deposits of predominantly mid ninth-century date (Fig. 5.8), particularly the ditch fills, also contained the first significant quantities of dress accessories from the site, of which most of the closely datable pieces were manufactured between the late eighth and mid ninth centuries (Fig. 5.15).

Fig. 5.15. Late eighth- to early ninth-century disc brooch from mid ninth-century refuse dump (3758).

Mid and late ninth century to early tenth century

The major changes in the spatial and structural character of the settlement during the mid to late ninth century (Fig. 5.9) are accompanied by changes in craft-working practices, trading patterns, and access to imported luxuries.

As in the first half of the ninth century, the vast majority of finds relating to craft-working activities were associated with textile manufacture. However, the quantity of textile manufacturing remains deposited was smaller, and the debris from all stages of fibre preparation and cloth manufacture was mixed together within the refuse dumps to either side of the gravel pathways. Some evidence for wood-working, leather-working, ferrous and fine metalworking also remained in the form of tools and debris, but overall the refuse seems to reflect a decrease in the scale of production between the mid to late ninth and early tenth centuries.

It is also possible that some of the tools and the one mould fragment from this phase could be residual from earlier periods, since sherds of pottery vessels re-worked from earlier deposits were found in the dumps, together with early eighth-century Frisian *sceattas*. Other notable instances of residual artefacts manufactured between the eighth and early ninth centuries include an inscribed lead plaque bearing the names of seven individuals, both male and female (Fig. 5.16; Brown and Okasha forthcoming), together with diagnostic dress accessories. These artefacts were recovered from late ninth- to early tenth-century deposits containing early Torksey and Late Saxon local pottery wares.

Despite these changes, the species composition patterns amongst the main domesticated livestock remained broadly similar to the preceding period, although cattle numbers rose again to the approximate level of the first half of the eighth century. Sheep continued to predominate, perhaps relating to the provision of wool for textiles, but the proportion of sheep to cattle fell by the early tenth century. Preliminary results also indicate that exploitation of the nearby wetlands altered significantly between the mid ninth and early tenth century, with numbers of waterfowl bones gradually increasing in comparison with the first half of the ninth century (Dobney *et al.* forthcoming). Numbers of chickens and domestic geese also decreased. However, the small quantities of roe deer and hare bones seem to have remained consistent with eighth- and earlier ninth-century levels.

It is difficult to establish whether the settlement continued to be integrated within inter-regional and long-distance exchange networks during this period. Fragments of imported Continental glass vessels and lava querns were still deposited, and a very small number of white-ware pottery sherds, ultimately from the Rhineland or Northern France, was also recovered. Unfortunately, the evident level of artefact residuality from the eighth and early ninth centuries suggests that the majority of continental imports found in deposits of this period could be residual. If participation in North Sea trading networks did continue, it appears to have been much decreased compared with the period between 700 and 850.

Fig. 5.16. Inscribed lead plaque with the names of seven individuals. Late eighth/early ninth century.

The impression gained from the combined evidence of the faunal remains, craft-working debris, and the probable absence of new imports from southern England and the Continent, is one of considerable change. The buildings from this period were much smaller and more ephemeral than at any other time. In addition, the inhabitants no longer appear to have exploited the nearby wetlands extensively. The range of craft activities decreased significantly, and trade and exchange links appear to have operated on a regional level only, witnessed by the receipt of Early Lincoln fine-shelled ware pottery from the mid ninth century, and Torksey ware from the late ninth century.

This evidence may reflect dislocation of trading patterns along the east coast of England during the mid to late ninth century and, as a corollary, disruption in the production and demand for specialist commodities which may have been bound for proto-urban trading centres. In addition, the structural character of the site, the recovery of only one residual eighth- to early ninth-century stylus (Pestell forthcoming), and the changes in the exploitation of the Trent wetlands, could also reflect a change in the character of the settlement during the mid to late ninth century.

Early tenth century to early eleventh century

During the early tenth century the structural character and use of the excavated area changed radically, as described above (Fig. 5.10). The period saw the construction of the largest buildings within the occupation sequence, followed by massive animal bone and refuse dumping, and indications of a settlement shift to the east.

The evidence from this, the Late Saxon or Anglo-Scandinavian period, provides a contrast to that from the eighth and early ninth centuries, in that the large buildings and massive animal bone dumps were accompanied by a dearth of decorated metalwork. Nevertheless, diagnostic types of tenth- to early eleventh-century pottery were present, including Torksey ware, Torksey-type ware, Lincoln kiln-type ware, Lincoln fine-shelled ware, and Late Saxon local wares. These were widespread throughout deposits from this period, especially in the southern and eastern parts of the site. They cannot be dismissed as intrusive due to their number, the limited degree of contamination of early to mid tenth-century deposits, and the typological developments of Torksey ware seen in the tenth-century sequence. Intrusion of medieval pottery occurred only in small quantities in the upper deposits.

The contrast between the tenth-century evidence on the one hand, and the eighth- to ninth-century evidence on the other, also has implications for assessing settlement wealth, status and character. The building foundations and vast quantities of animal bones from the tenth century demonstrate conspicuous consumption of timber and animal resources, yet demonstrable evidence for portable wealth and the importation of luxuries is extremely scarce. This contrast with circumstances in the eighth and ninth centuries may reflect different ways of expressing wealth and status. Larger buildings and increased consumption of animal resources reflect high social position at a time when luxuries and precious metals were rare or were unobtainable due to some social constraint.

In terms of the overall quantities of animal bones deposited, approximately three times as many cattle, sheep/goat, pig and horse bones were recovered from tenth century deposits in comparison with other periods. The majority came from the huge bone dump sealing building 7. In contrast, quantities of bones from geese, domestic chickens, wild geese, ducks and other waterfowl were significantly greater than for the period between the late eighth and mid ninth century. The tenth-century inhabitants were certainly exploiting the range of wetland bird species seen in earlier periods, as well as the roe deer and hare resources, and more rarely red deer and wild boar. Dolphins and porpoises were again utilized, as in the period between the late seventh and early eighth centuries (Dobney *et al.* forthcoming).

Despite the quantities of animals being consumed on the settlement, indications of specialist commodity production are more scarce than for the period between the mid eighth and ninth centuries. Textile production is reflected in quantities of loom-weights and other textile-related tools, but the numbers are relatively small: e.g. fewer than 40 loom-weights were recovered (Walton Rogers forthcoming a). A limited range of tools also reflects wood-working, while slag and hammer-scale indicate iron smithing. It is uncertain whether the hoard of wood-working tools inside two lead tanks, recovered as a stray find, should be dated to the Middle or Late Saxon periods (Fig. 5.17). Most comparable lead tanks, however, date from the tenth century or later (Cowgill forthcoming; Fox 1923, 300; Nicholson 1997a, 390–1; Finney 1998, 16). Overall, whilst levels of consumption of animal resources were conspicuous, levels of production and specialist craft provision appear to relate to the needs of the inhabitants alone.

The tenth-century pottery wares from the site reflect integration within regional trade networks. The Torksey ware indicates incorporation within Lower Trent valley and Humber communications routes, whilst the Lincoln wares demonstrate the growing role of the city as a provider of commodities for its hinterland during the tenth century (Miles and Young 1989, 234–5). Other evidence showing that the inhabitants enjoyed links on an inter-regional or long-distance level is absent, although the identification of bones from the black rat in a tenth-century pit might provide a faunal indicator of direct contact with Anglo-Scandinavian York (Dobney and Harwood 1999, 377–8; Dobney forthcoming). Bones of this animal from Coppergate, in York, provide the only other findspot of black rats in northern England at this period (O'Connor 1989, 189–91).

The general absence of newly minted coinage at Flixborough during the first half of the tenth century may also reflect a low level of integration within inter-regional exchange networks, or a constraint on access to coinage. The Anglo-Scandinavian coin issues from York did not reach Flixborough; instead, late ninth-century silver coinage – predominantly West Saxon in origin – was recovered from tenth- to eleventh-century contexts, having either been reworked from earlier deposits, or deliberately kept in circulation at a time of silver shortage. The occurrence only in tenth-century deposits of lead weights possibly related to the exchange of bullion, together with the recovery of a silver ingot, also hint at a return to a system of bullion exchange in the absence of regular coin supply. From the 970s, however, an unstratified silver penny of Edward the Martyr suggests the resumption of a coin supply, possibly from the Lincoln mint.

To sum up, the tenth century saw the greatest affluence within the occupation sequence at Flixborough in terms of the massive consumption of domesticated livestock, some of which may have arrived from the linked landholdings of a larger, composite estate. At the same time, the size of the buildings also indicates ostentatious use of timber resources. In contrast, the scale and diversity of craft specialization had decreased significantly in comparison with the eighth and ninth centuries, and indications of trading contacts reflect only regional links. Interestingly, however, the evidence for trade links does reflect the emergence of the regional 'central place' functions of Lincoln and, perhaps, York.

Interpretation of settlement character and status

The issue of defining the character of the Anglo-Saxon settlement in Flixborough parish has already given rise to speculation, despite the lack hitherto of detailed analysis. Provisional interpretations of the nature of the settlement have focused on the similarity between artefacts recovered from excavations on documented monastic sites and those from Flixborough. As a consequence of this similarity, particularly regarding eighth- and ninth-century artefacts, the immediate assumption following excavation was that the Flixborough settlement represented an undocumented monastic centre (Whitwell 1991, 247; Yorke 1993, 146; Blair 1996 a, 9).

Such an interpretation was influenced by a number of factors. First, in the absence of detailed information about the changing structural character of the Flixborough settlement and changing patterns of artefact and animal bone deposition, it was assumed that the settlement had a single homogeneous character for its whole occupation sequence. Secondly, the trajectory of the development of Middle Saxon settlement studies, leading on from the work of pioneers like Rosemary Cramp, has resulted in a disproportionate number of excavations at the sites of documented monasteries, often known to have enjoyed the patronage of Anglo-Saxon royal clans. The archaeological remains from these settlements, such as Whitby, Monkwearmouth and Jarrow, seemed to corroborate textual descriptions of structures, practices and commodities present at these sites. Consequently, and perhaps inevitably, the finds associated with these sites were seen as characteristic of high-status monastic centres, in the absence of wider comparative information from a greater range of settlement types (Peers and Radford 1943, 27–88; White 1984, 37–8; Cramp 1969, 21–66).

This bias towards documented monastic centres amongst our sample of excavations on Middle Saxon settlements has resulted in certain traits in

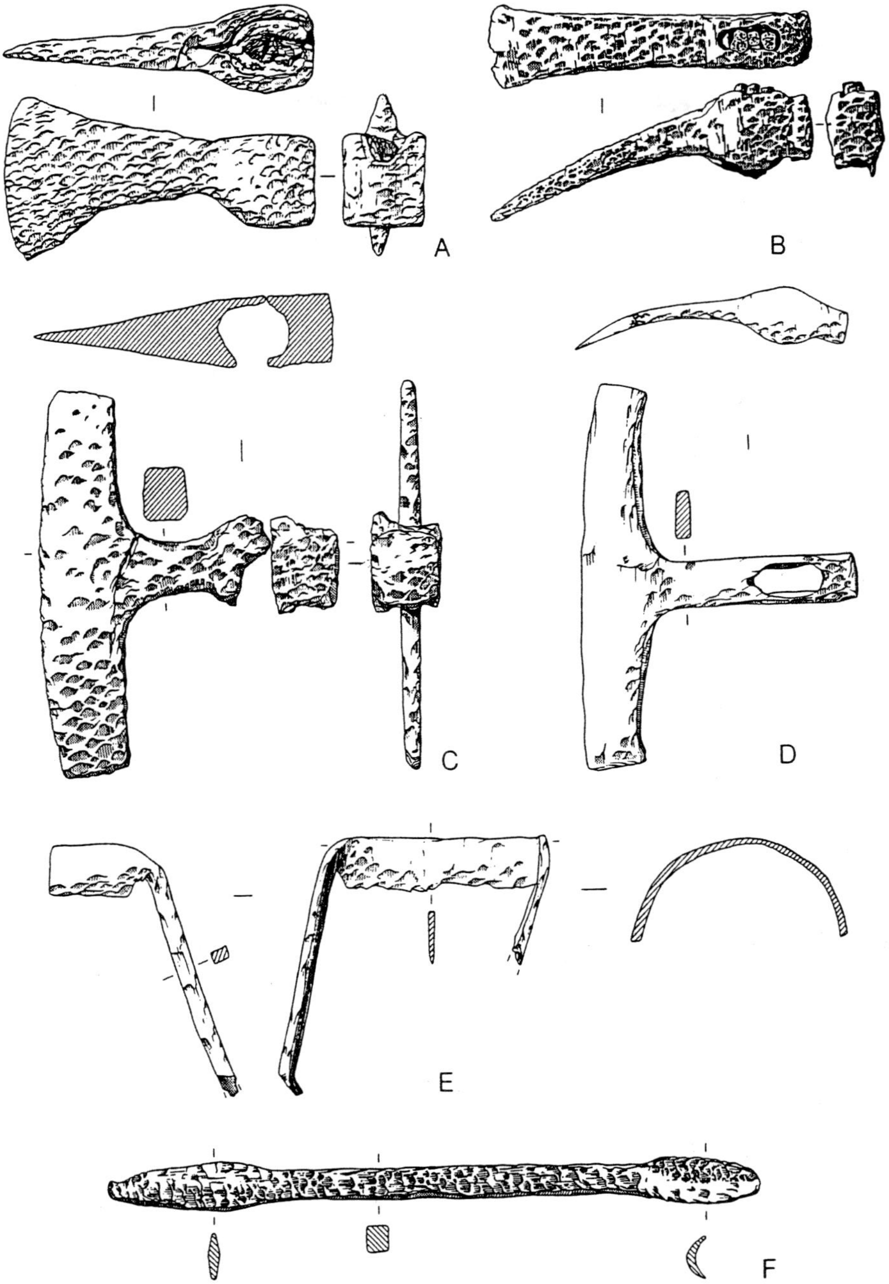

Fig. 5.17. Wood-working tools from Flixborough: a) axe (1:4); b) adze (1:4); c) T-shaped axe (1:4); d) T-shaped adze (1:4); e) shave (1:4); f) spoon-auger drill-bit (1:4).

settlement situation, structure and layout being viewed as typical of monasteries: for example, a riverine, coastal or promontory location; a formal planned layout with a central cult focus or foci, sometimes built in stone; small satellite buildings; and major enclosure ditches (Cramp 1976, 204–8; Stocker 1993, 101–14; Blair 1996a, 98–104). Similarly, certain types of finds relating to long-distance exchange contacts, craft-working, literacy, and certain dress accessories, have all been seen as indicative of monasteries (or *minsters*; Blair 1994, 65; Blair 1996, 9; Foot 1992, 222–5). It is not contested that combinations of the above traits are reflected at monastic centres, but it is far more difficult to ascertain to what extent some of these traits were exclusive to them.

The following discussion evaluates the evidence from Flixborough within a broader consideration of the extent to which these traits characterized monasteries, or whether they reflected wider trends within contemporary Anglo-Saxon settlements. Having exposed the limits of inference from the various categories of archaeological data, the changing structural and finds profiles within the Flixborough occupation sequence may now be assessed for their potential to illustrate changing settlement character, through the Middle and Late Saxon periods.

Settlement location, layout and structural character

Taking the issue of settlement location as a starting point, a number of points can be made. First, location of important settlements on the coast overlooking safe harbours and beaching sites, on riverine and road communication routes, or in insular or promontory situations, was not the preserve of monastic settlements alone. For example, the Northumbrian royal vill of Driffield was located at the navigable headwaters of the River Hull, with at least one possible waterfront mooring point known from nearby Skerne (Swanton 1996, 41; Loveluck 1998a, 45; Dent, Loveluck and Fletcher 2000, 242). Similarly, the West Saxon royal vill referred to as *Hamtun* (Southampton) was located at a strategic position between the mouths of the rivers Test and Itchen, at the head of Southampton Water. It is unclear, however, whether it was established at the same time, before or after the foundation of the trading and craft-working settlement at *Hamwic* (Morton 1992, 27).

Textual references to the location of monasteries cannot therefore be used to rule out the presence of other, important 'secular' settlements in such locations. Indeed, early donations to monasteries and their founders comprised vills or groups of vills, with their constituent settlements, in strategic situations. For example, the estates of the community of Lindisfarne along the River Tweed and in its hinterland, consisted of a range of vills on or in close proximity to this navigable waterway. Only two of the settlements within these landholdings are known to have become monasteries – Norham and Melrose (Smith 1984, 179–80).

In addition, when considering the issue of settlement location in badly drained ecological habitats, such as areas within and adjacent to floodplains, fenland, and marshes, the availability of areas of higher, well-drained land was at a premium for all types of settlement. Hence, in addition to the Anglo-Saxon settlement remains from Flixborough parish, two other recently discovered Middle Saxon settlements in the Trent valley, at Belton on the Isle of Axholme and at Girton near Newark, were also located on sand rises (Young pers. comm.; Leahy pers. comm.; Kinsley 1998, 46). The former, as its name suggests, was situated on a relatively large island, and the latter on a ridge or dune above the wetlands of the Trent floodplain.

On the basis of the survival of textual sources and the subjects which interested their writers, there is no doubt that insular and promontory locations in marshland environments were favoured topographical situations for monastic settlements. Examples of important monasteries situated on islands can be cited from across the southern Lincolnshire and Cambridgeshire fens, as well as on the Somerset Levels (Stocker 1993, 101–14; Hooke 1998, 173–8). Nevertheless, they were by no means the only documented settlements in these locations: monasteries sited in fenland-edge environments were also granted estates in their surrounding landscapes, comprising vills, land for seasonal grazing, and rights to resources such as fish and fowl (Hooke 1998, 175–9). These holdings provided food or commodity renders to the monastic estate centres, but there is no evidence to suggest that the subordinate settlements within estates should be regarded as distinctive from other contemporary, non-monastic settlements in fenland landscapes.

Indeed, monasteries were not the only significant 'high-status' settlements recorded in wetland edge locations; for example, the burghal fort of Lyng was situated on a promontory in the Somerset Levels, linked by a bridge to Athelney, with its monastery (Havinden 1981, 94–5). Fulcheri, the lord of the Flixborough estate in the time of Edward the Confessor, is also an example of a secular aristocrat who held lands in an insular location. In his case, he had a hall and, presumably, its attendant settlement, together with a range of other landholdings on the island and marshes of Axholme, situated on the opposite bank of the Trent from his estate centre Flixborough (Foster and Longley 1924, 192–3). Consequently, with increasing archaeological discoveries of undocumented Middle to Late Saxon settlements in wetland locations, and with the complexity of the settlement and exploitation patterns evident from textual sources, care must be taken in interpreting settlement character from topographical situation alone.

When examining the physical character of settlements, the problem of limited excavation immediately presents itself, yet some points can be made concerning settlement morphology and structures. With the increased numbers of excavations carried out in the past two decades, it has become apparent that a greater number of settlements exhibited evidence of planning in their layouts from the seventh century onwards (Hamerow 1995, 16; Loveluck 1998, 159).

This planning was manifested in a number of ways, one of which was the more frequent use of major enclosure ditches and palisades to define particular areas within settlements, and in rarer instances to surround settlements as a whole (Loveluck 1997, 191). Examples dating from between the seventh and tenth centuries span much of England: these include Yeavering and Milfield, in Northumberland (Hope Taylor 1977, 78–88; Gates and O'Brien 1988, 3); Cowage Farm, near Malmesbury, Wiltshire (Hinchliffe 1987; 240); Thwing, East Yorkshire (Manby pers. comm.); Riby Crossroads, north Lincolnshire (Steedman 1995, 221); Bramford, Suffolk (Reynolds 1999, 144); and the Raunds and Higham Ferrers settlements in Northamptonshire, amongst others (Windell, Chapman and Woodiwiss 1990, 17; Foard 1998, 77).

Other settlements, such as Goltho, Lincolnshire, in its Middle Saxon phase, North Elmham, Norfolk, and Wicken Bonhunt, Essex, were planned with particular reference to linear ditches and, in the case of the former two settlements, to linear trackways or 'streets' (Beresford 1987, 23; Wade-Martins 1980, 54–5; Wade 1980, 96–7). At Flixborough, the Middle Saxon ditch also seems to have been linear, heading down towards the Trent wetlands. The use of enclosure ditches, however, whether linear or otherwise, was not ubiquitous on settlements throughout the Middle and Late Saxon periods. At Flixborough, North Elmham, and Catholme in Staffordshire, the later phases of these settlements were either not enclosed or greater use was made of fences and hedging (Figs. 5.9 and 5.10; Wade-Martins 1980, 136 and 140; Losco-Bradley and Wheeler 1984, 111).

Set alongside the evidence for widespread use of ditches and other boundary markers on Middle to Late Saxon settlements, enclosure features suggested to have marked out monastic precincts can be seen in their wider contemporary context. Without documentary references describing the nature of a settlement, or topographical study showing the association of an enclosure with a church or churches, extreme caution should be exercised before suggesting that a Middle to Late Saxon boundary feature could represent a *vallum monasterii*, especially under circumstances of partial excavation. For example, the tentatively identified monastic boundary ditches and fences at Beverley, East Yorkshire, and Hartlepool, County Durham, cannot be distinguished from their counterparts found on contemporary non-monastic settlements (Armstrong, Tomlinson and Evans 1991, 8–11; Daniels 1989, 161). It is their assumed association with textually-attested monasteries and their proximity to churches that gives such interpretations credence.

Another common trend seen in settlement layout from the seventh century onwards is the more frequent occurrence of the superimposition of buildings on long-lived plots. This phenomenon can be observed on a wide range of sites around England, especially when elements of a settlement plan were maintained for an extended period. Thus, on sites where linear or 'axial' plans existed, whether defined by building orientation or ditch systems, buildings were often constructed on the same plots as their predecessors. This is not to say that they were always constructed on exactly the same foundations: the settlements of Yeavering, Wicken Bonhunt, North Elmham, Whithorn (Dumfries and Galloway) and Flixborough – for part of its occupational history – all possessed linear or axially planned elements, and building superimposition is a constant feature of these sites (Hope-Taylor 1977, 46–66; Wade 1980, 97–8; Wade-Martins 1980, 54–5; Hill 1997, 139–56). All are furthermore thought to represent the remains of high-status settlements, both secular estate centres and monasteries.

Likewise, superimposed buildings are also features of other planned settlements where structures were organized around central foci, whether churches or other large buildings. Examples have been excavated on such sites at Hartlepool (Daniels 1989, 205); Cheddar (Rahtz 1979, 49–61); Cowage Farm, near Malmesbury (Hinchliffe 1987, 245–7); Dunbar, East Lothian (Holdsworth 1991, 315); and Saint Peter's, Northampton (Williams *et al.* 1985; Blair 1996a, 101–3). Again all these settlements are recorded or interpreted as Middle and Late Saxon aristocratic or ecclesiastical centres. Nevertheless, superimposed buildings have also been uncovered on settlements which are not deemed to have been in any way extraordinary, as in the housing zone at West Heslerton (Powlesland 1997, 110–3). However, neither the housing zone nor the main Middle Saxon area of occupation within the West Heslerton settlement seem to present the same intensity of building superimposition as witnessed on the aforementioned settlements. Consequently, the maintenance of a planned layout, partially by long-term superimposition of buildings, seems to be a reflection of high status and of control by an individual or collective authority (James, Marshall and Millett 1985).

Like certain traits in Middle and Late Saxon settlement morphology, building size and certain architectural features have also been viewed as indicative of monastic settlements. It has been suggested that small buildings found at Hartlepool, Whitby and Whithorn were representative of monastic cells (Daniels 1989, 206; Blair 1996, 9–10). This view, however, needs some amendment, since the majority of the excavated Anglo-Saxon buildings at Whithorn were much larger than those from Hartlepool and Whitby, dating between the early eighth and mid ninth centuries (Hill 1997, 172–8). During this period, the Whithorn 'halls', and other examples at the suggested monastery at Hoddom (Dumfries and Galloway) were of a similar size to contemporary buildings from Flixborough and Wicken Bonhunt (see above; Lowe 1991, 14–19; Wade 1980, 97). On the basis of the various campaigns of excavation conducted at Whithorn, it is suggested that the structures discussed above were not located near to the main cult focus or communal buildings of the monastery (Hill 1997, 41–4). Smaller buildings existed alongside the 'halls' at Whithorn, but they did not predominate until the second half of the ninth century, with the onset of the Hiberno-Norse period (Hill 1997, 183–208).

In addition, particular styles of building foundation, notably gravel and dry-stone foundations for sill-beam based structures, have also been viewed as indicative of monasteries in Middle Saxon contexts. Again examples have been found at Whitby (Rahtz 1976, 461; Cramp 1993, 65), Hartlepool (Daniels 1989, 178–81), and Whithorn (Hill 1997, 178–9), but their occurrence on documented secular sites such as Dunbar, and on undocumented settlements such as Flixborough, suggests that this architectural style was more widespread, albeit seemingly reserved for higher status settlements (Holdsworth 1991, 315).

Consequently, it has become evident that large, earth-fast timber buildings as well as buildings with stone footings are found on both monastic and secular settlements, in addition to other small ancillary buildings. Nevertheless, a greater number of smaller buildings, possibly to be interpreted as 'cells', are found on monastic sites; and conversely, large, earth-fast buildings may be more characteristic of secular estate centres. In addition, temporal trends in building size also occur, and this is demonstrated clearly when Middle Saxon settlements are compared with their Late Saxon counterparts (Loveluck 1998, 159). In their tenth-century phases, the settlements at Flixborough, North Elmham (Wade-Martins 1980, 137), Goltho (Beresford 1987; 31–58), Faccombe Netherton (Hampshire) (Reynolds 1999, 136), and Raunds (Cadman and Foard 1984, 84–5; Windell, Chapman and Woodiwiss 1990, 23–5) all possessed either a single large rectangular building or a small number of such buildings often 20 m or more in length. In the case of the three former sites, these buildings, which may justifiably be called 'halls', were significantly larger than their Middle Saxon predecessors.

The final problem relating to the interpretation of buildings concerns the identification of churches or chapels prior to their relatively widespread construction in stone. Significant problems exist both in deciding how to recognize timber churches from archaeological remains and in understanding what the presence of a church or chapel on a settlement might represent (Morris 1989, 75). At Flixborough, building 1a – dating from the early to mid eighth century – was associated with six, east-west aligned graves (Figs. 5.6 and 5.7). The possible social differentiation reflected by burial in association with this building as opposed to interment in the cemetery, could indicate burial in the chapel of an elite household (Morris 1989, 133). A similar but slightly later example can be suggested at nearby Burnham, North Lincolnshire (Coppack 1986, 39–41). At other settlements in the Humber region, graves are also associated with possible churches. At Thwing, a building interpreted as a chapel or oratory was located in an enclosure with a small cemetery of 68 graves, though no graves were placed within the building itself (Manby forthcoming).

In the absence of a larger excavation area at Flixborough, it is not possible to draw a definitive conclusion as to whether or not the graves in the possible mortuary chapel relate to the leading family of the settlement. There are also similarities with the eighth-century mortuary chapel at Whithorn, although there are significant differences in the age of the individuals buried (Mays forthcoming; Cardy 1997, 556–60). At Whithorn, the mortuary chapel is viewed as peripheral to the main cult focus of the monastery; at Flixborough, it is not possible to draw any conclusions on this subject. Nevertheless, despite centuries of grave-digging in the areas of the Middle Saxon, Late Saxon and medieval settlements near All Saints' Church and North Conesby, no sign of any Middle Saxon sculpture or structural evidence which might indicate the presence of an earlier church has yet been discovered.

Artefacts and faunal remains as indicators of settlement status and character

Just as many of the structural traits formerly associated exclusively with monastic settlements can be shown to have had a much wider occurrence on Middle to Late Saxon settlements, so a broad assessment of finds profiles suggests a wider distribution of artefacts previously viewed as characteristic of monasteries. In addition to preservation and taphonomic factors, it would appear that the status and geographical location of settlements sometimes had as great an influence on the character of artefacts found as the nature of a settlement itself, whether monastery, secular estate centre or otherwise.

The occurrence of rare, imported luxury commodities at monasteries has been seen as characteristic of these sites, and indeed it may be. Nevertheless, if the distribution of imported luxuries on Middle Saxon settlements is studied for the area of eastern England, it is clear that monastic settlements were not the exclusive beneficiaries of access to east-coast trade routes. Instead, they formed part of a much wider network of settlements which were in receipt of luxuries, presumably dependent on the high status of at least some of their inhabitants, as well as their geographical location (Loveluck 1994, 312).

In major trading zones such as the Humber estuary, the question of whether access to imported commodities was limited to the highest echelons of society is unclear. It has been assumed that access to luxuries was controlled by social elites, both secular and ecclesiastical, for the purposes of emphasizing their control over resources and enhancing their social prestige (Malinowski 1922, 350–65; Hodges and Moreland 1988, 82–5). Around the Humber estuary, however, every excavated Middle Saxon settlement has yielded imported commodities, in varying quantities. Their common occurrence on settlements in this region indicates that not only the social elite but also possibly wider elements of society had ready access to imports, whether via direct reciprocal exchange with traders, gift exchange, or redistribution through lord-client relations (Mauss 1925, 1954 edn, 59; Gregory 1982, 42–55).

As a consequence, possession of small quantities of imported luxuries may not have displayed social rank to the same extent amongst Middle Saxon societies in different regions of England. Around the Humber, for example, the occurrence of imports on settlements may not reflect exceptionally high status, whereas the rarity of luxury imports in areas distant from major trading zones, such as the upper Trent valley or Northumberland, would have enhanced the social value of possessing and displaying them, alongside alternative methods of status-display, such as conspicuous amassing of livestock (Loveluck 1998a, 46; Loveluck forthcoming).

Hence, in areas poorly integrated into east – and south – coastal trade networks, imports do seem to occur only on settlements of the highest status. For example, in eastern Northumbria, north of the River Tyne, luxury imports from the Middle Saxon period have been recovered only from major monasteries, such as Jarrow and Monkwearmouth, and from royal centres, such as Yeavering and Bamburgh (Cramp 1976, 240; Cramp 1994, 292; Hope Taylor 1977, 181–2, 370). At Flixborough and other sites in 'entry point' regions, such as the Humber and Thames estuaries, Kent and East Anglia, the extent to which imported luxuries reflected the high status of a settlement, or an element of its population, must be considered alongside other archaeological indicators.

In addition to evidence of long-distance exchange contacts, another artefactual trait that has been (and still is) linked to monasteries is the presence of specialist craft-working and industrial evidence. Again, however, the use of such evidence to draw conclusions concerning settlement character has been heavily influenced by the bias towards the excavation of documented monastic sites. With the larger body of archaeological evidence now available, it has become apparent that indications of specialist craft-working activity are generally found on wealthier settlements, although the extent and diversity of craft-working does seem to change on some settlements, between the Middle and Late Saxon periods.

Due to the exceptional nature of the deposits and preservation conditions, the Flixborough settlement has yielded a vast collection of craft-working tools and industrial debris. In its range of craft-working activities, Flixborough shows similarities with Wharram Percy, East Yorkshire (Bayley 1992, 59–64; Lang 1992, 65–6; Richards 1997, 238), Riby Crossroads, North Lincolnshire (Steedman 1995, 222), Shakenoak, Oxfordshire (Brodribb, Hands and Walker 1972), Wicken Bonhunt, Essex (Wade 1980, 98), and also the documented monastery of Whithorn (Hill *et al.* 1997). Evidence for certain types of craft-working, however, is still found exclusively, or predominantly, at major monastic centres during the Middle Saxon period: for example, glass-working at Jarrow and Barking, Essex, and stone sculpture (Cramp 1994, 292–3; Webster 1991, 88; Cramp 1984). Indications of these activities are absent from Flixborough.

Evidence for literacy has generally been viewed as an unambiguous pointer towards the character of a settlement. As a consequence of the undoubted concentration of inscriptions – in Roman and sometimes runic script – at documented monasteries, evidence for literacy on settlements of Middle Saxon date has generally been equated with a monastic character (Peers and Radford 1943, 40–47; Cramp 1984, 124–203; Page 1995, 307–9 and 317–25). The occurrence of styli on the sites of the documented monasteries at Whitby,

Jarrow and Barking reinforced the impression that literacy was restricted to monastic settlements (Peers and Radford 1943, 64–5; Cramp 1976, 238; Webster 1991, 90).

Nevertheless, problems of interpretation surround the issue of the exclusivity of literacy to monasteries during the Middle Saxon period. The extent to which small numbers of literate clerics may have been resident at major secular and ecclesiastical vill centres in this period is unknown. Documentary evidence from the eighth century, indicating that laymen were prohibited from ministering in their own churches suggests that priests may have been resident at such settlements intermittently, if not permanently (Morris 1989, 75). Similarly, the extent to which a small element of the secular aristocracy was literate is also impossible to estimate, but a proportion may have been educated at monasteries, like Aldfrith, King of Northumbria between 685 and 705 (Farmer 1983, 201). Therefore, the presence of styli at an undocumented Middle Saxon settlement is not proof of a monastic community.

At Flixborough, styli were not deposited before the end of the eighth or early ninth century and, where it is possible to gauge, the few stratified examples recovered from contexts after the mid ninth century were residual. In addition, the inscribed lead plaque has its closest palaeographic affinities with the late eighth-century charters of Offa of Mercia (Brown and Okasha forthcoming). It would therefore appear that the population of the settlement possessed a significant literate element for a relatively short period of time, between the end of the eighth and the mid ninth centuries. This concentration of the evidence for literacy may well equate with some sort of monastic phase in the occupation of the settlement (see below). Such an interpretation based on evidence for literacy may, however, be too simplistic without the support of other forms of evidence. Conversely, the absence of styli until *c*. 800, and their very limited residual occurrence after the mid ninth century, might also reflect the non-monastic nature of the settlement for much of the period between the seventh and tenth centuries.

A much-neglected form of evidence which may give important insights into the status and character of settlements, are faunal remains. In the case of Flixborough, the bones of domesticated and wild animals yielded by far the largest source of data, and provisional findings suggest distinct patterns in the exploitation of species during different periods of the settlement's history (Dobney *et al*. forthcoming). Previously, broad patterns of animal husbandry regimes and wild faunal exploitation have been used to draw general conclusions regarding the agricultural and provisioning practices of settlements (Rackham 1989, 201; Crabtree 1990, 28 and 75–93). For example, at West Stow, Suffolk, the fifth- to seventh-century settlement was seen to show signs of self-sufficiency in its cattle husbandry regime, with both very young and old animals and a slaughtering peak in adolescence. In contrast, the much higher proportion of mature cattle at Middle Saxon Southampton, and during the Middle Saxon phases of rural settlements at North Elmham, Wicken Bonhunt, and Portchester (Hampshire) suggested provisioning by means of food renders (Bourdillon 1994, 123–4; Crabtree 1990, 75; Crabtree 1994, 50).

If a high proportion of mature animals and a commensurate lack of young and neonatal animals did reflect the provisioning of high-status settlements via renders from linked landholdings, then the high proportion of adult and sub-adult cattle at Flixborough might also reflect its status as a 'consumer' settlement. In addition, the exceptional size of a large number of the cattle at Flixborough, and the maintenance of that size through time, might also suggest specialist breeding for traction, within the context of a large composite estate (Dobney pers. comm.). Again taking cattle as an example, other indications of settlement character may also be reflected in the occurrence of large numbers of neonatal or very young calves, as a proportion of cattle populations. Such a pattern may relate to vellum production within Middle to Late Saxon monastic estates. This is possibly reflected at Lindisfarne, in eighth- to ninth-century contexts, but detailed analysis has yet to take place (O'Sullivan pers. comm.). A similar relationship between an abundance of neonatal calves and vellum production has also been suggested for eleventh- to thirteenth-century contexts at the episcopal settlement at Vanern, Sweden (Hagberg pers. comm.).

Nevertheless, despite the fact that some traits in livestock provision and breeding may reflect high-status consumption rather than production, not all husbandry practices may coincide. Consequently, a complex mix of animal rearing and importation should be expected. At Flixborough, the exceptional nature of the stratigraphy is providing an unprecedented picture of changing patterns in animal husbandry practices across all the main domesticated species during the Middle and Late Saxon periods. Provisional observations suggest that patterns of domesticated livestock consumption coincided with the predominance of certain craft activities, and also with possible changes in the character of the settlement (see below).

In addition, patterns in the exploitation of wild species may also reflect settlement status and character. A recent review of historical sources and archaeological finds of porpoises, dolphins and other whales during the medieval period, has indicated that access to these marine mammals was controlled by royal prerogative from immediately after the Norman conquest (Gardiner 1998, 179–84). Rights of access were then often granted to monasteries or the secular elite, and consumption of porpoises and dolphins, usually at feasts, was a high-status activity on account of their rarity. Due to the scarcity of evidence, it is less certain whether the occurrence of cetaceans on Anglo-Saxon settlements is also a reflection of high status. Small numbers, however, are recorded as tributes paid to elites in the Late Saxon period (Gardiner 1998, 175; Hooke 1998, 51). It is likely, therefore, that access to cetaceans as a food source was subject to some control, and as such their discovery on Middle and Late Saxon settlements may reflect the elite character of some of their inhabitants. Their occurrence at Flixborough in some numbers may, therefore, be an indicator of status, but the location and environment of settlements should never be forgotten and, in the case of Flixborough, porpoises and dolphins still penetrate the River Trent today (Buck 1997, 100.3): some of these animals could have been caught by accident, in fish traps.

Other wild fauna may also reflect settlement character or the high status of inhabitants, for example, the large quantities of cranes, wild geese, and the occurrence of hawks and lead net-weights at Flixborough might indicate falconry and the netting of wild birds. Such practices are attested in Middle and Late Saxon documentary sources and are associated with both secular and ecclesiastical elites, often in wetlands (Swanton 1975, 111; Hooke 1998, 179–81). In addition, cranes appear to have been a particular target for hawking amongst the highest social strata, as reflected in a letter of 748–54 from King Ethelbert of Kent to St Boniface, in which he requests a pair of falcons that would attack cranes (Emerton 1940, 179). Cranes were also a luxury component of the diet, and were a feast food like porpoises (Rackham 1986, 37).

A high proportion of fowl and fish might also reflect the observance of early dietary rules by monastic communities. The ecological situation of settlements must, however, be considered before drawing firm conclusions regarding status from faunal remains. For example, the situation of Flixborough and any other settlements above the Trent and Humber wetlands would have ensured a plentiful supply of fish and wildfowl.

Indications of changing settlement character at Flixborough

The review of archaeological traits used to assist in the interpretation of settlement character has demonstrated that many features previously associated with monastic settlements were in fact more widespread. In many cases, characteristics widely thought to signify monasteries can be seen to be more general indicators of high social status. This ambiguity is compounded by our reliance on the recovery of partial samples of settlements, site formation processes and preservation conditions. Fortunately, however, the organization of waste disposal at Flixborough, with what appears to be a central refuse dumping zone for much of the Middle and Late Saxon periods, allows for an attempt at the interpretation of settlement character.

It is immediately evident that radically different structural and finds profiles existed within different phases of the occupation sequence, despite similar waste disposal strategies. Following the review of the characteristics which have been used to classify Middle and Late Saxon high-status settlements, it is possible to suggest provisionally four major changes in the character of the settlement.

Between the late seventh and late eighth centuries, the archaeological remains are consistent with those of an aristocratic estate centre. The buildings were consistently large, averaging between 12 and 14 m in length, with their closest parallels at Wicken Bonhunt. The presence of a possible church or chapel need not be seen as an exclusively 'monastic' trait, but rather as symptomatic of family or household churches, known to have been built by secular aristocrats at their estate centres (Morris 1989, 131–3). Deposition patterns of luxuries and faunal resources also reflect a settlement characterized by a significant degree of conspicuous consumption. This can be seen in the access to imported commodities, such as glass vessels, pottery, silver *sceattas*, lava querns and, potentially, livestock. With regard to imports, Flixborough resembles all the other settlements known from this date on the south bank of the Humber: all have yielded imports, although the concentration at Flixborough may be exceptional.

The high percentage of adult and sub-adult cattle, and the peak in their slaughter as a proportion of other domesticated livestock during the mid to late eighth century, may also reflect renders from subordinate landholdings to the estate *caput* (Dobney *et al.* forthcoming). In addition, the consumption of porpoises and dolphins may also be an indication of the centrifugal pull of luxury foodstuffs. Craft production to supply most needs of the settlement is also reflected in the evidence for iron smithing, textile production, woodworking, limited leatherworking and non-ferrous metalworking.

During the first half of the ninth century, a series of changes potentially indicative of a different settlement character are apparent. Conspicuous consumption of imported commodities and the products of the agricultural economy continued, although provisional results suggest changes in the patterns of consumption. Between *c.* 800 and 850, the number of cattle slaughtered decreased dramatically, and the exploitation of domesticated fowl, particularly chickens and geese, reached a peak (Dobney *et al.* forthcoming). At the same time, new specialist artefacts were deposited, including styli and window glass. Similarly, the palaeography of the inscribed lead plaque suggests a date for its production at the end of the eighth or early ninth century.

These changes were accompanied by a dramatic increase in the evidence for craft production, seen across all craft-working activities, and particularly in the evidence for specialist textile manufacture, possibly for export (Walton Rogers forthcoming b). A commensurate dominance of sheep amongst the domesticated livestock at this period may be directly related to the provision of wool for textiles. The impression provided during this period is of a settlement with elements of its population involved in both conspicuous consumption and intensive production. The styli and window glass may be suggestive of a minster, and of an estate involved in the supply of finished commodities to nascent urban centres, probably within a socially-embedded context. A proportion of the settlement's inhabitants may have been part of a monastic community during the first half of the ninth century, although cautionary notes have previously been sounded as to whether minsters were always 'monastic' in character (Morris 1989, 131).

From the mid ninth until the early tenth century, a primary characteristic of the settlement is textile production, though not on the scale reflected in the preceding period. At the same time, buildings were much smaller, and evidence for the conspicuous consumption of luxuries and resources contemporary with this stage in the settlement's history is all but absent. In the late ninth century, however, signs of integration within regional exchange networks are again apparent, with the arrival of small quantities of Torksey and Lincoln wares. The appearance of the latter may reflect the establishment of new links between the emerging Late Saxon or Anglo-Scandinavian town of Lincoln and its rural hinterland. Overall, however, it is difficult to interpret Flixborough as a high-status settlement at this time.

By the early decades of the tenth century, conspicuous consumption had returned to Flixborough, although not in the form of portable, intrinsically valuable metalwork or exotic luxuries. Instead, the new media of display comprised ostentatious use of timber in the largest buildings within the occupation sequence, and also massive consumption of animal resources. Provisional indications show that species associated with luxury feasting, such as porpoises and cranes, were again present, in contrast to the period between the ninth and early tenth centuries. These traits in the structural and faunal remains are consistent with the emergence of an Anglo-Scandinavian 'manor', probably associated with the name Conesby – 'King's settlement'.

The evidence for craft specialization during the tenth century was far less diverse, with tools and debris limited to iron-working, small-scale textile production, and wood-working. This decrease in the apparent scale and range of craft practices may reflect a change in the relationship between urban and rural centres during the tenth century. Towns such as Lincoln and York appear to have acted as regional central places for their rural hinterlands, in a way that Middle Saxon emporia or *wics* had not. The evidence from Coppergate in York (Hall 1997, 1694; Walton Rogers 1997, 1824–5), and from the Flaxengate and Silver Street sites in Lincoln (Perring 1981, 41–3; Miles and Young 1989, 234) reflects concentration of craft production and possibly the emergence of regional market centres. This can be seen at Flixborough in the presence of Lincoln pottery wares. The town also began to supply coinage to its hinterland from the later decades of the tenth century – a trend reflected at Goltho, and possibly at Flixborough (Archibald 1987, 188). Consequently, the more limited patterns of craft and industry observable amongst the tenth-century remains probably reflect the level of specialist services required to furnish the needs of a secular estate or 'manorial' centre, set against the background of change in the roles of urban settlements.

Artefact discard patterns and archaeological visibility

The understanding of artefact discard patterns and taphonomy within different phases of the occupation sequence at Flixborough is fundamental to the interpretation of the settlement, and the lessons from their analysis have much wider implications. This is particularly the case for the recognition of tenth-century occupation in certain regions, and for interpreting changing settlement character through time. In addition, the provisional results of the integrated analysis of the different kinds of archaeological data have demonstrated that over-reliance on particular types of evidence can produce erroneous interpretations.

At Flixborough, certain periods of activity – for example, the periods between the late seventh and mid ninth centuries – are archaeologically more visible, in the sense that they contain a profusion of artefact types which are thought, as a consequence of previous typological and stratigraphic research, to be datable. On many sites, the datable artefacts tend to include dress accessories, diagnostic imports, such as specific pottery types or glass vessels, and coins. In the case of Flixborough, however, the close dating of the sequence was enhanced by previous study of regional developments in pottery types through the Anglo-Saxon period (Vince forthcoming; Young forthcoming). In contrast, after the late ninth century, dress accessories decorated in Late Saxon or Anglo-Scandinavian art styles (demonstrably contemporary imports) and coins minted between the 890s and 970s were all but absent. Without the exceptional stratigraphic sequence at Flixborough, together with the diagnostic tenth- to early eleventh-century pottery types, it would have been difficult to recognize the major tenth-century phases.

If the site had been located on good arable land, the large tenth-century buildings and bone dumps would have been largely ploughed out. Archaeologists would then have been faced with a plough soil assemblage which contained a profusion of datable eighth- to ninth-century artefacts, together with a smaller number of tenth-century pottery types. In such a situation, the conclusion might have been drawn that the remains represented those of an eighth- to ninth-century settlement, and that occupation declined in the tenth century. Any interpretation of this kind would have been completely erroneous, bearing in mind the wealth expressed in the size of the buildings and in the consumption of domesticated and wild animals. Nevertheless, without the survival of vertical stratigraphy and an appreciation of all the forms of evidence, the significance of tenth-century material can be underestimated.

This is amply illustrated by the coin list from Flixborough, which has already been published in summary form (Blackburn 1993, 82–3). The coinage was presented as an isolated artefact type, in the complete absence of any information relating to stratigraphy or assorted artefacts. Consequently, consideration of the spectrum of coinage from the site gave a misleading impression with regard to the demise of occupation in the excavated area, and did not take into account a coin of Edward the Martyr, struck between 975 and 978. The coins actually reflect patterns of coin supply, loss and subsequent re-deposition. They do not provide the *termini post quos* for the tenth-century occupation, which are provided by the pottery. It would have been equally misleading to use decorated metalwork in this manner.

The high archaeological visibility of eighth- and ninth-century finds may have had an especial impact on the interpretation of the large collections of metalwork and coins recovered through metal-detecting on Anglo-Saxon settlements in recent years. Sites such as Bawsey, Norfolk (Webster 1991, 231–2) and South Newbald, East Yorkshire (Leahy 2000, 51–71) have yielded quantities of decorated jewellery and coins, similar to those from the eighth and ninth centuries at Flixborough. The exotic nature of the finds has inevitably focused attention on the Middle Saxon phases of these sites. Where archaeological evaluation has taken place, for example at Bawsey, both Middle and Late Saxon phases are evident, yet the metalwork gives the impression that the *floruit* of the settlement was in the Middle Saxon period (Reynolds 1999, pl. 12). Such a conclusion could also be drawn for Flixborough, if the metalwork alone were to be considered. Yet consideration of the full range of evidence from the site shows that there was a change in the character of the settlement in the tenth century, involving different media of expressing wealth which were less archaeologically visible. The same could also be the case for the tenth- to eleventh-century phases of other settlement sites which are currently labelled as Middle Saxon due to a reliance on the recovery of metalwork without associated excavation.

It is also possible that the significance of Late Saxon finds has been missed from predominantly metal-detected (and even from some excavated) assemblages, due to an unrealistic expectation that equivalent quantities of datable artefacts would be discarded from the Middle and Late Saxon periods. This relates mainly to the use of decorated metalwork but also, to a certain extent, to pottery. Taking Flixborough as an example, far greater quantities of pottery were deposited during the eighth and ninth centuries – mostly Maxey-type ware. In comparison, the quantity of tenth- to early eleventh-century pottery was much smaller. Nevertheless, much of the tenth-century pottery comprised imported Torksey and Lincoln wares, and the smaller quantities could reflect fluctuating and changing relationships with urban centres. Yet if this assemblage had been recovered from the plough soil in association with metal-detected finds, the smaller quantity of tenth-century pottery may have been interpreted as evidence of settlement decline.

A final problem relating to changing patterns of artefact discard, concerns the issue of the ethnic affiliation of the inhabitants of Flixborough during the tenth century. Up until the mid ninth century, the form and decoration of dress accessories reflects the use of contemporary Anglo-Saxon motifs and art styles, for example Trewhiddle-style decoration on strap-ends (Thomas 1998, 85; Thomas forthcoming). From the late ninth century, however, diagnostic art styles disappear at Flixborough: the most visible tenth- to early eleventh-century artefact type is the pottery, but this cannot be used to suggest ethnic affiliation.

The absence of decorated metalwork with Scandinavian motifs, such as the Mammen or Borre styles, in this area of known Scandinavian settlement can be explained by a combination of factors. When pieces of decorated Anglo-Scandinavian metalwork have been recovered from excavated settlements such as Wharram Percy, they represent only a very small number in comparison to other Anglo-Saxon finds, despite over 40 years of excavations (Richards 1997, 239). If this were to prove a widespread pattern, then the absence of diagnostic Anglo-Scandinavian metalwork at Flixborough could be accounted for by a combination of the infrequent discard of such artefacts and the settlement shift to the east during the tenth century. An alternative hypothesis is that members of the existing Anglo-Saxon elite maintained their position, and actively chose not to associate themselves with a new Scandinavian elite. Detailed linguistic research, however, on both major place-names, topographical names and minor names (such as field-names) indicates that the vast majority of names in the Flixborough area are derived from Old Danish and Old Norse. This is suggestive of extensive Scandinavian affiliation, if not settlement, in the locality (Cameron 1998, 33; Cameron forthcoming).

Conclusion

Within the confines of this interim discussion of the Anglo-Saxon settlement remains from Flixborough parish, it has been possible to present a provisional picture of the changing lifestyles evident within the occupation sequence, and to set the results within their broader context. Although it is too early to draw definitive conclusions, it has already been possible to demonstrate the value of integrating the information from different forms of evidence. This is especially true for the reconstruction of different aspects of the settlement's economy through time, and for the identification of its changing character and status.

The changing patterns of consumption and production, observable because of the exceptional vertical stratigraphy and the centralized waste disposal strategies, have also shown the danger of seeking to ascribe all-embracing labels of settlement character to complex Middle to Late Saxon sequences. In the absence of clear vertical stratigraphy, archaeological and historical interpretation of settlement character has often tended towards the assumption of single labels, often coinciding with textually-derived terms, such as minster, monastery, manor, *caput* or vill centre. At Flixborough, however, the evidence suggests radical change in settlement status and character within the second half of the first millennium, and also changes in the ways of displaying status. It is possible that such labels may be appropriate to certain phases in the settlement's occupation sequence, but reflections of dynamic change in the archaeological record mitigate against the ascription of a single term, derived from historical nomenclature.

The acceptance of such terminology also relies on the assumption that archaeological reflections of settlements, such as 'monasteries' or 'vill' centres, are unambiguous. Unfortunately, this does not seem to be the case.

Consequently, the provisional association of certain archaeological profiles within the Flixborough sequence with historical labels is entirely subjective. It is also over-simplistic to suggest a model of high-status settlement evolution from a secular centre to a monastery, and back to a secular centre or nascent 'manor'. The complex series of archaeological profiles identified include an episode of relative poverty between the mid ninth and early tenth centuries. This suggests a more complex sequence of settlement change, reflecting fluctuations in both the presence and the character of elites, and also variation in the media of social display.

Nevertheless, it is possible that some of the changes in the archaeological character of the settlement reflect historically observable phenomena: for example, the take-over of Middle Saxon monasteries as secular centres and the sub-division of their estates during the Late Saxon or Anglo-Scandinavian period. In north Lincolnshire, in 1066, the former monastic settlements and estates that had existed at West Halton, Barrow, and possibly Barton, had all become secular centres with associated territories. They were held by leading aristocrats, namely King Harold Godwinson, Earl Morcar, and the thegn Ulf Fenisc respectively (Foster and Longley 1924; Everson 1984, 123–5). The transformation of monastic settlements and estates into secular counterparts is also reflected epigraphically, and possibly archaeologically, at Kirkdale, North Yorkshire (Page 1995, 309–10; Rahtz and Watts 1998, 6–7).

The essential problem remains, however, that it is seldom possible to marry textual and archaeological evidence. Textual evidence may provide 'snap-shots' around which models of settlement evolution can be constructed, but such models may overlook settlement changes during historically less 'visible' periods. Archaeological evidence, on the other hand, may allow the observation of changes over a longer term. Yet due to the complexities of interpreting data from re-worked settlement deposits, and the frequent lack of vertical stratigraphy, it is rarely possible to identify settlement phases which equate with textual descriptions. Without special pleading, no textual references can be directly associated with the Flixborough remains. Despite this, the settlement may provide the exception to the rule and it may prove possible to equate archaeological profiles with documented phenomena, during certain phases. The fact that these tentative associations can be linked only to certain phases also highlights the limitations of the practice: they do not explain the complex range of changes seen throughout the whole of the settlement's history, based on the sample excavated.

Rather than force historical labels on to archaeological evidence, it may be more appropriate to attempt to characterize the Flixborough remains on the basis of the evident patterns of consumption and production. Thus, the character and status of the settlement and its inhabitants can be interpreted above all through changes in the exploitation of animal resources, and through fluctuations in patterns of craft-working, exchange, portable wealth, and other specialist activities. Such settlement characterization also has to be undertaken in tandem with analysis of changing structural trends, attitudes to burial, and evidence of ritual and religion. The different archaeological characteristics of the various phases of the settlement can then be compared with other settlements, in both Britain and mainland Europe. It may be useful to compare patterns of consumption and production with other high-status settlements in north-western Europe from the same period, such as Höxter (Grothe and König 1999, 374–9), Soest (Melzer 1999, 365–73) and Paderborn (Gai 1999, 183–96) in Germany; Tissø, in Denmark (Jørgensen 1998); Petegem and Gent, in Belgium (Callebaut 1994, 93–110); and Hamage (Louis 1997, 55–63) and Saleux les Coutures (Catteddu 1997, 143–8), in northern France.

Depending on the availability of high quality information, the different patterns in consumption and production, and in the other traits outlined above, can then be utilized to build a more comprehensive understanding of both the economy and character of settlements. In such a way, a picture of relationships within rural settlement hierarchies, and between rural settlements and urban centres, can be constructed from the archaeological evidence. Following the excavation – and the analysis and publication – of a greater range of settlements from the seventh to eleventh centuries, it is now possible to begin to undertake such studies, not only for Anglo-Saxon England, but also for Carolingian Europe.

Acknowledgements

I am grateful to English Heritage for providing the funding which has enabled the analysis of the Flixborough Anglo-Saxon remains and I am extremely grateful to my colleagues who have further enhanced the results being produced by working beyond their funded remit. I must offer especial thanks to Rosemary Cramp who has provided guidance and constant encouragement throughout my time associated with the Flixborough Anglo-Saxon settlement project and as a student. I also thank those colleagues who have provided comments on a draft of this paper, and colleagues in Humber Field Archaeology – Mike Frankland, David Atkinson, Leś Turner, Rebecca Smith and Bill Marsden for producing the plans, line drawings and photographs.

References

Addyman, P., with Fennel, K. R. and Biek, L. 1964. A Dark-Age settlement at Maxey, Northants, *Medieval Archaeology*, 8, 20–73

Archibald, M. M. 1987. Medieval coins, in G. Beresford, *Goltho: The Development of an Early Medieval Manor, c.850–1150*, 188, English Heritage Archaeological Report No. 4, J. Geddes (ed), London: Historic Buildings & Monuments Commission for England

Archibald, M. M. forthcoming. Sceattas and pennies, in Loveluck (ed), forthcoming (a).

Armstrong, P., Tomlinson, D. and Evans, D. H. (eds) 1991. *Excavations at Lurk Lane, Beverley, 1979–82*, Sheffield Excavation Reports No. 1, Sheffield

Barratt, J. forthcoming. The fish remains, in K. Dobney (ed), *Pigs, Porpoises and Power: the biological remains from Flixborough*, Excavations at Flixborough, Vol. 2, Oxford: Oxbow Books

Bayley, J. 1992. The metalworking evidence, in G. Milne and J. D. Richards, *Two Anglo-Saxon Buildings and Associated Finds: Wharram: A study of settlement on the Yorkshire Wolds*, VII, 59–65, York University Archaeological Publications 9, York

Bencard, M. and Bender Jørgensen, L. 1990. Excavation and stratigraphy, in M. Bencard (ed), *Ribe Excavations 1970–76*, J. Hines (trans), Vol. 4, 15–168, Esbjerg: Sydjysk Universitetsforlag

Bendixen, K. 1981. Sceattas and other coin finds, in M. Bencard (ed), *Ribe Excavations 1970–76*, Vol. 1, 63–101, Esbjerg: Sydjysk Universitetsforlag

Beresford, G. 1987. *Goltho – The Development of an Early Medieval Manor, c.850–1150*, English Heritage Archaeological Report No. 4, J. Geddes (ed), London: Historic Buildings & Monuments Commission for England

Blackburn, M. 1993. Coin finds and coin circulation in Lindsey, in A. Vince (ed), *Pre-Viking Lindsey*, 80–90, Lincoln Archaeological Studies No. 1, Lincoln: City of Lincoln Archaeological Unit

Blair, J. 1994. *Anglo-Saxon Oxfordshire*, Oxford: Sutton Publishing / Oxfordshire Books

Blair, J. 1996 (a). Churches in the early English landscape: social and cultural contexts, in J. Blair and C. Pyrah (eds), *Church Archaeology: research directions for the future* (CBA Res Rep 104), 6–18, York

Blair, J. 1996 (b). Palaces or minsters? Northampton and Cheddar reconsidered, in *Anglo-Saxon England*, 25, 97–121

Blinkhorn, P. forthcoming. Ipswich ware, in C. P. Loveluck (ed), forthcoming (a).

Bourdillon, J. 1994. The animal provisioning of Saxon Southampton, in J. Rackham (ed), *Environment and Economy in Anglo-Saxon England* (CBA Res Rep 89), 120–25, York

Brodribb, A. C. C., Hands, A. R. and Walker, D. R. 1972. *Excavations at Shakenoak Farm, near Wilcote, Oxfordshire*, Part III, *Site F*, Oxford: privately printed

Brown, M. and Okasha, E. forthcoming. Inscribed objects, in Loveluck (ed), forthcoming (a).

Buck, A. L. 1997. *An Inventory of UK Estuaries, 5, Eastern England*, Peterborough: Joint Nature Conservation Committee

Cadman, G. and Foard, G. 1984. Raunds: manorial and village origins, in M. L. Faull (ed), *Studies in Late Anglo-Saxon Settlement*, 81–100, Oxford: Oxford University Department for External Studies

Callebaut, D. 1994. Residences fortifiées et centres administratifs dans la vallée de l'Escaut (IXe–XIe siècle), in P. Demolon, H. Galinié and F. Verhaeghe (eds), *Archéologie des villes dans le Nord-Ouest de l'Europe (VIIe–XIIIe siècle)*, 93–112, Actes du IVe Congrès International d'Archéologie Médiévale (Douai 1991), Douai: Société d'Archéologie de Douai

Cameron, K. 1998. *A Dictionary of Lincolnshire Place-names*, Nottingham: English Place-name Society

Cameron, K. forthcoming. The settlement in its landscape – the place-name evidence, in Loveluck (ed), forthcoming (a).

Canti, M. 1992. *Research into Natural and Anthropogenic Deposits from Excavations at Flixborough, Humberside*, Ancient Monuments Laboratory Report 53/92, London: English Heritage

Canti, M. forthcoming. Soil conditions and analysis of anthropogenic deposits, in Loveluck (ed), forthcoming (b).

Cardy, A. 1997. The human bones, in P. Hill, *Whithorn and St Ninian: The excavation of a monastic town 1984–91*, 519–562, Whithorn and Stroud: The Whithorn Trust and Sutton Publishing

Carrot, J. forthcoming. The mollusc remains, in K. Dobney (ed), forthcoming, *Pigs, Porpoises and Power: The biological remains from Flixborough*, Excavations at Flixborough, Vol. 2, Oxford: Oxbow Books

Catteddu, I. 1997. Le site médiéval de Saleux 'Les Coutures': habitat, nécropole, et églises du haut Moyen Age, in G. De Boe and F. Verhaeghe (eds), *Rural Settlements in Medieval Europe*, Papers of the 'Medieval Europe Brugge 1997' Conference, Vol. 6, 143–8, I. A. P. Rapporten 6, Zellik

Chandler, J. 1993. *John Leland's Itinerary – Travels in Tudor England*, Stroud: Sutton Publishing

Coppack, G. 1986. St. Lawrence Church, Burnham, South Humberside – The excavation of a parochial chapel, *Lincolnshire History and Archaeology*, 21, 39–60

Cowgill, J. forthcoming. The carpentry tool hoard: the lead tanks, in Loveluck (ed), forthcoming (a).

Crabtree, P. J. 1990. *West Stow Early Anglo-Saxon Animal Husbandry* (East Anglian Archaeol Rep 47), Ipswich: Suffolk County Planning Department

Crabtree, P. J. 1994. Animal exploitation in East Anglian villages, in J. Rackham (ed), *Environment and Economy in Anglo-Saxon England* (CBA Res Rep 89), 40–54, York

Cramp, R. J. 1969. Excavations at the Saxon monastic sites of Wearmouth and Jarrow, Co. Durham: an interim report, *Medieval Archaeology*, 13, 21–66

Cramp, R. J. 1976. Monastic sites, in D. M. Wilson (ed), *The Archaeology of Anglo-Saxon England*, 201–52, Cambridge: Cambridge University Press

Cramp, R. J. 1984. *Corpus of Anglo-Saxon Stone Sculpture*, 1, *County Durham and Northumberland*, Oxford: British Academy / Oxford University Press

Cramp, R. J. 1993. A re-consideration of the monastic site of Whitby, in R. M. Spearman and J. Higgit (eds), *The Age of Migrating Ideas: Early Medieval Art in Northern Britain and Ireland*, 64–73, Edinburgh: National Museums of Scotland

Cramp, R. J. 1994. Monkwearmouth and Jarrow in their continental context, in K. Painter (ed), *Churches Built in Ancient Times: recent studies in early Christian archaeology*, 279–94, Society of Antiquaries Occasional Paper 16, London

Daniels, R. 1988. The Anglo-Saxon monastery at Church Close, Hartlepool, Cleveland, *Archaeological Journal*, 145, 158–210

Darby, H. C. 1987. Domesday Book and the geographer, in J. C. Holt (ed), *Domesday Studies*, Woodbridge: Boydell Press

Dent, J., Loveluck, C. P. and Fletcher, W. 2000. The early medieval site at Skerne, in R. Van De Noort and S. Ellis (ed), *Wetland Heritage of the Hull Valley – An Archaeological Survey*, 214–242. Humber Wetlands Project (English Heritage), Hull: University of Hull

Didsbury, P. forthcoming. The Roman pottery, in Loveluck (ed), forthcoming (a).

Dobney, K. and Loveluck, C. P. 1998. Flixborough 5, in Chapter 9: The archaeological survey of the lower Trent valley and Winterton Beck, in R. Van De Noort and S. Ellis (eds), *Wetland Heritage of the Ancholme and Lower Trent Valleys – An Archaeological Survey*, 159–63, Humber Wetlands Project (English Heritage), Hull: University of Hull

Dobney, K. and Harwood, J. 1999. Here to stay? Archaeological evidence for the introduction of commensal and economically important mammals to the North of England, in N. Benecke (ed), *The Holocene History of the European Vertebrate Fauna – Modern Aspects of Research*, Archäologie in Eurasien, Band 6, 373–87, Rahden: Verlag Marie Leidorf

Dobney, K., Jacques, D. and Johnstone, C. forthcoming. The vertebrate remains, in K. Dobney (ed), forthcoming, *Pigs, Porpoises and Power: the biological remains from Flixborough*, Excavations at Flixborough, Vol. 2, Oxford: Oxbow Books

Dudley, H. 1931. *The History and Antiquities of the Scunthorpe and Frodingham District*, Scunthorpe

Emerton, E. (trans) 1940. *The Letters of Saint Boniface*, New York: Columbia University Press

Ervynck, A. 1999. Possibilities and limitations of the use of archaeozoological data in biogeographical analysis: a review with examples from the Benelux region, *Belgian Journal of Zoology*, 129, issue 1, 125–38

Everson, P. 1984. The pre-conquest estate of Aet Bearuwe in Lindsey, in M. Faull (ed), *Studies in Late Anglo-Saxon Settlement*, 123–7, Oxford: Oxford University Department of External Studies

Evison, V. forthcoming. Glass vessels, in Loveluck (ed), forthcoming (a).

Farmer, D. H. 1983. Bede: Lives of the Abbots of Wearmouth and Jarrow, trans, in D. H. Farmer (ed), *The Age of Bede*, 183–208, Harmondsworth: Penguin Books

Finney, A. 1998. St Saviourgate, York, in *CBA Forum*, 15–17, Annual Newsletter of CBA Yorkshire, York

Foard, G. 1998. The Saxon landscape: a regional perspective, in P. Everson and T. Williamson (eds), *The Archaeology of Landscape*, 67–94, Manchester: Manchester University Press

Foot, S. 1992. Anglo-Saxon minsters: a review of terminology, in J. Blair and R. Sharpe (eds), *Pastoral Care Before the Parish*, Leicester: Leicester University Press

Foster, C. W. and Longley, T. 1924. *The Lincolnshire Domesday and the Lindsey Survey*, Lincoln Record Society, Vol. 19, Gainsborough: Belton

Fox, C. 1923. *The Archaeology of the Cambridge Region*, Cambridge: Cambridge University Press

Gai, S. 1999. Die Pfalz Karls des Großen in Paderborn, in Stiegemann and Wemhoff, 183–96

Gardiner, M. 1997. The exploitation of sea mammals in medieval England: bones and their social context, *Archaeological Journal*, 154, 173–95

Gates, T. and O'Brien, C. 1988. Cropmarks at Milfield and New Bewick and the recognition of *Grubenhäuser* in Northumberland, *Archaeologia Aeliana*, 5th ser., 16, 1–9

Gaunt, G. 1976. The artificial nature of the River Don, north of Thorne, Yorkshire, *Yorkshire Archaeological Journal*, 47, 15–21

Gaunt, G. forthcoming (a). The present environmental setting – geology and topography, in Loveluck, forthcoming (a).

Gaunt, G. forthcoming (b). The Anglo-Saxon topographical situation, in Loveluck, forthcoming (b).

Gregory, C. 1982. *Gifts and Commodities*, London: Academic Press

Grothe, A. and König, A. 1999. Das frühmittelalterliche Höxter, in Stiegemann and Wemhoff (eds), 374–9

Hall, A. forthcoming. The botanical remains, in K. Dobney (ed), forthcoming, *Pigs, Porpoises and Power: the biological remains from Flixborough*, Excavations at Flixborough, Vol. 2, Oxford: Oxbow Books

Hall, R. A. 1997. The excavation at 16–22 Coppergate, in P. Walton Rogers, *Textile Production at 16–22 Coppergate*, 1689–1708, The Archaeology of York, P. V. Addyman (ed), Vol. 17, The Small Finds 17/11, York

Hamerow, H. F. 1995. Shaping settlements: early medieval communities in northwest Europe, in J. Bintliff and H. F. Hamerow (eds), *Europe Between Late Antiquity and the Middle Ages: Recent Archaeological and Historical Research in Western and Southern Europe* (Brit Archaeol Rep, Int Ser, 617), 8–37, Oxford

Havinden, M. 1981. *The Somerset Landscape*, London: Hodder & Stoughton

Hill, P. 1997. *Whithorn and St Ninian: the excavation of a monastic town 1984–91*, Whithorn and Stroud: The Whithorn Trust and Sutton Publishing

Hinchliffe, J. 1986. An early medieval settlement at Cowage Farm, Foxley, near Malmesbury, *Archaeological Journal*, 143, 240–59

Hines, J. forthcoming. Great square-headed brooch, in Loveluck, forthcoming (b).

Hodges, R. 1981. *The Hamwih pottery: the local and imported wares from 30 years' excavations at Middle Saxon Southampton and their European context* (CBA Res Rep 37), London

Hodges, R. and Moreland, J. 1988. Power and exchange in Middle Saxon England, in S. T. Driscoll and M. R. Nieke (eds), *Power and Politics in Early Medieval Britain and Ireland*, 79–95, Edinburgh: Edinburgh University Press

Holdsworth, P. 1991. Dunbar, *Current Archaeology*, no. 127, (Vol. 11, No. 7), 315–17

Hooke, D. 1998. *The Landscape of Anglo-Saxon England*, Leicester: Leicester University Press

Hope Taylor, B. 1977. *Yeavering – An Anglo-British Centre of Early Northumbria*, London: HMSO

James, S., Marshall, A. and Millett, M. 1984. An early medieval building tradition, *Archaeological Journal*, 141, 182–215

Jensen, S. 1991. *Ribes Vikinger*, Ribe: Den Antikvariske Samling

Jørgensen, L. 1998. *Vikingerne Ved Søen*, Interim report on the excavations at Tissø, Copenhagen: National Museum of Denmark

Kemp, R. L. 1996. *Anglian Settlement at 46–54 Fishergate*, The Archaeology of York, P. V. Addyman (ed), Vol. 7: Anglian York, 7/1, York: CBA

Kinsley, G. 1998. Interim report on archaeological watching briefs and excavations at Girton Quarry Extension, Newark, 1997–98, in R. W. D. Fenn (ed), *Tarmac Papers*, Vol. 2, 41–50, Llandysul: Gomer Press

Lang, J. T. 1992. The stylistic evidence of the moulds, in G. Milne and J. D. Richards (eds), *Two Anglo-Saxon Buildings and Associated Finds: Wharram: a study of settlement on the Yorkshire Wolds*, VII, 65–6, York University Archaeological Publications 9, York

Leahy, K. 2000. Middle Anglo-Saxon metalwork from South Newbald and the 'Productive Site' phenomenon in Yorkshire, in H. Geake and J. Kenny (eds), *Early Deira: Archaeological Studies of the East Riding in the fourth to ninth centuries AD*, 51–82, Oxford: Oxbow Books

Lillie, M. and Parkes, A. 1998. The palaeo-environmental survey of the lower Trent valley and Winterton Beck, in R. Van De Noort and S. Ellis (eds), *Wetland Heritage of the Ancholme and Lower Trent Valleys: An Archaeological Survey*, Humber Wetlands Project (English Heritage), Hull: University of Hull

Losco-Bradley, S. and Wheeler, H. M. 1984. Anglo-Saxon settlement in the Trent valley: some aspects, in M. L. Faull (ed), *Studies in Late Anglo-Saxon Settlement*, 101–14, Oxford: Oxford University Department for External Studies

Louis, E. 1997. Archéologie des bâtiments monastiques, VIIème-IXème siècles: Le cas de Hamage (France, Département du Nord), in G. De Boe and F. Verhaeghe (eds), *Religion and Belief in Medieval Europe*, Papers of the 'Medieval Europe Brugge 1997' Conference, Vol. 4, 55–63, I. A. P. Rapporten 4, Zellik

Loveluck, C. P. 1994. *Exchange and Society in Early Medieval England, 400–700 AD*, unpublished Ph.D thesis, University of Durham

Loveluck, C. P. 1997. Flixborough – the character and economy of a high-status Middle Saxon settlement in northern England, in G. De Boe and F. Verhaeghe (eds), *Rural Settlements in Medieval Europe*, Papers of the 'Medieval Europe Brugge 1997' Conference, Vol. 6, 179–94, I. A. P. Rapporten 6, Zellik

Loveluck, C. P. 1998 (a). A high-status Anglo-Saxon settlement at Flixborough, Lincolnshire, *Antiquity*, 72, 146–61

Loveluck, C. P. 1998 (b). The development of the Anglo-Saxon landscape, economy, and society, 'on Driffield', East Yorkshire, AD 400–750, *Anglo-Saxon Studies in Archaeology and History 9*, 25–48, Oxford University Committee for Archaeology 1996, Oxford

Loveluck, C. P. forthcoming (a). The Romano-British to Anglo-Saxon transition: social transformations from the Late Roman to early medieval period in northern England, AD 400–700, in R. Daniels and M. McCarthy (eds), *Past, Present, and Future: The archaeology of northern England*, Monograph of the Society of Antiquaries of Newcastle, Newcastle

Loveluck, C. P. (ed) forthcoming (b). *Flixborough: A high-status Middle to Late Saxon settlement, in North Lincolnshire, AD 600–1000*, Excavations at Flixborough, Vol. 1, Oxford: Oxbow Books

Loveluck, C. P. (ed) forthcoming (c). *Flixborough: The character, environment and economy of the high-status, Middle to Late Saxon settlement, AD 600–1000*, Excavations at Flixborough, Vol. 3, Oxford: Oxbow Books

Lowe, C. E. 1991. New light on the Anglian minster at Hoddom, *Trans Dumfriesshire Galloway Natur Hist Antiq Soc*, 3rd ser., 66, 11–35

Mainman, A. J. 1990. *Anglo-Scandinavian Pottery from Coppergate*, The Archaeology of York, P. V. Addyman (ed), Vol. 16: The Pottery, 16/5, London: CBA

Mainman, A. J. 1993. *Pottery from 46–54 Fishergate*, The Archaeology of York, P. V. Addyman (ed), Vol. 16: The Pottery, London: CBA

Malinowski, B. 1922. *Argonauts of the Western Pacific*, London: George Routledge & Sons

Manby, T. forthcoming. *Excavations at Thwing, East Yorkshire.*

Mauss, M. 1925. *Essai sur le don / The Gift*, trans, 1954 edition, London: Routledge

Mays, S. forthcoming. The human burials – the skeletal remains and pathology, in Loveluck (ed), forthcoming (a).

Melzer, W. 1999. Soest zur Karolingerzeit, in Stiegemann and Wemhoff (eds) (b), 365–73

Miles, P. and Young, J. 1989. Conclusion, in P. Miles, J. Young and J. Wacher, *A Late Anglo-Saxon Kiln Site at Silver Street, Lincoln*, The Archaeology of Lincoln, Vol. XVII, 3, City of Lincoln Archaeological Unit, London: CBA

Morris, R. 1989. *Churches in the Landscape*, London: J. M. Dent
Mortimer, C. forthcoming. Analysis of crucibles and moulds, in Loveluck (ed), forthcoming (a).
Mortimer, J. R. 1905. *Forty Years' Researches in British and Saxon Burial Mounds of East Yorkshire*, London: A. Brown and Sons
Morton, A. (ed) 1992. *Excavations at Hamwic*, Vol. 1, (CBA Res Rep 84), London
Nicholson, A. 1997 (a). Objects of lead?, in P. Hill, 1997, 389–97
Nicholson, A. 1997 (b). The iron, in P. Hill, 1997, 405–33
O'Connor, T. P. 1989. *Bones from Anglo-Scandinavian Levels at 16–22 Coppergate*, The Archaeology of York, P. V. Addyman (ed), Vol. 15: The Animal Bones 15/3, London: CBA
O'Connor, T. P. 1991. *Bones from 46–54 Fishergate*, The Archaeology of York, P. V. Addyman (ed), Vol. 15: The Animal Bones 15/4, London: CBA
Ottaway, P. J. 1996. The ironwork, in R. A. Hall and M. Whyman, Settlement and monasticism at Ripon, North Yorkshire, from the seventh to eleventh centuries AD, *Medieval Archaeology*, 40, 99–113
Ottaway, P. J. forthcoming. Agricultural tools; Carpentry tools; Iron-working tools; Non-ferrous metalworking tools; in Loveluck (ed), forthcoming (a).
Page, R. I. 1995. *Runes and Runic Inscriptions: Collected Essays on Anglo-Saxon and Viking Runes*, D. Parsons (ed), Woodbridge: Boydell Press
Payne, A. forthcoming. Geophysical survey, in Loveluck (ed), forthcoming (a).
Parkhouse, J. 1997. The distribution and exchange of Mayen lava quernstones in early medieval north-western Europe, in G. De Boe and F. Verhaeghe (eds), *Exchange and Trade in Medieval Europe*, Papers of the 'Medieval Europe Brugge 1997' Conference, Vol. 3, 97–106, I. A. P. Rapporten 3, Zellik
Peers, C. and Radford, C. A. R. 1943. The Saxon monastery of Whitby, *Archaeologia*, 89, 27–88
Perring, D. 1981. *Early Medieval Occupation at Flaxengate, Lincoln*, The Archaeology of Lincoln, Vol. IX, 1, Lincoln Archaeological Trust, London: CBA
Pestell, T. forthcoming. The styli, in Loveluck (ed), forthcoming (a).
Powlesland, D. 1997. Early Anglo-Saxon settlements, structures, form and layout, in J. Hines (ed), *The Anglo-Saxons from the Migration Period to the Eighth Century – An ethnographic perspective*, 101–17, Studies in Historical Archaeoethnology, Vol. 2, Woodbridge: Boydell Press
Rackham, J. 1988. Synthesis of the vertebrate remains, in R. Daniels, The Anglo-Saxon monastery at Church Close, Hartlepool, Cleveland, 201, *Archaeological Journal*, 145, 158–210
Rackham, O. 1986. *The History of the Countryside*, London: J. M. Dent
Rahtz, P. 1976. Appendix C: The building plan of the Anglo-Saxon monastery of Whitby Abbey, in D. M. Wilson (ed), *The Archaeology of Anglo-Saxon England*, 459–62, Cambridge: Cambridge University Press
Rahtz, P. 1979. *The Saxon and Medieval Palaces at Cheddar* (Brit Archaeol Rep, Brit Ser, 65), S. M. Hirst (ed), Oxford
Rahtz, P. and Watts, L. 1998. *Kirkdale Archaeology, 1996–1997*, Supplement to the *Ryedale Historian*, no. 19, Helmsley: Helmsley Archaeological Society
Reynolds, A. 1999. *Later Anglo-Saxon England – Life and Landscape*, Stroud: Tempus
Richards, J. 1997. Anglian and Viking settlement in the Yorkshire Wolds, in G. De Boe and F. Verhaeghe (eds), *Rural Settlements in Medieval Europe*, Papers of the

'Medieval Europe Brugge 1997' Conference, Vol. 6, 233–42, I. A. P. Rapporten 6, Zellik

Smith, I. M. 1984. Patterns of settlement and land use of the late Anglian period in the Tweed Basin, in M. L. Faull (ed), *Studies in Late Anglo-Saxon Settlement*, 177–96, Oxford: Oxford University Department for External Studies

Starley, D. forthcoming. Iron-working evidence: smelting evidence, smithing slag and hammerscale, in Loveluck (ed), forthcoming (a).

Steedman, K. 1994. Excavation of a Saxon site at Riby Crossroads, Lincolnshire, *Archaeological Journal*, 151, 212–306

Steuer, H. 1999. Handel und Wirtschaft in der Karolingerzeit, in Stiegemann and Wemhoff (eds) (b), 406–16

Stiegemann, C. and Wemhoff, M. (eds) 1999 a. *799 – Kunst und Kultur der Karolingerzeit: Karl der Große und Papst Leo III in Paderborn*, Katalog der Ausstellung Paderborn 1999, Katalog Teil 1, Mainz: Verlag Philipp von Zabern

Stiegemann, C. and Wemhoff, M (eds) 1999 b. *799 – Kunst und Kultur der Karolingerzeit: Karl der Große und Papst Leo III in Paderborn*, Beiträge zum Katalog der Ausstellung Paderborn 1999, Mainz: Verlag Philipp von Zabern

Stocker, D. 1993. The early Church in Lincolnshire, in A. Vince (ed), *Pre-Viking Lindsey*, 101–22, Lincoln Archaeological Studies No. 1, Lincoln: City of Lincoln Archaeology Unit

Stuart-Macadam, P. 1989. Nutritional deficiency diseases: a survey of scurvy, rickets and iron deficiency anaemia, in M. Y. Iscan and K. A. R. Kennedy (eds), *Reconstruction of Life from the Skeleton*, 202–22, New York: Alan Liss

Swanton, M. J. (ed and trans) 1975. *Anglo-Saxon Prose*, London: Dent

Swanton, M. J. (trans) 1996. *The Anglo-Saxon Chronicle*, London: Dent

Thomas, G. 1998. Silver wire strap-ends from East Anglia, in D. Griffiths (ed), *Anglo-Saxon Studies in Archaeology and History 9*, Oxford: Oxford University Committee for Archaeology

Thomas, G. forthcoming. The strap-ends and hooked tags, in Loveluck, forthcoming (a).

Vince, A. forthcoming. The imported pottery, in Loveluck, forthcoming (a).

Wade, K. 1980. A settlement site at Bonhunt Farm, Wicken Bonhunt, Essex, in D. G. Buckley (ed), *Archaeology in Essex to AD 1500* (CBA Res Rep 34), 96–9, London

Wade-Martins, P. 1980. *Excavations in North Elmham Park, 1967–1972*, Norfolk Museums Service, (East Anglian Archaeol Res Rep 9), Vol. 1, Norwich: Norfolk Archaeological Unit

Walton Rogers, P. 1997. *Textile Production at 16–22 Coppergate*, The Archaeology of York, P. V. Addyman (ed), Vol. 17: The Small Finds 17/11, York

Walton Rogers, P. forthcoming (a). Textile production, in Loveluck, forthcoming (a).

Walton Rogers, P. forthcoming (b). The importance and organization of textile production, in Loveluck, forthcoming (b).

Wastling, L. forthcoming. Crucibles and moulds, in Loveluck, forthcoming (a).

Watkins, G. 1991. The pottery, in P. Armstrong, D. Tomlinson and D. H. Evans (eds), *Excavations at Lurk Lane, Beverley 1979–1982*, Sheffiels: Sheffield Excavation Reports Series No. 1

Webster, L. 1991. Selected finds from Barking Abbey, Essex, and Selected finds from a Middle/Late Saxon site at Bawsey, Norfolk, in L. Webster and J. Backhouse (eds), *The Making of England. Anglo-Saxon art and culture AD 600–900*, 88–94, 231–2, London: British Museum Press

White, A. 1984. Finds from the Anglian monastery at Whitby, *Yorkshire Archaeological Journal*, 56, 33–40

Whitwell, J. B. 1991. Flixborough, *Current Archaeology*, no. 126, Vol. XI, No. 6, 244–7

Williams, D. and Vince, A. 1997. The characterization and interpretation of Early to Middle Saxon granitic tempered pottery in England, *Medieval Archaeology*, 41, 214–20

Williams, J., Shaw, M. and Denham, V. 1985. *Middle Saxon Palaces at Northampton*, Northampton: Northamptonshire County Council

Windell, D., Chapman, A. and Woodiwiss, J. 1990. *From Barrows to By-pass: Excavations at West Cotton, Raunds, Northants, 1985–89*, Northampton: Northamptonshire County Council

Yorke, B. 1993. Lindsey: the lost kingdom found?, in A. Vince (ed), *Pre-Viking Lindsey*, 141–50, Lincoln Archaeological Studies 1, Lincoln: City of Lincoln Archaeology Unit

Young, J. forthcoming. Early Saxon wares; Maxey-type wares; Other Middle Saxon wares; Late Saxon wares; in Loveluck, forthcoming (a).

6
From Isidore to Isotopes
Ivory Rings in Early Medieval Graves

Catherine Hills

My interest in Anglo-Saxon archaeology owes its origin partly to the lectures I attended at Durham so long ago that Roman Britain and Anglo-Saxon England were part of a course on modern history. My introduction to cruciform brooches, Anglo-Saxon manuscripts, and Hadrian's Wall came from Rosemary Cramp, Professors Birley and Mann in the Old Fulling Mill, into which they, and miscellaneous others, were squeezed in the days before Rosemary took over and made the archaeology department into one of the best and largest in England. At first sight, the pagan cremation burials I went on to dig up in an Anglo-Saxon grave-field might seem to have little to do with the Mediterranean Christian milieu which has inspired much of Professor Cramp's own research, but in this contribution I shall explore some evidence for at least an indirect connection between the two.

To a degree this represents a response to the thesis that long-distance trade in early Anglo-Saxon England was mostly channelled through Kent (Huggett 1988), a suggestion which finds support in the obvious continental connections of much Kentish material and in the wealth of graves in Kent relative to the rest of Anglo-Saxon England. Some materials and artefact types do concentrate in Kent, with sparse distributions elsewhere. However, the relative emptiness of eastern England in older distribution maps is due partly to the prevalence of cremation there in the early Anglo-Saxon period, and partly to the failure of earlier excavators to recover more than a few fragments of artefacts from cremation urns. Careful examination of the bones and finds from cremation cemeteries, especially those from Spong Hill, Norfolk (Hills and Penn 1994), has, by contrast, produced a large number of certain or probable imports. There are, for example, more glass vessels known from this site than any other Anglo-Saxon cemetery (Evison 1994a). It is not always possible to distinguish the melted glass remains of vessels and beads, but a minimum of 100 cremations contained the remains of glass vessels, with 29 identifiable to type. Bronze sheet, definitely or probably identifiable as the remains of bowls, was found in 123 cremations. The same range of objects has been found at other cremation cemeteries, for example Sancton (Timby 1993) and Newark (Kinsley 1989). However, not all of the glass and bronze vessels need have been imports: some could have been produced in England, even fairly locally, although there is no direct evidence for this. Those which were imported are likely to have come from no further afield than the Rhineland or northern France, possibly via Kent. Some other possible imports – crystal and amber beads – could have come from a variety of sources, some local, and cannot be used easily to reconstruct patterns of trade.

There is one group of material which, if correctly identified, must have arrived in England as the result of long-distance trade via the Mediterranean, namely ivory. Ivory was used to make rings, and is found in both cremation and inhumation burials dating from the fifth to the seventh centuries in England and from the fourth to the seventh centuries on the Continent. These rings have been recognized in Anglo-Saxon graves since the nineteenth century (Thomas 1887) and, as T. C. Lethbridge pointed out (1952, 17) in connection with finds from Lackford they 'indicate a considerable trade in expensive foreign imports'. Barbara Green discussed this material in the report on Caistor-by-Norwich, and identified it as comprising the remains of elephant ivory rings used as bag-handles (Myres and Green 1973, 100–103). Discussion since then has been based on Green's account, with updated lists of sites producing ivory; at least 70 such sites are now known (e.g. Evison 1987). New evidence can also be found from as far afield as Schleswig-Holstein, Rome and Ethiopia which allows the English finds to be put into a wider context. How, when and why did African ivory arrive in northern Europe during the first millennium AD?

It has, in fact, sometimes been doubted that the material in question is indeed elephant ivory. Because the pattern of its distribution fails to conform with the idea of transmission through Kent, it has been suggested that this ivory derives not from elephant, but from walrus, the predominant source of ivory in the later Anglo-Saxon period (Huggett 1988; Kennett 1991). Those who have examined much of the material have not supported the walrus identification (e.g. MacGregor 1985) and it has most recently been refuted by Julie Bond in her report on ivory from Spong Hill (Bond 1994). It is worth restating here the reasons for rejecting alternative identifications.

The burnt ivory from cremations is a very distinctive material, identical in all the examples examined at Spong Hill, and it is clearly recognizable from its description in reports on other sites where it occurs. It is a bluish grey, soft, dense, homogeneous substance, usually fractured into small, flat, rectangular pieces. This pattern of breakage arises from the 'cone within cone' structure of elephant ivory, which is quite distinct from that of walrus (Penniman 1952). Another diagnostic feature is the size of the rings – difficult to establish

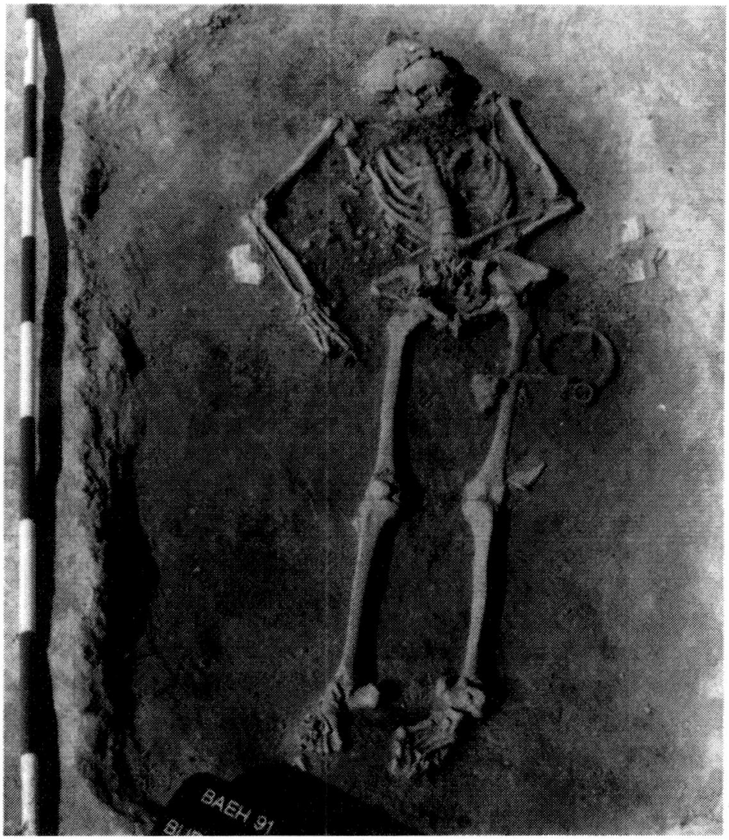

Fig. 6.1. Barrington, Cambridgeshire: inhumation with ivory ring. (Photo: Archaeological Field Unit, Cambridgeshire County Council).

for most cremations but often measurable in inhumations: each has been formed by cutting across a tusk near its base in order to create a one-piece ring. Many rings are complete, or were so when first recorded (Fig. 6.1). Where metal fittings exist they are either remains of attachments, probably to a bag, or they are repairs to a ring which split in antiquity. I have seen no ring which could plausibly be explained as a composite, made from more than one piece, and, even if such examples exist, the separate elements would be sections of rings of comparable diameter to the complete examples. The diameter of each ring is that of the tusk from which it was cut, ranging from 100 to 150 mm. Examples from recent publications include: Berinsfield grave 107, 110 mm (Boyle *et al.* 1995, 53); Lechlade grave 18, 145–150 mm (Boyle *et al.* 1998 63); Castledyke grave 112, *c.*131 mm (Drinkall and Foreman 1998, 66); Barrington, grave 69, 121 mm (Malim and Hines 1998, 72). Older finds give comparable measurements, as do continental examples: for example, the 86 listed by

Renner (1970), mostly from southern Germany, have diameters of between 100 and 150 mm.

Walrus tusks are typically only 30–40 mm in diameter. Although some male walruses have very long tusks, of up to 1 m in length, these tusks are not significantly greater in diameter than shorter tusks. Walruses have heads which are small relative to their bodies and which could never sustain tusks of a diameter even approaching 100 mm. Walrus ivory was utilized in England, especially in the late Anglo-Saxon period, when craftsman used all available resources, including antler for combs, horn for handles, horses' teeth for playing pieces and whale bone – the material used for the Franks Casket. Most of these materials have been found on the settlement sites where they were worked, as well as in graves. But the rings discussed in this paper were not made from walrus tusks.

An alternative proposal is that this was fossil mammoth ivory. Green argued against this, on the grounds that the fossil ivory she had examined was too friable and could not have been worked. However, fossil ivory from Siberia has been and continues to be worked successfully. To test this proposition, Arthur MacGregor submitted three samples of ivory from Anglo-Saxon graves to the Oxford Research Laboratory for radiocarbon dating (Gowlett *et al.* 1987, 144; I am grateful for permission to use this information). These gave the following results (errors are quoted as one standard deviation):

Chatham Lines	1705 ± 100 B.P. (OxA–479)
Fairford	1575 ± 60 B.P. (OxA–648)
Sancton	2330 ± 70 B.P. (OxA–649)

Two of these dates clearly fall within the mid first millennium AD, the date to be expected for ivory contemporary with the Anglo-Saxons. The third date, from the first millennium BC, is still far too recent for fossil ivory, but too early for the Anglo-Saxons. The explanation here may be either reuse of an old object or, more probably, contamination of the sample. Re-use as an explanation might work for some types of objects but is not satisfactory for others. Ivory was used in the Roman period to make a variety of objects, from ornaments such as hair-pins and inlays to large objects including furniture, as well as diptychs – pairs of carved plaques which some scholars have argued were sometimes re-carved in the Carolingian period. However, these are flat objects: even if the medieval recipes for flattening curved ivory tusks were reliable (which is doubtful), re-curving would surely be impractical, and would have resulted in two-piece, not one-piece rings. There exist round containers – pyxides – usually elaborately carved, some of sufficiently large diameter: northern barbarians were capable of melting down silver classical statues and could easily have sliced across elaborately carved ivories, but they would then have had to go to the trouble of removing the carving to arrive at the smooth rings usually recorded. Most of these objects belong to Late Antiquity, so their reuse would not, in any case, explain the earlier radiocarbon date. While the occasional reuse of ancient ivory cannot be ruled out and could, conceivably, be the explanation of the anomalous radiocarbon date, the scale and duration of the use of ivory rings discussed below seems far too great to have been supplied on a regular basis through the slicing-up of old boxes. For most of these objects the original, simple identification is to be preferred: the material is elephant ivory, not walrus; it is contemporary with the Anglo-Saxons and is not fossil ivory; the rings have been made simply by cutting transverse slices across the upper end of elephant tusks.

Is it possible to be more precise as to its origins? Did it come from African or Indian elephants? Ivory from Schmalstede, Schleswig-Holstein, has been identified with a 70% probability as African elephant ivory (Bode 1998a, 95–6). African elephants produce larger tusks than Indian, and both males and females have tusks. Cutler has argued that the large, Late Antique diptychs could only have been made from African elephant tusks (Cutler 1998, 82). African ivory was more highly valued than Indian, and in the tenth century Arab writers record the export of African ivory to India (Phillipson forthcoming). It has been claimed that during the Roman period the appetite for beasts for the arena exhausted the supply of African elephants, and it has sometimes been argued that the ivory used in late antiquity came from India, not Africa. This has been taken to be confirmed by the statement by Isidore of Seville (d. 636) that elephants formerly came from both Africa and India but in his day only from India (*Etymologies*, bk 12, 2). It might be asked whether Isidore really knew the ultimate source of exotic materials such as ivory. It is true, however, that it was during Isidore's lifetime that the old trade routes were disrupted by Arab expansion. He might have been reporting accurately, but on a very recent situation, which should not be assumed to apply in earlier centuries. Alternatively, it has been suggested that 'India' actually meant Ethiopia to medieval writers. Clearly, elephants did continue to exist in sub-Saharan Africa, whether known to European writers or not.

It is not an easy matter to distinguish visually – even microscopically – between ancient objects made from African or from Indian ivory, especially when dealing with small, burnt fragments. Isotopic analysis has been used with some success in an attempt to distinguish between bones and ivory from elephants living in different parts of Africa (van der Merwe *et al.* 1990) which holds out some hope that in future it will also be possible to distinguish definitively between African and Indian ivory. For the present, an African rather than an Indian source seems much more probable.

African ivory could have reached the Mediterranean by a number of routes, but there is little evidence for contact between West Africa and the Mediterranean before the ninth century AD (Insoll 1996, 60–62). There is, however, good reason to suppose that the route from the Indian Ocean up the Red Sea into the Mediterrean survived as a flourishing trade-route until the seventh century, when it was blocked by Arab expansion.

The kingdom of Aksum in Ethiopia was known in the ancient world as a source of ivory, and there is now good archaeological evidence to support this tradition. Aksum was the subject of a recent research project directed by David Phillipson, which has confirmed that its main period of prosperity lay between the third and the seventh century AD, and that ivory was worked there on some scale (Phillipson 1998 and forthcoming). Such ivory could have come either across the Indian Ocean from India or from southern Africa, but it is more likely to be local to Aksum. From the fourth century, Aksum was a Christian kingdom with close contacts to the Mediterranean world. With the expansion of Islam in the seventh century, contact became more difficult but was never entirely lost, even after the Arab conquest of Egypt in 642 which cut the transport routes up the Red Sea. Before that date, in the fifth and sixth centuries as in earlier times, ivory from southern African elephants (or, less probably, from India) was collected and shipped on to the Mediterranean. The continued prosperity of Aksum shows that its established trading activities continued until the seventh century.

Cutler has shown that the size and thickness of ivory plaques increased during the late Antique period, when the price of ivory was also low, suggesting that it was in relatively large supply (Cutler 1984). Phillipson has pointed out that this increase in the supply of ivory coincides with the time of Aksum's prosperity, while the reduction in the seventh century coincides with its decline (Phillipson forthcoming).

Contact between Europe, the Red Sea region and the Indian Ocean is confirmed by finds of cowrie shells and amethyst beads in graves. In England both occur occasionally in female inhumations, predominantly of the seventh century (Evison 1987, 122; Geake 1997, 62–3). On the Continent the distribution of cowries shows a concentration in Alamannia and Bavaria, again in graves chiefly of the later sixth and seventh centuries (Martin 1976, 95–6; Arends 1978). They are generally identifed as amulets (Meaney 1981, 123–8). There may be some contradiction between the European evidence and that from Aksum for the date of the decline in trade, since cowries and amethysts in inhumation graves are dated to the seventh century, and ivory rings also seem to be deposited well into that century and even occasionally into the next. Cessation of supply would have had a rapid impact on production, but of course use of ivory artefacts and their eventual deposition in graves would have continued for some time afterwards.

It has sometimes been assumed that the decline of the Western Empire in the fifth century entailed the rapid and complete end of large-scale manufacture of all types of goods. That this was not the case has been shown by the history of glass and pottery production in the Rhineland, where industries continued from the Roman into the Merovingian period, albeit with diminished variety and technical sophistication, and on a smaller scale. In the case of luxuries such as ivory it might seem reasonable to suppose that production continued only in the Eastern Empire. That this is not entirely the case is shown by recent evidence from Rome, where excavations on the Palatine have produced offcuts and finished objects made from bone and ivory in association with late fourth- to fifth-century pottery (St Clair 1996). This material is interesting for several reasons. Firstly, workshop debris is rare at any period. Also, a variety of objects were made here from several materials, including some which combined two or more materials, namely pins with bone shanks and ivory heads. The craftsmen evidently were not specialized as to material or type of artefact. There is very little ivory waste (less than that derived from bone), as might be expected for a rare and valuable material. Ivory working might therefore be expected to leave few traces, even apart from the problems of preservation of organic material, but clearly the raw material was reaching western Europe at the time when it was occurring in northern burials. An economical ivory worker might have cut rings from the ends of the tusk while selecting the central parts for more elaborate carved panels.

The distribution and date of ivory in graves provides the most substantial evidence for the nature of the trade, although its precise character is not easy to establish. General surveys of archaeological material, from regional or chronological perspectives, tend not to include ivory as a significant artefact type. As an organic material, it is preserved only in certain environmental contexts. Only where there are cemeteries with good organic preservation but no ivory can it be argued with conviction that it was not buried. In all the 6,000 published graves from Krefeld-Gellep (North Rhine-Westphalia) no trace of ivory was recorded, but organic preservation was poor at Krefeld. At Stockum (also in the Rhineland) preservation was better, and many graves contained combs (Siegmund 1998): here the absence of ivory looks genuine, as it does at Frénouville (Normandy) where none was recorded (Pilet 1980). There seems to be a relative absence of ivory from cemeteries west of the Rhine, but it is beyond the scope of this paper to establish that situation securely. Finds apparently concentrate in southern Germany, in Alamannia and Bavaria, where recent chronological schemes confirm a sixth- to seventh-century date, as they do for the examples from Lombardic graves in Italy (Jørgensen 1992, 3,7).

In England, ivory rings are lacking from inhumations in Norfolk, where organic preservation is very poor. They are, however, found in cremations in the same region. Since the range of grave-goods placed in female burials is similar, whether the body was cremated or inhumed, I would argue that some inhumations in this area are likely to have been accompanied by ivory rings, but that these have not survived. None the less, there are cemeteries in other parts of the country which have adequate or even good bone preservation but where no graves are found containing ivory. Here the absence seems real, but no clear distribution pattern emerges: there are sites close to each other where one has produced ivory, the other not. In Yorkshire for example, ivory was found at West Heslerton (Powlesland forthcoming), but not at Sewerby (Hirst 1985), while in Kent it occurred at Dover Buckland (Evison 1987) but not at Mill Hill, Deal (Parfitt and Brugmann 1997). The cemeteries without ivory, like Sewerby, tend to be smaller than those were it does occur but even this trend can be contradicted – for example at Norton there was none from 120 excavated graves (Sherlock and Welch 1992). Older excavations tended to produce only one grave with an ivory ring in each cemetery but more recent reports list more – three at Beckford (Evison and Hill 1996), Lechlade (Boyle *et al.*1998) and Barrington (Malim and Hines 1998), five at Broughton Lodge (Kinsley 1993), Dover Buckland and Heslerton, and as many as nine at Empingham (Timby 1996). Overall, the distribution pattern within Anglo-Saxon England does not produce a concentration in any one region (Huggett 1988, fig. 3; Evison 1987, fig. 118). The date-range of inhumations with ivory is the same as that for furnished Anglo-Saxon burials in general, namely from the later fifth to the end of the seventh century, or even into the early eighth century (Geake, 1997, 81). For example, at Beckford and Great Chesterford (Evison 1994b) graves with ivory are dated to the later fifth century, at Lechlade they seem to belong to the sixth century while at Dover several are dated later than 650. If there is a concentration, it is in the sixth century, but probably this reflects no more than the greater number of furnished burials attributed to that period.

The main factor to be accounted for in establishing the incidence of ivory in cremations is the care with which the cremated bones have been excavated. Small pieces of burnt ivory are occasionally found during post-excavation processing by bone specialists, even amongst bones which have been carefully excavated (McKinley 1994, 86). Only cremation cemeteries where there is a complete bone report can be regarded as reliable sources of information. Where it is recorded, carbonized ivory from cremation burials, although fragmented, can survive better than it does in inhumations.

The earliest graves so far recorded with ivory rings are those most remote from the source of the ivory. These are cremations of fourth- and fifth-century date in northern Germany. At Pritzier and at Perdohl, both in Mecklenberg, Schuldt (1955, 86) identified what he described as bone arm-rings in cremations, associated with brooches of fourth- and fifth century types. The description and illustration of the Pritzier material, however, shows it to be ivory. At Pritzier many of the cremated bones were examined, and Schuldt lists burials as of adults, children or multiple burials. In Schleswig-Holstein several cremation cemeteries have now produced remains of ivory rings. Only one example was found at Bordesholm, where not much of the cremated bone appears to have been examined, associated with a fifth-century brooch and a bossed pot (Saggau 1986, 50). A cemetery only 1 km away from Bordesholm, at Schmalstede, which was in use only for the duration of the fifth century (Bode 1998a, 1998b), has produced ten cremations with ivory. It has been argued that these two sites were used by the same community, and it would be interesting to see whether further investigation of the bones at Bordesholm would produce more ivory. For Süderbrarup, in the same region, a thorough bone report has been published, but no ivory was found (Wahl 1988). At Issendorf, south of Hamburg, a cemetery with many similarities to English sites, ivory has been identified in 26 cremations, associated with brooches of

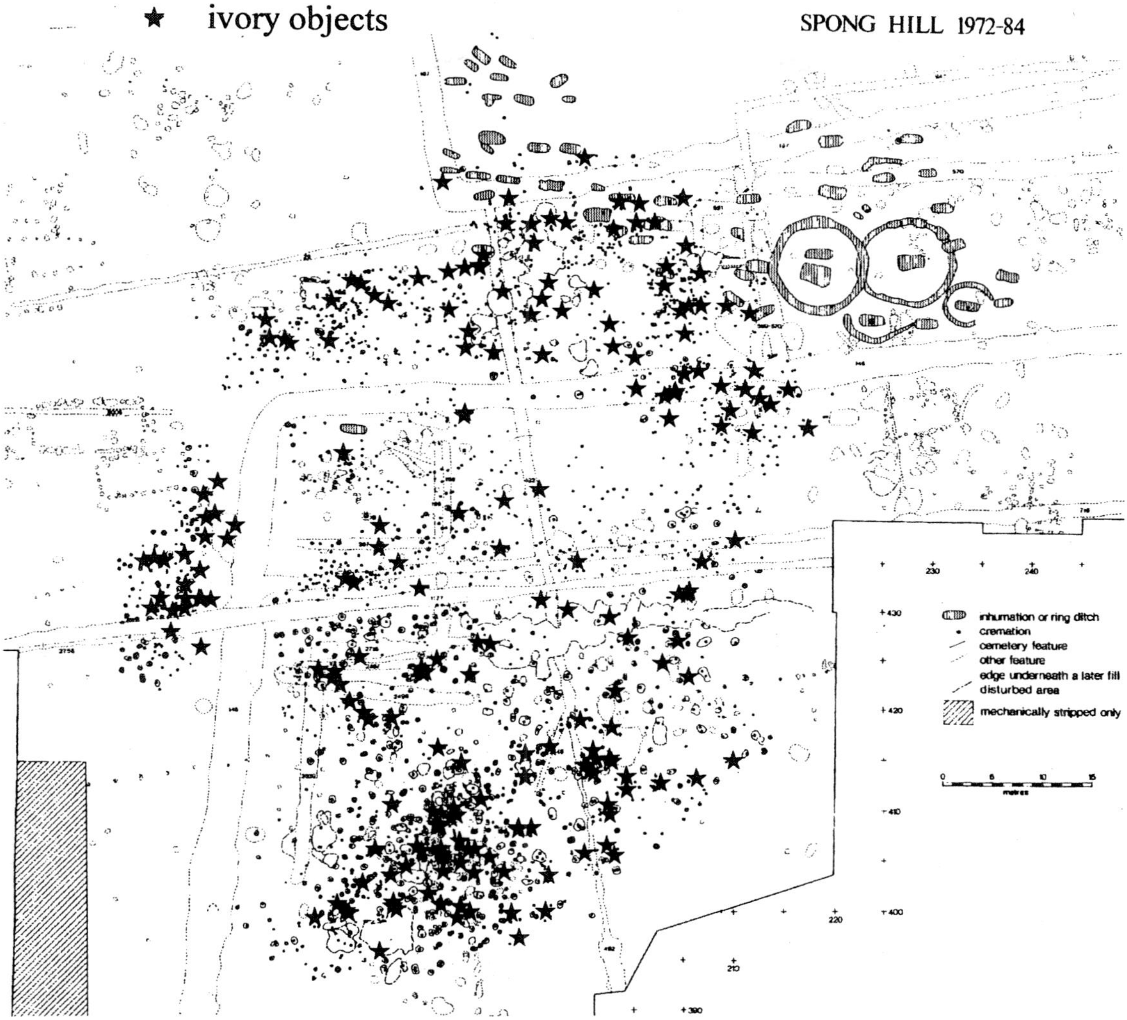

Fig. 6.2. Spong Hill, Norfolk: distribution of ivory.

fourth- and fifth-century date (Weber 1996, 36). The presence of ivory in north German cemeteries, especially those contemporary with English early Anglo-Saxon cremations (in the case of Issendorf in use into the sixth century) represents yet another feature linking both sides of the North Sea.

In English cremations, ivory occurs in burials of fifth- and sixth-century date. At Spong Hill, it was found throughout the cemetery (Fig. 6.2), associated with pottery of all types, and with brooches from the chronological range covered by the cemetery as a whole, namely the later fifth and sixth centuries, including an equal-armed brooch and later cruciforms. The picture from other cremation cemeteries is comparable. The ivory in German and English cremations is very unlikely to have arrived via Kent. The routes which brought glass, bronze vessels and gold coins to the north from the Mediterranean could also have brought the ivory. The Roman buckles which find their way into graves in north Germany during the fourth and fifth centuries are further evidence of this connection, perhaps with the Rhineland rather than directly with the Mediterranean.

In cremation cemeteries the numbers of graves with ivory are larger than in inhumation cemeteries, but since the total numbers of burials is also larger the proportion remains small (Fig. 6.3). At Schmalstede ten cremations out of 300 had ivory and at Issendorf, 26 of 3,000, which amounts respectively to only 3% and 1%. Although more information is available from English cremation cemeteries it is still difficult to extract a clear picture of the incidence of ivory. Clearly this has been underestimated in older reports, where the bones were not kept for examination, or where only a sample was examined. The picture from more recent excavations which remain, as yet, unpublished, is also difficult to assess. Percentages may be misleading if the proportion of the recorded urns which were reasonably complete and undisturbed is unclear, or if the proportion of the contents kept for analysis is unknown. Time-lapse between excavation and publication may lead to further confusion and loss. Some still-unpublished sites were analysed by Julian Richards, whose tables remain the best source for these, although some of his figures have been superseded by published reports (Richards 1987). Published sites include Lackford, with ivory recorded in 13 of 500 cremations, Illington, with 13 from 200 and Caistor-by-Norwich, with only five from about 300 more or less complete urns. At Newark, a site with confused records where, of more than 400 listed cremations, only 220 urns still contained cremated bones by the time the report came to be written, there were 39 with ivory. At Sancton 15 of 73 urns available for study from the 1976–80 excavations contained ivory – 20% – as well as 24 of those from earlier excavations. Amongst unpublished sites, according to Richards, ivory occurred in 13.7% of 205 urns at Elsham, but only in 2.8% of 251 urns at Loveden Hill and little or none was found at Mucking (Richards 1987, table 18). At Spong Hill, of 2,400 cremations, 205 contained ivory, amounting to about 8.5%, but rather more if only the reasonably complete burials are counted. The variation in quantity may be largely due to bias in recovery, since the sites for which a detailed report on all (or a large sample of) the bones has been compiled – Elsham, Sancton, Newark, Spong Hill – are those with larger numbers of graves with ivory. The exception to this generalization seems to be Mucking, a fact which may lend support to other evidence that the material from Mucking is less closely related to East Anglia than to other parts of southern England.

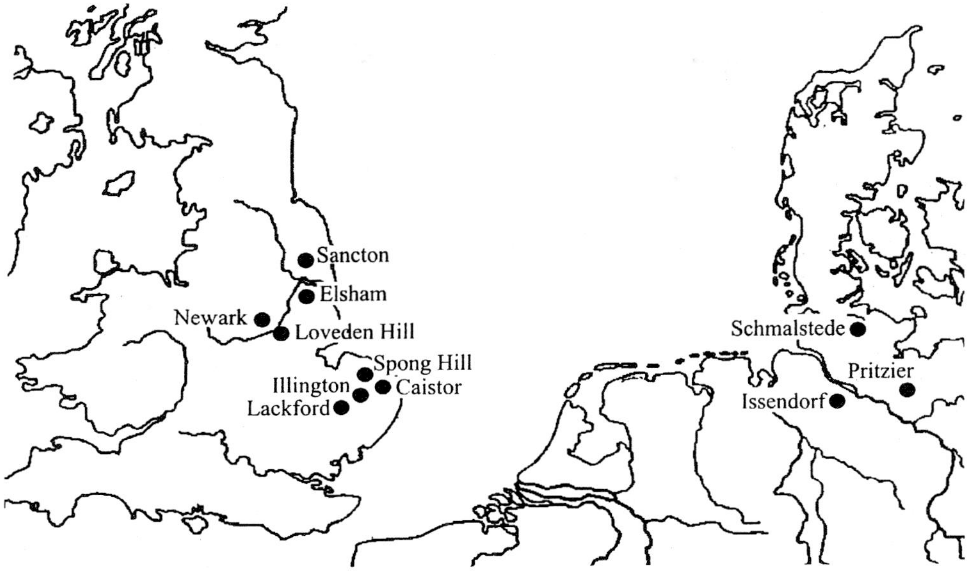

Fig. 6.3. Cremation cemeteries with ivory in England and northern Germany.

What were these ivory rings for and who was using them? It is usually assumed that these items were buried with women, and evidence from inhumations appears to bear this out, both in England and on the Continent, although two of the nine Empingham graves were skeletally sexed as male. Although the dichotomy between burial of men with weapons and women with jewellery may not have applied universally, it remains a general rule and the association of ivory with the latter rather than the former is clear. For cremations the picture is not so clear-cut. Schuldt asserted that bone arm-rings were associated with women and children, but although some of the cremated bones at Pritzier were examined, they were only aged, not sexed; this was also true at Newark. Where sexing has been attempted there is a bias towards female association, but also a significant number of males associated with ivory artefacts. Richards found four males as opposed to 17 females in his sample. In Germany, at Schmalstede, of the ten cremations with ivory all were adult burials, but three were male and three female. At Issendorf, of 26 burials, ten were female, four male and one contained the double burial of a male and female. All sexed graves containing ivory from Sancton were female. The largest number for analysis, giving perhaps the clearest picture, comes from Spong Hill. There, discounting multiple burials, 71 were definite or probable female burials with ivory as opposed to 18 males. Only five infant burials were associated with ivory, apart from six multiple burials of adults with infants. It is of course difficult to sex cremations (McKinley 1994, 19–21) and these identifications are given by McKinley with varying estimates of confidence. But even if only those without queries are listed, the same pattern appears: three definite males and 17 females. A similar result has now been obtained by several bone specialists, and McKinley found different patterns, using the same techniques, at Sancton and Spong Hill, which increases confidence in her results. It does seem to be the case that ivory was sometimes buried with cremated men, although in general this is a female-linked grave-good, as Richards's analysis suggested.

Other associated grave-goods confirm this picture. In inhumations, ivory is found in graves with jewellery, not with weapons. In cremations, ivory is again associated with brooches and glass beads, also with spindle-whorls and combs, but seldom with miniature tweezers, razors or shears, or with playing pieces. Weapons are seldom found in cremations, and there is not a clearly male-linked group of cremated grave-goods, but miniatures and playing pieces are found more often in male than female graves, so their infrequent association with ivory is consistent with its female linkage.

What are these rings for? Schuldt's description of them as arm-rings cannot be accurate since those which can be measured are too big: bracelets do not have diameters of more than 100 mm. Also, recorded excavated examples are found most often by the hip or leg, not on or near the arm. Recent English finds are very consistent in this feature: a majority are found not only near the leg, but on the left side. They were clearly suspended from a belt or girdle or, occasionally, put into the grave separately beside the body. The most widely accepted interpretation is that they were bag-handles. This was suggested in England in the nineteenth century by Akerman and Thomas (Thomas 1887, 386–7). Vogt (1960) argued that rings of ivory or metal formed the opening to a bag which, in the examples he knew in Switzerland, usually had a decorative openwork bronze disc as a kind of lid. Renner (1970) argued against this, and maintained that the discs, with protective outer rings made of ivory or metal, were purely decorative. Some of her arguments have some force – for example that the discs are decorated on both sides, and so were purely decorative. Several reconstructions of the use of the disc have been proposed, all of which might at times have been employed, and which do not all involve bags or ivory rings. The discs hardly occur in England and interpretation of the rings need not depend on them. Many ivory rings have been found close to an assortment of objects which might well have been contained in a bag. Some graves contained items such as mounted teeth, ammonites and cowries, all of which have been interpreted as amulets, most probably kept in a bag (Meaney 1981). Recently recorded examples have been found together with keys, latch-lifters and small metal fittings, which might have been in a bag or may have formed part of it. Green (Myres and Green 1973) followed Vogt (and earlier English archaeologists) in her reconstruction of the rings as bag-handles, and other English scholars have agreed with her, influenced, perhaps, by the use of pairs of large rings as handles for knitting bags in the recent past. The ancient bags cannot have been formed like those of more recent date, however, since they had only one ring, not two. Recent finds at Heslerton have included preserved remains of leather and textile which seem to confirm the bag thesis (Walton-Rogers forthcoming). One was associated with remains of an unusual textile which might itself have been imported, prompting the suggestion that the rings were in fact traded as parts of already made-up bags (Drinkall and Foreman 1998, 285); alternatively, a piece of valuable cloth might have been kept in a bag. There are still problems with this interpretation. For example, why was a valuable, imported item – an ivory ring – used only as an almost concealed part of a utilitarian item such as a bag? Could not bags have been made much more simply with draw strings or as pouches? Presumably many bags were indeed made more simply, since only a few had rings.

Whether ivory rings were a sign of status is a question subject to all the usual caveats in attempting to extract social information from burial evidence. Most of them occur in graves which are also equipped with a variety of other objects, nearly always brooches and beads, often wrist-clasps, buckles, knives, keys and girdle-hangers. Their relative rarity might also indicate wealth and/or status. Cremations also tend to be equipped with other items, including brooches, beads, spindle-whorls and sheet-bronze fragments, which might suggest relative status. The very rich, female Anglo-Saxon grave at Swallowcliffe Down did not have an ivory ring, although it did have an elaborately ornamented bag or satchel (Speake 1989). Perhaps ivory rings were not part of the equipment of women at the top of society but of the next stratum of society.

What this analysis has shown is that ivory rings, probably parts of bags, were a small but persistent part of the equipment buried with women in England and on the Continent over a period of some centuries. They derive from an established trade, not the occasional gift of an unusual object, and the period of their occurrence coincided largely with the time when supply of ivory to the Mediterranean, probably via Aksum, was at its greatest. The ivory in cremations on both sides of the North Sea in the fifth century certainly did not travel via Kent. It seems most likely that it went up the Rhine, whether as rough or finished rings or bags, and was then taken either east along the Frisian and German coast or west to East Anglia. The westerly route continued in use after there had ceased to be a market for ivory in northern Germany, but since the distribution is so widespread amongst sixth-century inhumations in England, a variety of routes and mechanisms can be postulated. If the apparent distribution on the Continent is real, it suggests connections between northern Germany, Alamannia, Lombard Italy and England which might be supported by other material, for example the use of hand-made, stamped pottery. This might be set against a more westerly Frankish/Kentish axis, and would make it even less likely that Kent was the main source for at least this class of imports. The latest of the English graves, and many of those on the Continent, come from a Christian context, thus forming at least a tenuous connecting thread between pagan burial practice and Mediterranean Christianity.

References

Arends, U. 1978. *Ausgewählte Gegenstände des Frühmittelalters mit Amulettcharakter*, dissertation, University of Heidelberg

Bode, M.-J. 1998 (a). *Schmalstede: Ein Urnengräberfeld der Kaiser- und Völkerwanderungszeit* (Offa-Bücher 78), Neumünster: Wachholtz

Bode, M.-J. 1998 (b). Verbindungen zwischen England und dem Kontinent an einem Beispiel aus Schleswig-Holstein, *Studien zur Sachsenforschung*, 11, 5–17

Bond, J. 1994. An explanatory note on the identification of the ivory fragments, in Hills, Penn and Rickett, 1994, 35–6

Boyle, A., Dodd, A., Miles, D. and Mudd, A. 1995. *Two Oxfordshire Anglo-Saxon Cemeteries: Berinsfield and Didcot* (Thames Valley Landscapes Monogr 8), Oxford

Boyle, A., Jennings, D., Miles, D. and Palmer, S. 1998. *The Anglo-Saxon Cemetery at Butler's Field, Lechlade, Gloucestershire*, Vol. 1, (Thames Valley Landscapes Monogr 10), Oxford

Cutler, A. 1984. The making of the Justinian diptychs, *Byzantion: Revue Internationale des Etudes Byzantines*, 54, (repr in Cutler 1998)

Cutler, A. 1993. Five lessons in late Roman ivory, *Roman Archaeol*, 167–92

Cutler, A. 1998. *Late Antique and Byzantine Ivory Carving*, Aldershot: Ashgate

Drinkall, G. and Foreman, M. 1998. *The Anglo-Saxon Cemetery at Castledyke South, Barton on Humber* (Sheffield Excav Rep 6), Sheffield: Sheffield Academic Press

Evison, V. 1987. *Dover: The Buckland Anglo-Saxon Cemetery* (HBMC Archaeol Rep 3), London: HBMC

Evison, V. 1994 (a). Anglo-Saxon glass from cremations, in Hills, Penn and Rickett, 1994, 23–30

Evison, V. 1994 (b). *An Anglo-Saxon Cemetery at Great Chesterford, Essex* (CBA Res Rep 91), London: CBA

Evison, V. and Hill, P. 1996. *Two Anglo-Saxon Cemeteries at Beckford, Hereford and Worcester* (CBA Res Rep 103), London: CBA

Geake, H. 1997. *The Use of Grave-Goods in Conversion-Period England, c.600–c.850* (Brit Archaeol Rep, Brit Ser, 261), Oxford: BAR

Gowlett, J., Hedges, R., Law, I. and Perry, C. 1987. Radiocarbon dates from the Oxford AMS system: Archaeometry datelist 5, *Archaeometry*, 29, 1, 125–55

Hills, C., Penn, K. and Rickett, R. 1994. *The Anglo-Saxon Cemetery at Spong Hill, North Elmham Part V* (East Anglian Archaeol Rep 67), Gressenhall: Norfolk Museums Service

Hirst, S. 1985. *An Anglo-Saxon Inhumation Cemetery at Sewerby, East Yorkshire* (York Univ Archaeol Pub 4), York: University of York

Huggett, J. 1988. Imported grave goods and the early Anglo-Saxon economy, *Medieval Archaeology*, 32, 63–96

Insoll, T. 1996. *Islam, Archaeology and History* (Brit Archaeol Rep, Int Ser, 647), Oxford: BAR

Jørgensen, L. 1992. Castel Trosino and Nocera Umbra. A chronological and social analysis of family burial practices in Lombard Italy (6th–8th cent. AD), *Acta Archaeol*, 62, 1–58

Kennett, D. 1991. Elephant and walrus: ivory and cultural relationships in the fifth and sixth centuries: a summary of the evidence from the South Midlands, *South Midlands Archaeol*, 21, 31–4

Kinsley, G. 1989. *The Anglo-Saxon Cemetery at Millgate, Newark-on-Trent, Nottinghamshire* (Nottingham Archaeol Monogr 2), Nottingham:

Kinsley, G. 1993. *Broughton Lodge* (Nottingham Archaeol Monogr 4), Nottingham:

Lethbridge, T. 1936. *A Cemetery at Shudy Camps, Cambridgeshire* (Cambs Antiq Soc Quarto Pub, new ser V), Cambridge: Cambridge Antiquarian Society

Lethbridge, T. 1951. *A Cemetery at Lackford, Suffolk* (Cambs Antiq Soc Quarto Pub, new ser VI), Cambridge: Cambridge Antiquarian Society

MacGregor, A. 1985. *Bone, Antler, Ivory and Horn*, London: Croom Helm

McKinley, J. 1994. *Spong Hill Part VIII: The cremations* (East Anglian Archaeol Rep 69), Gressenhall: Norfolk Museums Service

Malim, T. and Hines, J. 1998. *The Anglo-Saxon Cemetery at Edix Hill (Barrington A), Cambridgeshire* (CBA Res Rep 112), London: CBA

Martin, M. 1976. *Das fränkische Gräberfeld von Basel-Bernerring*, Basel: Philipp von Zabern

Meaney, A. 1981. *Anglo-Saxon Amulets and Curing Stones* (Brit Archaeol Rep, Brit Ser, 96), Oxford: BAR

Meaney, A. 1998. Girdle groups with ivory bag rings, in Malim and Hines, 1998, 268–9

Myres, J. and Green, B. 1973. *The Anglo-Saxon Cemeteries of Caistor-by-Norwich and Markshall, Norfolk* (Soc Antiq Res Rep XXX), London: Society of Antiquaries

Parfitt, K. and Brugmann, B. 1997. *The Anglo-Saxon Cemetery on Mill Hill, Deal, Kent* (Medieval Archaeol Monogr Ser 14), London: Society for Medieval Archaeology

Penniman, T. 1952. *Pictures of Ivory and other Animal Teeth, Bone, and Antler* (Pitt Rivers Museum Occasional Paper on Technology 5), Oxford: Pitt Rivers Museum

Phillipson, D. 1998. *Ancient Ethiopia: its antecedents and successors*, London: British Museum Press

Phillipson, D. forthcoming. Aksum: an African civilization in its world contexts, *Proceedings of the British Academy*

Pilet, C. 1980. *La nécropole de Frénouville* (Brit Archaeol Rep, Int Ser, 83) Oxford: BAR

Powlesland, D. forthcoming. *West Heslerton: The Anglian cemetery*

Renner, D. 1970. *Die durchbrochene Zierscheiben der Merowingerzeit*, Mainz: Römisch-Germanischen Museum

Richards, J. 1987. *The Significance of Form and Decoration of Anglo-Saxon Cremation Urns* (Brit Archaeol Rep, Brit Ser, 166), Oxford: BAR

Saggau, H. 1986. *Bordesholm. Der Urnenfriedhof am Brautberg bei Bordesholm in Holstein 1: Text und Karten*, Neumünster: Wachholtz

St Clair, A. 1996. Evidence for Late Antique bone and ivory carving on the northeast slope of the Palatine: The Palatine East excavation, *Dumbarton Oaks Papers*, 50, 369–74

Schuldt, E. 1955. *Pritzier, Ein Urnenfriedhof der späten römischen Kaiserzeit in Mecklenberg*, Berlin: Akademie-Verlag

Sherlock, S. and Welch, M. 1992. *An Anglo-Saxon Cemetery at Norton, Cleveland* (CBA Res Rep 82), London: CBA

Siegmund, F. 1998. *Merowingerzeit am Niederrhein: Die frühmittelalterliche Funde aus dem Regierungsbezirk Düsseldorf und dem Kreis Heinsberg*, Cologne: Rheinland Verlag

Speake, G. 1989. *A Saxon Bed Burial on Swallowcliffe Down* (English Heritage Arch Rep 10), London: English Heritage

Thomas, G. 1887. On excavations in an Anglo-Saxon cemetery at Sleaford, in Lincolnshire, *Archaeologia*, 50, 383–406

Timby, J. 1993. Sancton I Anglo-Saxon cemetery. Excavations carried out between 1976 and 1980, *Archaeol J*, 150, 243–365

Timby, J. 1996. *The Anglo-Saxon Cemetery at Empingham II, Rutland* (Oxbow Monograph 70), Oxford: Oxbow Books

Van der Merwe, N., Lee Thorpe, J., Thackeray, J., Hall-Martin, A., Kruger, F., Coetzee, H., Bell, R. and Lindeque, M. 1990. Source-area determination of elephant ivory by isotopic analysis, *Nature*, 346 (23 Aug 1990), 747–9

Vogel, J.C., Eglington, B. and Auret, J. M. 1990. Isotopic fingerprints in elephant ivory and bone, *Nature*, 346 (23 Aug 1990), 747–9

Vogt, E. 1960. Interpretation und museale Auswertung alamannischer Grabfunde, *Zeitschrift für Schweizerische Archäologie und Kunstgeschichte*, 20, 70–90

Wahl, J. 1988. *Süderbrarup II: Anthropologische Untersuchungen* (Offa Bücher 64), Neumünster: Wachholtz

Walton-Rogers, P. forthcoming. The Textiles, in Powlesland forthcoming

Weber, M. 1996. *Das Gräberfeld von Issendorf, Kreis Stade*, dissertation, University of Hamburg

Weber, M. 1998. *Das sächsische Gräberfeld von Issendorf, Kreis Stade: Katalog der Funde*, Hamburg

7

From *Beowulf* to Binford
Sketches of an Archaeological Career

Christopher D. Morris

It was a great privilege for me to be asked to give the opening address at the conference in honour of Rosemary Cramp – but also a frightening experience.[1] We were there to wish her well as she approached her seventieth birthday, but also to celebrate her achievements. In compiling this text, I could imagine Rosemary in front of me, fixing me with her beady eye, and I was immediately transformed back into the challenging role of being one of her tutorial students struggling to say something coherent: 'Tell me, Mr Morris, do you have anything to say on this subject?'

What I have to contribute on this subject – that is, Rosemary herself – comes from the perspective of having begun as a well-meaning, but at times rather puzzled, History student who took the route of Anglo-Saxon studies as a means of entering Archaeology. It was Rosemary's achievement to take a motley collection of individuals from a variety of backgrounds and interests – students from History, English, and some doing a general degree in Archaeology in the days before an honours course existed – and to instil in them a different perspective upon the study of the past, through a focus upon what was rather quaintly called in those days 'Anglo-Saxon Antiquities'. Like Miss Brodie's 'gals', those of us who ventured to Rosemary's lair in the Old Fulling Mill had to be prepared to offer a level of commitment to the subject which was quite unknown in our 'parent' departments. If that meant a Historian learning Old English, or an English student undertaking excavation experience (at Jarrow or Monkwearmouth of course), then you just got on with it: 'no' was not an option. There was a further expectation of being seen to work in the Department on the subject for next week's class, but that duly carried with it the privilege of access to Rosemary's and Eric Birley's private libraries: both were incredibly generous and trusting in their support to students – undergraduate as well as postgraduate – in terms of access to books and journals, and they instilled in us the value of browsing widely in a subject as well as focusing upon the particular topic of concern. This is a characteristic which continued throughout Rosemary's career as a University teacher, and which was also of inestimable value to colleagues in the Department.

In those days, Rosemary still had links with the English Department and her own brand of Old English teaching helped many a bemused student through dark nights of studying *Beowulf*, when what they really wanted to do was to read Shakespeare or Milton. She was a valued member of St Mary's College and a much-loved 'moral tutor' there at the time of Mary Holdsworth's Principalship and she therefore had a reputation among the student body that stretched far beyond History, Archaeology and English. In part, that reputation proceeded from the impression she made on new students during Freshers' Week, as she informed and entertained them as part of their induction. Amid the sardonic comments came serious information, most notably the parting shot that struck terror into many a quivering soul 'and if you don't work, then you fail and you just get thrown out!'

Of course, *Beowulf* is the formal starting-point of Rosemary's academic career, although her archaeological beginnings go back to her time on her father's farm in Leicestershire, where she decided to explore some Roman remains.[2] Then, academically nurtured in the Oxford University environment of the late 1940s and 1950s, she had no opportunity for archaeological study at the undergraduate level. However, the Oxford University Archaeological Society and the Ashmolean Museum provided foci for earnest undergraduates such as Rosemary, and she then developed these interests at postgraduate level, through contact with Professor Christopher Hawkes of the Institute of Archaeology. Rosemary undertook her B.Litt. thesis, relating the foremost Anglo-Saxon poem to the emerging archaeological evidence, while she was a tutor in English at St Anne's College. Her acknowledgements to Hawkes and to Professor Dorothy Whitelock in her seminal paper on the subject (deriving from her thesis) in the inaugural volume of *Medieval Archaeology* in 1957 reflect this background.

> In the Anglo-Saxon period, where both the written and the archaeological evidence have so many gaps and difficulties of interpretation, the picture of Anglo-Saxon society given in *Beowulf* must be fully acknowledged by archaeologists while on the other hand no critic of the poem can afford to neglect the new material evidence that is constantly being produced. *Beowulf* is the only poem that gives a full picture of secular life in this period and as such it has constantly been used to articulate the archaeologist's dumb evidence (Cramp 1957a, 57).[3]

Thus the opening of her paper, and at the end she concluded:

> As W. P. Ker said: 'The poem of *Beowulf* has been sorely tried; critics have long been at work on the body of it to discover how it is made.' It is a measure of the poem's strength that it emerges alive from this continual vivisection, but the newest archaeological evidence has transfused new vigour into the body. The recent analyses of literary critics have shown the careful artistry of the poem, its lack of empty statement and vain allusion, and archaeologists must equally have examined the work as a whole before criticising a unit of its statement.
>
> What archaeology brings to the poem is not yet a solution of its date... The archaeological evidence that is now available, however, can enrich considerably the study of the poem; it can supply relevant illustrations so that simple words such as 'hall' or 'sword' conjure up a precise picture in the mind of the modern reader. Moreover a knowledge of the excellencies and refinements of Anglo-Saxon craftsmanship enables us to appreciate what governed the poet's choice of epithet in stressing the features that he did stress in more complicated passages of description (Cramp 1957a, 77).

Twenty-six years later, Rosemary reconsidered part of the subject of this paper and gently chided both archaeologists and students of this early literature:

> The dichotomy between [James] Earl's thought-provoking exploration of the function of images in the poem, especially the hall image, and the partial archaeological evidence that he invokes to support his views is unfortunate, but no more unfortunate perhaps than the unsubtle way archaeologists have used the words 'hall' and 'bur' to describe structures that they have excavated. Perhaps it is not possible to communicate the diversity and subtle differences that exist between the material and written cultural vestiges, but at least one should be aware of them (Cramp 1993b, 334–5).

There are others, such as Richard Bailey and our late-lamented friend Jim Lang, who would have been better able than I to articulate how Rosemary's approach at this time did indeed bring together these two worlds of scholarship for the student of English in the later 1950s; certainly for me as a History student in the 1960s she opened both of these worlds.

The fledgling Archaeology Department in Durham was established under Eric Birley, and Rosemary has described to several of us how he showed her the building of the Old Fulling Mill almost as if it were the new house for a bride. However, because it did not have honours degree students of its own, Archaeology tended to be viewed by others with a degree of suspicion. Eric Birley, John Mann and Rosemary (assisted in early days by Edwina Proudfoot) embodied this upstart Department down by the River Wear, widely seen in those days by fellow students (and, I suspect, a number of staff) as a refuge for eccentrics. However, many good students were attracted to both Roman and Anglo-Saxon studies because of the advocacy of the staff for their specialisms in the few grudgingly allotted lectures in the first-year courses. If there was a benign indifference in the History Department to the oddball students who chose to take courses in Archaeology, there was much less encouragement to English Language students to seek courses with Rosemary, and it was a comment upon her reputation that students did, indeed, seek her out to take 'Anglo-Saxon Antiquities' – and not just in penny-numbers.

It should be emphasized that Rosemary always expected students to engage with the primary material and, as a true pedagogue, expected more from students than they could necessarily give at a particular stage. For most students, the experience in tutorials was that they responded to the expectation and 'raised their game'. Of course, Rosemary would then simply expect an even greater improvement, but any one who experienced this sort of education through personal expectation, could not but improve. In essence, of course, this experience is based in part upon the labour-intensive system of tutorials, and in part upon time spent handling material or going out on field-visits. Its foundation was also the philosophy of the fundamental interaction of personal research and teaching which, while by no means unique to Rosemary, was exemplified at its best in her.

It is also a comment upon her reputation that, almost from the beginning of her time at Durham, Rosemary attracted research students. The long, distinguished line of these postgraduates is headed by Richard Bailey. She established over a period of more than 30 years a distinguished and distinctive postgraduate school in all aspects of Anglo-Saxon studies, particularly archaeology and art, and early medieval archaeology more generally, especially in relation to the early Christian world.

Rosemary was, as the Scots say, 'well-kent' around Durham and, even as a young lecturer, her reputation preceded her. Along with other 'Young Turks' of the time, she managed to get the University to establish an Academic Electoral Assembly to enfranchize the younger staff through election to the Senate – an institution that still survives. There is an unfortunate view peddled by many academics that getting involved in the institutions of the University is not a legitimate activity for a research-orientated academic. If there is one thing I have learned above all else from Rosemary, it is that if you want to have any influence over your own or your Department's destiny in a university, then you have to join in and get your significant lines of communication clear. Whether in the academic community of the university, or in the wider archaeological world, Rosemary has never been one to stand aside from being involved in an organization, especially if she feels that change is needed.

Rosemary ensured, both during the 1960s before she was appointed to the Chair and subsequently in the 1970s, that she did join in 'University politics', if you like, but no less important for all that the description has acquired a pejorative ring. She has never been afraid of a challenge or the need to address a problem straight on. Although Rosemary has had the good fortune to be spared the excesses of Teaching Quality Assurance and Research Assessment, her own academic career is an example of how teaching, administration and research have become so thoroughly meshed together as to produce a self-evidently successful result that requires no formal criteria of assessment.

While the Department of Archaeology which I knew as a student in the 1960s provided a good academic environment, Rosemary knew all along that much more could be done with the subject in Durham. By the late 1960s, Dennis Harding had joined Eric Birley, John Mann and Rosemary, and at last the Department could offer, in theory at least, a respectable coverage of Archaeology in chronological terms – even if at that time its focus was very much on England, especially the North of England with extensions into the classical Roman world. But the real transformation of Durham Archaeology came with her appointment to the Chair in 1971.

***

Rosemary was determined to weld the Department into a team that collectively could stand comparison with any other in the country. That, I believe, was achieved simply because she was prepared to put faith in her younger colleagues. As with her students, Rosemary expected her staff to aim higher and achieve more. By judicious prodding and above all by a belief in us, she pushed us to think laterally and held faith with myself, John Casey, Anthony Harding, Janey Cronyn (later replaced by Chris Caple), Colin Haselgrove (who replaced Dennis Harding on his elevation to the Abercromby Chair at Edinburgh), and later on Martin Jones and Martin Millett (who replaced John Mann, on his early retirement). We were all individualists, much in her own image, and she treated us as (presumably) she felt she and others of her generation should have been treated. There was a 'rein' but it was a loose and long one, and I for one am grateful to her for the faith she placed in us over the years.

People like myself can look back fondly to the rather more relaxed atmosphere of the Department at the Old Fulling Mill, but Rosemary was only too well aware that change had to occur. The student base from 'optional' and 'special' subjects in other honours courses, the general degree, and the admittedly committed postgraduate cohort, was just not enough either to provide the basis in terms of student numbers for expansion within the University, or the clout in terms of the outside world as regards academic standing. It became a major priority, once she took over the Chair, to establish a single honours degree in Archaeology, and two joint degrees with Ancient History and Anthropology (regrettably, it took much longer to achieve the joint degree with History), not to mention the upgrading of the postgraduate taught diploma courses to Master's status. By the mid–1970s this was all achieved, and student numbers began to rise to the extent that Rosemary could indeed achieve the staffing increases and space allocation that I have already described. It is, however, deeply ironic to remember concern amongst the staff at the 'quite unacceptable' increase of our student-staff ratio figures into double figures, which threatened, as I remember, in a bad year to be 'as high as 13:1' [*sic*]!

Many were the animated debates amongst us as to what was the most appropriate format for the honours degree, how we should teach it, what practical requirements we should expect, etc. However irritated Rosemary became with her younger colleagues' wilder flights of fancy and assertions of greater insight, she never lost sight of the main aim. This was to establish, alongside a re-energized postgraduate school, an undergraduate school that could compete for students wishing to take Archaeology on equal terms with the longer established centres such as London, Cambridge, Cardiff, Edinburgh, and the newer Departments of repute such as Sheffield and Southampton. Durham was later on the scene in this respect than most other universities, but in this main aim, she triumphantly succeeded – as evidenced by the audience at the conference and the even larger number of Durham Archaeology graduates (both undergraduate and postgraduate) who have taken significant jobs in academic and professional archaeological and museum institutions throughout the British Isles and beyond. In this peopling of the academic and archaeological establishments by Durham archaeologists is the true measure of Rosemary's achievement as Professor of Archaeology and as the Department's leader.

***

All this was achieved while Rosemary threw herself wholeheartedly into the wider world of archaeology. It is a matter of public knowledge how much she contributed in this wider arena: simply to list her involvement with bodies at every level would be a lengthy undertaking. She made a very real contribution to public archaeology, and some things really do stand out. These include her immense amount of work on behalf of the former Science-Based Archaeology Committee as Chairman of the SERC Committee; her services to the British Museum as a Trustee; and her appointment to English Heritage as a Commissioner, and the Royal Commission on the Ancient and Historical Monuments of Scotland (for which she was a Commissioner for 25 years). After she retired in 1990, she became an extremely active President of the Council for British Archaeology, travelling from one end of the country to the other to appear in person to speak to the reforms being initiated under her Presidency. 'Inconvenience' has never come into it with Rosemary as an excuse: if she had to be in London, shall we say, at English Heritage or SERC one day, and then in Edinburgh at the Royal Commission the next, that was what she did. Saturdays would as often as not see Rosemary on the early train to London for a British Museum Trustees' meeting, and for a significant period she would be in the Department early on a Monday morning attending to paperwork, then taking a 10 o'clock class, before dashing to the station to catch the train to Edinburgh to attend the Scottish Antiquaries' Council meeting in the afternoon. Sometimes this hectic lifestyle just got the better of her. I do not think people in the various societies and institutions to which Rosemary has given her time so generously have always appreciated just how much sheer toil and nervous energy were involved.

In the North-East of England, Rosemary was one of the earliest Cathedral Archaeological Consultants appointed, and in Durham she has ensured that the World Heritage Site is cared for in a manner befitting its unique importance. This was achieved firstly, by her personal inspection of plans for changes or of the work itself, and secondly, by getting the Chapter's agreement to the appointment of a resident archaeologist—one of only (I believe) two such full-time posts in England. Similarly, she then worked towards the re-establishment of the University Museum, which had been in the Old Fulling Mill, but had subsequently been abandoned by the University and the collections dispersed. It required the commitment of others – notably Anthony Harding in the early years – to ensure that this project really worked, but without her vision, and her ability to use her lines of communication it would never have got off the ground. Now Durham City has an additional resource for its citizens, and a valuable supplementary tourist attraction to go with the more obvious one towering overhead. It was also largely due to Rosemary's personal interest, commitment and drive that the Bede Monastery Museum at Jarrow Hall was established in the 1970s, and nurtured through the 1980s. She conceived her own role as extending to smoothing the way for successive Curators with the local councillors and other trustees. The establishment and maintenance of this prime tourist attraction, which retains academic credibility while contributing to the regeneration of a depressed area and to the education of generations of school children in the heritage of their birthplace, owes almost everything to Rosemary's vision and determination. In its way, it represents the combination of academic standing, regional commitment and outreach to the wider audience that we associate with her.

Rosemary's work at Jarrow-Wearmouth had always involved people outside the immediate world of her Department (indeed several joined in as a result of her work in the extra-mural sphere), and she has always been generous in talking to local societies about her work. I doubt there is any archaeological or local historical society in the North of England which she has not addressed. Of course, being on so many committees away from Durham meant that occasionally there were incompatibilities and impossible conflicts of obligation entered into over the phone or in conversation, and somehow not entered into the diary – or the *right* diary...! Nevertheless, Rosemary always maintained her obligations, in relation to professional archaeologists assisting the local societies and amateurs in the region. Apart from innumerable lectures and talks, she trekked regularly across to Cumbria to be an active President of the Cumberland and Westmorland Archaeological and Architectural Society; she gave of her time to attend the meetings of the Durham and Northumberland Architectural and Archaeological Society in Durham; and she took an active part in the CBA Regional Group covering the whole of the North, vigorously asserting the need for the western part of the region to be equally involved and represented in the group's activities.

Rosemary has welcomed into the Department those who had a serious interest in its work. Initially, a group originally from an extra-mural class came in with the Jarrow-Wearmouth project. But it also included those who simply wanted to find out about their local archaeology: the Local Information Room, the Northern Archaeological Survey, the Durham Archaeological Survey (even if they have now been superseded) all related to this. As in Eric Birley's day, so in Rosemary's, the Department was a 'home' for local archaeologists. Some of those who came in to do one thing, then found themselves involved by Rosemary in other things: Fred Bettess, for instance, contributed to the raising of standards of practical work in the Department – as exemplified by his book *Surveying for Archaeologists*, first published in 1984 through the University. Others, such as the late David Burkitt, joined as Honorary Research Fellows and established new areas of academic enquiry (in his case, palaeopathology) from the initial base of Rosemary's own material from her research projects (cf. Cramp 1983c).

***

What of Rosemary's own research projects and her own achievement in academic terms? As indicated above, Rosemary began her research career with Anglo-Saxon archaeology and *Beowulf* at Oxford. When she came to Durham, she took the opportunity to begin her life's work on Early Christian archaeology, focusing especially upon Anglo-Saxon monumental stone sculpture and the remains of Bede's monastery at Wearmouth-Jarrow. Recognition of her lifetime achievement in this field has been appropriately acknowledged by her receipt of the Frend Medal of the Society of Antiquaries of London.

Actually, Rosemary's first substantial article after '*Beowulf* and Archaeology' was one concerned with Scotland, and which arose directly out of both her teaching of 'Anglo-Saxon Antiquities' and her life-long concern to link east and west within Northumbria. It has also been the subject of wry humour over the years, since 'The Anglican Sculptured Crosses of Dumfriesshire' has such a marvellous slip concealed in the typo of the title.[4] There is, furthermore, within the body of the text that characteristic and not-so-gentle warning to others that this is but the beginning of her study, that there is more to come, and that she expected to be left to undertake it in her own time: 'It should be stressed that Ruthwell is a highly individual monument, and its total conception, *which I intend to discuss elsewhere*' has the stamp of a single mind (Cramp 1960a, 12).

In the forty years since that article, Rosemary has, indeed, carved out her own territory and developed a distinctive research voice. While there have been several other scholars in the field of Anglo-Saxon sculpture and/or Anglo-Saxon art (and of these not a few have come from her Durham stable), it is undeniable that, as stated recently by a publisher, 'Professor Cramp's work on Anglo-Saxon sculpture... has transformed our knowledge of the subject' (*Pindar Press Catalogue, Spring 1999*). She has consequently been accorded the distinction of having her journal articles and contributions to books on this subject brought together in the distinguished 'Select Studies in the History of Art' series (Cramp 1992), which states:

> The crosses and sculptural fragments surviving, particularly in the region of Anglo-Saxon Northumbria, had previously been known through the result of antiquarian research. To the author belongs the credit of bringing this body of work into the perspective of contemporary European and Insular art, and establishing a context for their creation with the help of archaeological methods.

Several other such studies, whether of an individual stone or a group of sculptures, have been produced, like the article on the Dumfriesshire sculpture, in the relevant local archaeological journal or in regionally-produced publications. While this has, perhaps, been of some inconvenience to some fellow-scholars, it has ensured that those for whom they have the most immediate resonance in the local area, have had a chance to gain access to modern scholarship concerning their own material. This scholarship has been displayed not only in the articles about particular stones but also in catalogues, such as those from the exhibition on 'A Century of Anglo-Saxon Sculpture' mounted jointly with Jim Lang in the DLI Museum & Arts Centre and the Moot Hall at Hexham (Cramp and Lang 1977), and the catalogue produced jointly by Rosemary and Roger Miket for the permanent display of the Anglo-Saxon and Viking collections in the University of Newcastle upon Tyne Museum of Antiquities (Cramp and Miket 1982). Even her *Short Guide to the Pre-Conquest Sculptured Stones in the Dormitory of Durham Cathedral* contained pithy comments worthy of more than a privately published pamphlet (Cramp 1965a/1971c), but it has enabled many a casual visitor to the Cathedral to appreciate some of the significance of these battered bits of stone collected by Canon Greenwell from various locations around the North of England. Similarly, her Appendix on pre-Conquest sculpture in a church guide at Jarrow and her joint authorship of the church guide to Monkwearmouth has presented scholarship lightly and with relevance to their readers (Cramp 1962a; Colgrave and Cramp 1965). Two other 'collectors' items' of exhibition catalogues are further examples of this lightly-worn and generously-shared scholarship: *The Monastic Arts of Northumbria* held in Hexham and Middlesborough, before travelling to Cardiff under the auspices of the Arts Council (Cramp 1967c), and

Anglo-Saxon Connections, mounted by her with the blessing of the Dean and Chapter in the Cathedral Treasury, on the occasion of the International Society of Anglo-Saxonists Conference in Durham (Cramp with Entwhistle 1989). All of these texts remain of considerable value to student and scholar alike.

Detailed early sculptural studies from around Northumbria – Monkwearmouth (Cramp 1964c), St Oswald's Church, Durham (Cramp 1966a), Lancaster (Cramp 1966b) and Tynemouth Priory (Cramp 1967b) – together with her keynote Jarrow Lecture in 1965 on *Early Northumbrian Sculpture*, set the style and agenda for her work:

> When one looks today at the remnants of stone carving in these main centres [such as the monasteries of Lindisfarne, Wearmouth-Jarrow, Hexham and York] or the fragments of crosses in many of our remote parish churches, one should not forget what an immense achievement it was for the English to step outside their tradition of abstract non-monumental decorative art, and to produce under the stimulus of Mediterranean and late antique models what Kendrick calls justly 'a premature variety of Romanesque art'. It was indeed the love of earlier Christian culture such as Bede related of Benedict Biscop which produced that special contribution from the British Isles, that so early brought Christ and his Saints out of the surroundings of the Church and majestically mounted them as a symbol of Christ's Victory in the wild open places of Northumbria (Cramp 1965, 12–13).

The range of Rosemary's publications on Anglo-Saxon sculpture, increasingly through the 1970s and 1980s at international venues, is considerable and wide-ranging in geographical and chronological terms. Successive papers at colloquia at Mainz brought to an international audience 'The position of the Otley crosses in English sculpture of the eighth to ninth centuries' (Cramp 1971d) and 'Tradition and Innovation in [Southern] English stone sculpture of the tenth and eleventh centuries' (Cramp 1972a). Similarly, 'Mediterranean elements in the early medieval sculpture of England' were laid out to the UISPP Congress at Nice (Cramp 1976c) and 'Anglo-Saxon and Italian sculpture' at a Spoleto seminar (Cramp 1986a). British audiences and readers meanwhile were treated to mature reflections on 'Anglo-Saxon sculpture of the Reform period' (Cramp 1975a); 'Early Northumbrian sculpture at Hexham' (Cramp 1974a & b); 'Schools of Mercian sculpture' (Cramp 1977c); and 'The Pre-Conquest sculptural tradition in Durham' (Cramp 1980c). Rosemary returned to her Ruthwell theme in considering 'The Evangelist symbols and their parallels in Anglo-Saxon Sculpture' at the 1300th anniversary celebrations of the birth of Bede at Cornell University in the USA (Cramp 1978b). Durham was itself host to an international symposium in 1977 to celebrate the fiftieth anniversary of the publication of W.G. Collingwood's major book on *Northumbrian Crosses of the pre-Norman Age*. Rosemary's contribution to the symposium and publication was to tackle the most difficult aspect – that of 'The Anglian tradition in the Ninth century', i.e. the period of overlap (Cramp

1978a). Alongside these papers, Rosemary has contributed generously to *Festchriften* for colleagues (1974d; 1983a; 1983b; 1986c).

But these articles and papers were side issues alongside the ultimate goal of *The Corpus of Anglo-Saxon Stone Sculpture,* which was established in Durham under the auspices of the British Academy. The gestation period for this enormous project was long, and at times it must have seemed to Rosemary and her devoted Research Assistants (especially Betty Coatsworth) that it would never come to fruition. But faith and hard work prevailed and 1984 was the landmark year with the publication of the General Introduction and Volume I (appropriately enough, for County Durham and Northumberland) in two parts (Cramp 1984a & b). Professor Fred Holliday, the Vice-Chancellor of Durham University at the time, wrote in his Foreword, as follows:

> The University of Durham has felt privileged to have housed this important project, not only for its significant contribution to scholarship, but because the work has captured interests and imaginations far beyond academic walls (Cramp 1984, v).

Succinct this may be, but it encapsulates the essence of Rosemary's work, while the subsequent volumes, both by her and her collaborators – particularly Richard Bailey and Jim Lang, whose lives have been equally bound up with this project – have fully borne out Professor Holliday's observation (Bailey and Cramp 1988; and cf. Cramp 1997d). Bishop Browne, Baldwin Brown, Sir Thomas Kendrick – the list of Rosemary's predecessors who set out to undertake this enormous project is distinguished, yet she has got far further than any other in pursuit of the goal. Naturally, Rosemary's drive and determination continue to infuse energy and scholarship into this *magnum opus.* One must hope that present and future vice-chancellors of Durham University will continue to feel privileged to house this project until its culmination.

Rosemary's interests in Anglo-Saxon archaeology are catholic: she has contributed interesting perspectives on Anglo-Saxon architecture in her reviews of Harold Taylor's and Philip Rahtz's work (Cramp 1985a & 1998b), and provided a succinct and thought-provoking 'Introduction' to Janey Cronyn's and Velson Horie's important work on the St Cuthbert's Coffin (1985b). Her *Beowulf* beginnings have ensured her continued interest in, and involvement with, the archaeology of the pagan Saxon period: an excavation at Catterick (Cramp 1996b); studies of metalwork (e.g. Cramp 1964b); and an important early overview of the post-Roman archaeology of York all reflect this (Cramp 1967a). Her overview of Northumbrian settlement in 1983 is referred to above, and this had been prefigured by shorter articles on 'The early English' [in Northumberland] and 'The Anglo-Saxon Period' [in Co. Durham] (Cramp 1969a & 1970c). It has been followed up by 'Northumbria: the archaeological evidence' (Cramp 1988a) and, more recently, 'Bernicia before Wilfrid' in relation to Hexham and Tynedale (Corfe and Cramp 1997). In a different vein, her enthusiasm for communicating accurate information about the past is also reflected in a book for children on *The Earliest English* (Cramp and Gummer 1963).

Geographically, Rosemary's interests gravitated northwards (as exemplified initially by her work on 'New discoveries [of stone sculpture] at The Hirsel, Coldstream' (Cramp and Douglas-Home 1978), followed up by excavations there, reported promptly in the Universities' *Archaeological Reports* series and in *Discovery and Excavation in Scotland*). They also went westwards, as exemplified by her long-standing commitment to the Whithorn Trust and its excavations (see Hill, this volume), and her Whithorn lecture in 1994 on 'Whithorn and the Northumbrian Expansion Westwards' (Cramp 1995c), not to mention her contributions to the conference in 1992 and subsequent book on *Govan and its Early Medieval Sculpture* (Cramp 1994a & b).

The other great research achievement of her academic career is in respect of Anglo-Saxon monastic studies. Firmly grounded upon Rosemary's own excavations at Bede's monastery – begun over 40 years ago at Wearmouth and a few years later at Jarrow (cf. Cramp 1959a; Cramp 1964b) – yet encompassing the wider scene in both Northumbria and beyond, there is a substantial body of original material and discussion in the public domain. Notable are two fundamental general studies in the *Scottish Archaeological Forum* for 1973 and a major chapter on 'Monastic Sites' in the then-standard edited volume on *The Archaeology of Anglo-Saxon England* (Cramp 1973a; Cramp 1976d). These are chapters which remain of fundamental relevance and importance to the subject. Similarly, her Paul Johnstone Memorial Lecture on *The Hermitage and the Offshore Island* has an enduring quality. Ever one to get her retaliation in first, and not to miss the chance to make a relevant political point, Rosemary concluded this lecture with the following statement:

> Finally let me leave you with this sobering thought: that on the three islands I have looked at in detail [St Cuthbert's Isle, Lindisfarne; Farne Island; and Coquet Island], there is much better protection for the sea-birds than for the surviving archaeology (Cramp 1981a, 20).

Hardly less contentious is the subject of the excavations at Whitby Abbey – a key early medieval monastic site taken into Guardianship in 1920:

> This is still the most extensively excavated monastic site in Northumbria, and it is unfortunate that the excavations took place under such uncontrolled conditions. It seems to have been excavated by remotely supervised Ministry of Works workmen who maintained a record of the finds but little else. The account of the 1920–5 excavation, as summarised by Sir Charles Peers, was published in 1943... No proper account exists of the area explored, but a record of the finds and a gridded outline of the site are extant...The excavation report of the structures discovered follows a model constructed from the scanty documentary evidence for the site and Bede's account of... Coldingham (Cramp 1973, 112).

This is the academic language of barely suppressed anger at utter incompetence on the part of official authorities, even though it is written with the benefit of hindsight. In that light, it is amazing what both Rosemary and Philip Rahtz in several different articles over the years (Cramp 1993c; also see 1976d & e), have managed to salvage from this sorry tale, and we are all in their debt for this.

As is well-known, the situation was barely different at Lindisfarne itself, a place with which Rosemary has had a long association, and where her former student Deirdre O'Sullivan has undertaken much important new work over many years (see O'Sullivan, this volume). I have mentioned above Rosemary's consideration of St Cuthbert's Isle, but she has also – as with Whitby – focused upon the sculptural evidence which survived not just the Viking 'holocaust', but the activities of the Ministry of Works earlier this century. Some of Rosemary's more wide-ranging papers, such as 'The Artistic Influence of Lindisfarne within Northumbria' deriving from a Durham Conference in 1987 (Cramp 1989b), or 'Northumbria and Ireland' in one of the Kalamazoo volumes (Cramp 1986d), or the 'Insular tradition: an overview' in another (Cramp 1997a) have all delineated the cultural milieu within which this monastery existed, and its artistic output. These are complemented by her critical studies of individual churchmen in early Northumbria, such as *The Background to St Cuthbert's Life* (Cramp 1980a), 'Aidan – the pioneer' (Cramp 1993a) and 'The making of Oswald's Northumbria' (Cramp 1995a), which have all added much to our understanding of the historical context for this iconic place.

Other sites in which Rosemary has taken a deep interest for many years are those of Hartlepool and Tynemouth, and in addition to her discussion of them in her general articles, she has added important analyses of the excavated sculpture from George Jobey's excavations at Tynemouth (Cramp 1967b) and the carved stonework and moulds from Robin Daniels' excavations at Hartlepool (Cramp and Daniels 1987). Further, she has written about excavated stone furniture from Tim Potter's excavations at Heysham (Cramp 1994d), the window-glass and carved stone from Escomb (excavated by Mike Pocock and Hazel Wheeler: Cramp 1971a & b) and the window-glass from Whithorn (excavated by Peter Hill: Cramp 1997c).

But it is to Wearmouth-Jarrow that we return. When the final report on these sites is published, we shall all be able to appreciate the major logistical problems she overcame simply in getting access to these sites, and then in excavating them, and in managing the large teams that assisted her over the many years of excavation. A lesser person would have balked at the problems, or have given up after the terrible accident she suffered at Jarrow when she was photographing the site; a lesser person would certainly not have seen the black humour in being taken off the site in a wheelbarrow! A lesser person would certainly have despaired at the enormous scale of the post-excavation problem, and the difficulty of retrospective stratigraphic and structural analyses due to lack of available resources at the right time for such work.[5] The displays at Monkwearmouth Church, the Bede Monastery Museum (now 'Bede's World': cf. Cramp 1980b) and a clutch of fundamental articles on both the site itself and, particularly, the remarkable collection of glass recovered (about which Rosemary is herself an acknowledged expert) already testify to her achievement. The Interim report in *Medieval Archaeology* (Cramp 1969b); the report on the church excavation at St Paul's Jarrow in the CBA volume on *The Archaeological Study of Churches* (Cramp 1976i), followed by accounts of both churches and sites in the *Archaeological Journal* (Cramp 1976f & g); the updated summary account of the excavations in Gerald Bonner's edited volume *Famulus Christi* (Cramp 1976h); and, more recently, her account published in a Society of Antiquaries of London monograph of 'Monkwearmouth and Jarrow in their Continental Context' (Cramp 1994c) have pointed the way forward for assessment of these sites. Similarly, the artefactual articles on 'Glass finds from the Anglo-Saxon monastery of Monkwearmouth and Jarrow' in *Studies in Glass History and Design* (Cramp 1974a); on the 'Decorated window-glass and millefiori from Monkwearmouth' (Cramp 1970b); that on the 'Window-glass from the monastic site of Jarrow' in the *Antiquaries Journal* (Cramp 1971) and another article on the same theme in the *Journal of Glass Studies* (Cramp 1975d); and her joint article with Janey Cronyn on polychrome plaster (Cramp and Cronyn 1990. All of these have been rich appetizers. Our appetite is, indeed, whetted for the main course, but – as with the *Corpus* – we know it will be well worth the wait.

***

What of Binford, then? Well, when Rosemary became the Appointed Professor of Archaeology, rather than, as it were, achieving a Personal Chair in Medieval Archaeology, she felt that she had inherited a broader responsibility to the discipline as a whole. Certainly she felt she had to a duty to inculcate some of the more general concepts of archaeological thinking to the new Honours Archaeology students. Although I am sure she would be the first to admit that she does not have a great affinity with the various theoretical schools of archaeology, she did *some* reading on this area of the subject, even though it was not particularly congenial to her. One of my last conversations with her in Durham in September 1990, when I was packing up to go to Glasgow and she was packing up to go into retirement, concerned our personal libraries and the problems of boxing them up and then moving them out of the building in Saddler Street. We were chatting in her room, when she went over to her bookshelf, and took out Lewis Binford's *An Archaeological Perspective*, saying with a wicked smile – 'At least I won't have to look at this one ever again' – and she threw it on the floor. So much for that theoretical guru!

There is much still to come and plenty of time for it. In these incomplete sketches of Rosemary's archaeological career to date, I hope that I have managed at least to convey something of the nature of this whirlwind personality who touched the lives of so many of her pupils and of those who have been fortunate to be her colleagues.

Notes

1. Introductory address at *The View from Durham: A Conference in Honour of Rosemary Cramp*, 23 April 1999. This address has been somewhat amended from the form in which it was delivered, although hopefully it preserves some of the character of the immediacy of the occasion. Intended as a tribute to Rosemary as a person, rather than as an academic paper, a 'sanitized' version would not truly reflect the occasion on which it was delivered. However, as some parts of the address derive from 'oral tradition', I have decided that their transmission from the past to future is best ensured through that route. This is not a biography (official or otherwise). A great deal may yet be expected from Rosemary in terms of scholarship, and there will no doubt be many more stories to be told in future years. I simply offer this to her with affection and respect as a 'portrait' painted at a certain, if significant, time of life that reflects my own perspective on the nature and influence of a charismatic personality, whose life and career so far have been an inspiration to so many others – students, colleagues, and friends. I am proud and grateful to have made the transition through each of these states (along with many others, both present at the conference and unable to attend).
2. See note below by Derek Craig for published references to this.
3. Although I originally prepared references to Rosemary's published work for the address independently of Derek Craig's 'Interim Bibliography' below, I benefitted from sight of his work at a final stage of preparation of this text and have tried to ensure that it is consistent with it. I have been able to add to my text one or two references to her publications which were not mentioned in my lecture, thanks to Derek's listing, but I have not attempted to include all of them. It may well be that, as with most essays, mine has some serious omissions from the 'list of reading'. However, the 'feedback process' begun by receipt of Derek's bibliography will help to rectify this, and I look forward to reading a number of her papers, especially those which have come out in the past three years. Rosemary herself will be only too well aware that I have not kept up in her chosen fields of academic study, but I hope that she will feel that at least I have tried to characterize her contributions in them.
4. See Derek Craig's own 'Bibliographical footnote' on this matter.
5. However, as can be seen from the entries in Derek Craig's 'Interim Bibliography', she always made sure that notes were published on each season's work, whether as in the early days in the *University of Durham Gazette* or later in the 'Medieval Britain' section of *Medieval Archaeology*.

8

Rosemary Cramp
An interim bibliography

Derek Craig

Compiling a list of a scholar's published writings for a *Festschrift* has about it a spurious air of finality, reminiscent of the premature burial of the protagonist in an Edgar Allan Poe story. This is especially inappropriate when (as in Rosemary Cramp's case) the subject continues to bring out a flurry of new articles each year, and is busily working on a series of major excavation reports and sculpture surveys. However, Rosemary has published so many papers of importance, not always in obvious places, that it may be useful to provide a preliminary list. As her research assistant for the past few years, I have been in the privileged position of knowing what papers she was writing, and I have had the advantage of having some of her more obscurely-placed publications brought to my attention. I therefore offer this appreciation of her immense contribution to archaeology with the pleasurable awareness that it will be rendered out-of-date almost immediately. While it is as complete as possible, up to 1999 there are almost certainly items that I have missed.

***

The earliest published evidence of Rosemary Cramp's involvement in archaeology can be found in the *Journal of Roman Studies* 36 (1946), 142, and 38 (1948), 89, as a result of her excavations at Ivy House Farm, Glooston, Leicestershire, near to her family home, at the age of sixteen.

1957

Beowulf and archaeology, *Medieval Archaeol*, 1, 57–77 (reprinted in D. K. Fry (ed), *The 'Beowulf' Poet: a collection of critical essays*, 114–40, Englewood Cliffs, New Jersey: Prentice-Hall, 1968)

Review of: P. Hunter Blair, *Anglo-Saxon England*, Cambridge 1956, in *Medium Aevum*, 26, 117–20

1959

St Peter's church, Monkwearmouth, *Univ Durham Gazette*, new ser, 7 (2), 6–7

Review of: C. Clark, *The Peterborough Chronicle 1070–1154*, Oxford 1958, in *Antiq J*, 39, 309

1960

The Anglian sculptured crosses of Dumfriesshire, *Trans Dumfriesshire Galloway Natur Hist Antiq Soc*, 3rd ser, 38 (1959–60), 9–20 (reprinted in *Studies in Anglo-Saxon Sculpture*, 1992, 1–15)

Durham: Monkwearmouth, 139–40; in D. M. Wilson and J. G. Hurst (eds), Medieval Britain in 1959, *Medieval Archaeol*, 4, 134–65

Monkwearmouth, *Univ Durham Gazette*, new ser, 8 (2), 11

1961

Monkwearmouth, *Univ Durham Gazette*, new ser, 9 (2), 9–10

1962

Appendix I. Pre-Conquest sculpture at Jarrow, in B. Colgrave and T. A. Romans, *A Guide to St. Paul's Church, Jarrow, and its monastic buildings* (new edn), 30–1, Gloucester: British Publishing Co.

Review of: G. W. Dunleavy, *Colum's Other Island: the Irish at Lindisfarne*, Madison 1960, in *Medium Aevum*, 31, 137–9

1963

Durham: Monkwearmouth, 315; in D. M. Wilson and D. G. Hurst (eds), Medieval Britain in 1961, *Medieval Archaeol*, 6–7 (1962–3), 306–49

Monkwearmouth, *Univ Durham Gazette*, new ser, 10 (2), 12–13

Cramp, R. and Gummer, J. (illustrated by J. Lathey), *The Earliest English*, London: Edward Arnold (reprinted, New York: St Martin's Press 1964)

1964

Appendix II. The 'Viking Type' penannular brooch and torc from Orton Scar, 86–9; in E. Birley, The Orton Scar find, and Thomas Reveley of Kendal, *Trans Cumberland Westmorland Antiq Archaeol Soc*, new ser, 64, 81–9

An Anglo-Saxon pin from Birdoswald, *Trans Cumberland Westmorland Antiq Archaeol Soc*, new ser, 64, 90–3

A name-stone from Monkwearmouth, *Archaeol Aeliana*, 4th ser, 42, 294–8 (reprinted in *Studies in Anglo-Saxon Sculpture*, 1992, 16–20)

Durham: Jarrow, 232; in D. M. Wilson and D. G. Hurst (eds), Medieval Britain in 1962 and 1963, *Medieval Archaeol*, 8, 231–99

Durham: Monkwearmouth, 232, 241; in D. M. Wilson and D. G. Hurst (eds), Medieval Britain in 1962 and 1963, *Medieval Archaeol*, 8, 231–99

Review of: H. R. Ellis Davidson, *The Sword in Anglo-Saxon England*, Oxford 1962, in *Medieval Archaeol*, 8, 303–4

Review of: C. J. Godfrey, *The Church in Anglo-Saxon England*, Cambridge 1962, in *Medium Aevum*, 33, 133–4

1965

Durham Cathedral: a short guide to the pre-Conquest sculptured stones in the Dormitory, Durham: privately printed

Early Northumbrian Sculpture, Jarrow Lecture 1965, Jarrow: The Parish of Jarrow (reprinted in *Studies in Anglo-Saxon Sculpture*, 1992, 21–38; and in M. Lapidge (ed), *Bede and His World: the Jarrow lectures 1958–1993*, 2 vols, 133–52, Aldershot: Variorum 1994)

Durham: Monkwearmouth, 171; in D. M. Wilson and D. G. Hurst (eds), Medieval Britain in 1964, *Medieval Archaeol*, 9, 170–220

Monkwearmouth, *Univ Durham Gazette*, new ser, 12 (2), 5–6

Review of: N. K. Chadwick (ed), *Celt and Saxon: Studies in the Early British Border*, Cambridge 1963, in *Scot Hist Rev*, 44, 63–5

Review of: D. M. Wilson, *Anglo-Saxon Ornamental Metalwork, 700–1100, in the British Museum* (British Museum Catalogue of Antiquities of the Later Saxon Period, 1), London 1964, in *Medieval Archaeol*, 9, 229–30

Colgrave, B. and Cramp, R., *St Peter's Church, Wearmouth*, Gloucester: British Publishing Co.

1966

A cross from St Oswald's church, Durham, and its stylistic relationships, *Durham Univ J*, 58 (3), n ser 27 (3), 119–24 (reprinted in *Studies in Anglo-Saxon Sculpture*, 1992, 39–46)

The decoration, 148–9; in B. J. N. Edwards, A portion of an inscribed pre-Conquest cross-shaft from Lancaster, *Medieval Archaeol*, 10, 146–9

Durham: Jarrow, 169–70; in D. M. Wilson and D. G. Hurst (eds), Medieval Britain in 1965, *Medieval Archaeol*, 10, 168–219

Jarrow, *Univ Durham Gazette*, new ser, 13 (2), 10–11

1967

Anglian and Viking York, (Borthwick Papers 33), York: St Anthony's Press

Appendix B. Two newly discovered fragments of Anglo-Saxon sculpture from Tynemouth, 99–104; in G. Jobey, Excavation at Tynemouth priory and castle, *Archaeol Aeliana*, 4th ser, 45, 33–104 (reprinted in *Studies in Anglo-Saxon Sculpture*, 1992, 47–54)

The Monastic Arts of Northumbria, London: Arts Council of Great Britain

Catterick (Cataractonium), 208; in R. P. Wright (ed), Roman Britain in 1966. II. Inscriptions, *J Roman Stud*, 57, 203–10

Durham: Jarrow, 263–4; in D. M. Wilson and D. G. Hurst (eds), Medieval Britain in 1966, *Medieval Archaeol*, 11, 262–319

Durham: Monkwearmouth, 264; in D. M. Wilson and D. G. Hurst (eds), Medieval Britain in 1966, *Medieval Archaeol*, 11, 262–319

Review of: H. M. Taylor and J. Taylor, *Anglo-Saxon Architecture*, 2 vols., Cambridge 1965, in *Medium Aevum*, 36, 99–100

Review of: D. M. Wilson and O. Klindt-Jensen, *Viking Art*, London 1966, in *J Brit Archaeol Ass*, 3rd ser, 30, 161–2

1968

Bertram Colgrave, *Univ Durham Gazette*, new ser, 15 (2), 7–8

Durham: Jarrow, 155–6; in D. M. Wilson and D. G. Hurst (eds), Medieval Britain in 1967, *Medieval Archaeol*, 12, 155–211

Durham: Monkwearmouth, 156; in D. M. Wilson and D. G. Hurst (eds), Medieval Britain in 1967, *Medieval Archaeol*, 12, 155–211

Monkwearmouth (1967), *Univ Durham Gazette*, new ser, 15 (2), 18–19

1969

The early English, in J. Philipson (ed), *Northumberland* (National Park Guide 7), 53–7, London: HMSO

Excavations at the Saxon monastic sites of Wearmouth and Jarrow, co. Durham: an interim report, *Medieval Archaeol*, 13, 21–66

Durham: Hartlepool, Lumley Street, 231; in D. M. Wilson and D. G. Hurst (eds), Medieval Britain in 1968, *Medieval Archaeol*, 13, 230–87

1970

Glass finds from the Anglo-Saxon monastery of Monkwearmouth and Jarrow, in R. Charleston, W. Evans and A. E. Werner (eds), *Studies in Glass History and Design. Papers read to the Committee B sessions of the VIIIth International Congress on Glass held in London 1st–6th July 1968*, 16–19, Sheffield [publisher not named]

Decorated window-glass and millefiori from Monkwearmouth, *Antiq J*, 50 (2), 327–35

The Anglo-Saxon period, in J. C. Dewdney (ed), *Durham County and City with Teesside*, 199–206, Durham: Local Executive Committee of the British Association

1971

Appendix I. The window glass, 26–8; in M. Pocock and H. Wheeler, Excavations at Escomb church, County Durham, *J Brit Archaeol Ass*, 3rd ser, 34, 11–29

Appendix II. Fragment of carved stone, 28–9; in M. Pocock and H. Wheeler, Excavations at Escomb church, County Durham, *J Brit Archaeol Ass*, 3rd ser, 34, 11–29

Durham Cathedral: a short guide to the pre-Conquest sculptured stones in the Dormitory (revised edn), Durham: privately printed

The position of the Otley crosses in English sculpture of the eighth to ninth centuries, in V. Milojčić (ed), *Kolloquium über spätantike und frühmittelalterliche Skulptur* 2 (Institut für Ur- und Frühgeschichte, Universität Heidelberg, Vortragstexte 1970), 55–63, Mainz: Philipp von Zabern (reprinted in *Studies in Anglo-Saxon Sculpture*, 1992, 55–78)

1972

Tradition and innovation in English stone sculpture of the tenth and eleventh centuries, in V. Milojčić (ed), *Kolloquium über spätantike und frühmittelalterliche Skulptur*, 3 (Institut für Ur- und Frühgeschichte, Universität Heidelberg, Vortragstexte 1971), 139–48, Mainz: Philipp von Zabern (reprinted in *Studies in Anglo-Saxon Sculpture*, 1992, 79–94)

The Anglo-Saxon and medieval monastery of Jarrow, Co. Durham, *Archaeol Bull CBA. Regional Group 3*, 1 (May 1972), 5–6

The Anglo-Saxon and medieval monastery of Monkwearmouth, Co. Durham, *Archaeol Bull CBA Regional Group 3*, 1 (May 1972), 6

Durham: Jarrow, 148–50; in L. E. Webster and J. Cherry (eds), Medieval Britain in 1971, *Medieval Archaeol*, 16, 147–212

Durham: Monkwearmouth, 150–2; in L. E. Webster and J. Cherry (eds), Medieval Britain in 1971, *Medieval Archaeol*, 16, 147–212

Review of: E. Okasha, *Hand-list of Anglo-Saxon Non-runic Inscriptions*, Cambridge 1971, in *Archaeol Aeliana*, 4th ser, 50, 300–1

Review of: C. Thomas, *The Early Christian Archaeology of North Britain*, Oxford 1971, in *Antiquity*, 46, 250–1

1973

Anglo-Saxon monasteries of the north, *Scot Archaeol Forum*, 5 (1974), 104–24

1974

Early Northumbrian sculpture at Hexham, in D. P. Kirby (ed), *Saint Wilfrid at Hexham*, 115–40, Newcastle upon Tyne: Oriel Press (reprinted in *Studies in Anglo-Saxon Sculpture*, 1992, 95–139)

Appendix II. A hand-list of Hexham Anglo-Saxon sculpture, in D. P. Kirby (ed), *Saint Wilfrid at Hexham*, 172–9, Newcastle upon Tyne: Oriel Press (reprinted in *Studies in Anglo-Saxon Sculpture*, 1992, 140–7)

The Anglo-Saxon and medieval monastery of Jarrow, Co. Durham, *Archaeol Bull CBA Regional Group 3*, 7 (May 1974), 6–8

The Anglo-Saxons and Rome, *Trans Architect Archaeol Soc Durham Northumberland*, new ser, 3, 27–37

The post-Conquest monastic buildings, in M. A. S. Hickmore, *St Paul's Church, Jarrow*, 20–1, Newcastle: Frank Graham

1975

Anglo-Saxon sculpture of the reform period, in D. Parsons (ed), *Tenth-Century Studies: essays in commemoration of the millennium of the Council of Winchester and the 'Regularis Concordia'*, 184–99, 245–7, London and Chichester: Phillimore (reprinted in *Studies in Anglo-Saxon Sculpture*, 1992, 148–73)

Jarrow 1973, *Univ Durham Gazette*, new ser, 21, 16–17

Monkwearmouth excavations, 1974, *Univ Durham Gazette*, new ser, 21, 20–2

Window glass from the monastic site of Jarrow: problems of interpretation, *J Glass Stud*, 17, 88–96

1976

Beowulf: 15. *Beowulf* and archaeology, in J. Hoops *et al.* (eds), *Reallexikon der germanischen Altertumskunde*, 2nd edn, II. 2–3, 244, Berlin and New York: Walter de Gruyter

Historical and documentary background, in P. A. G. Clack and P. F. Gosling, *Archaeology in the North: report of the Northern Archaeological Survey*, (ed. D. W. Harding), 38–42, Gateshead: Northern Archaeological Survey

Mediterranean elements in the early medieval sculpture of England, in *Union internationale des sciences préhistoriques et protohistoriques, IXe congrès*, colloque XXX, *Les relations entre l'empire romain tardiff, l'empire franc et ses voisins*, 263–95, Nice: Parc Valrose de l'Université de Nice

Monastic sites, in D. M. Wilson (ed), *The Archaeology of Anglo-Saxon England*, 201–52, London: Methuen

Appendix B. Analysis of the finds register and location plan of Whitby Abbey, in D. M. Wilson (ed), *The Archaeology of Anglo-Saxon England*, 453–7, London: Methuen

Jarrow church, 220–8; in Report of the Summer Meeting of the Royal Archaeological Institute at Newcastle upon Tyne in 1976, *Archaeol J*, 133, 135–249

Monkwearmouth church, 230–7; in Report of the Summer Meeting of the Royal Archaeological Institute at Newcastle upon Tyne in 1976, *Archaeol J*, 133, 135–249

Monkwearmouth and Jarrow: the archaeological evidence, in G. Bonner (ed), *Famulus Christi: essays in commemoration of the thirteenth centenary of the birth of the Venerable Bede*, 5–18, London: SPCK

St Paul's Church, Jarrow, in P. V. Addyman and R. K. Morris (eds), *The Archaeological Study of Churches* (CBA Res Rep 13), 28–35, London: Council for British Archaeology

1977

The Brixworth archaeological research committee, *J Brit Archaeol Ass*, 130, 52–4

Northumbrian sculpture, in R. J. Cramp and J. T. Lang, *A Century of Anglo-Saxon Sculpture*, Newcastle upon Tyne: Frank Graham [not paginated]

Schools of Mercian sculpture, in A. Dornier (ed) *Mercian Studies*, 191–233, Leicester: Leicester University Press (reprinted in *Studies in Anglo-Saxon Sculpture*, 1992, 174–216)

University of Durham: Department of Archaeology, *Antiquity*, 51, 139–40

1978

The Anglian tradition in the ninth century, in J. T. Lang (ed), *Anglo-Saxon and Viking Age Sculpture and its Context: papers from the Collingwood Symposium on insular sculpture from 800 to 1066* (Brit Archaeol Rep, Brit Ser, 49), 1–32, Oxford: BAR (reprinted in *Studies in Anglo-Saxon Sculpture*, 1992, 217–46)

The evangelist symbols and their parallels in Anglo-Saxon sculpture, in R. T. Farrell (ed), *Bede and Anglo-Saxon England: papers in honour of the 1300th anniversary of the birth of Bede, given at Cornell University in 1973 and 1974* (Brit Archaeol Rep, Brit Ser, 46), 118–30, Oxford: BAR (reprinted in *Studies in Anglo-Saxon Sculpture*, 1992, 247–57)

Review of: R. Bruce-Mitford, *The Sutton Hoo Ship-Burial*, 1, London 1975, in *Antiq J*, 58 (2), 426–8

Review of: H. M. Taylor, *Anglo-Saxon Architecture*, 3, Cambridge 1978, in *British Book News*, 925

Cramp, R. and Douglas-Home, C., New discoveries at The Hirsel, Coldstream, Berwickshire, *Proc Soc Antiq Scot*, 109 (1977–8), 223–32

1980

The Background to St Cuthbert's Life. Delivered in the Prior's Hall at Durham, 14 March 1980, Durham Cathedral Lecture 1980, Durham: Dean and Chapter of Durham

The Bede Monastery Museum, Jarrow: St Paul's Jarrow Development Trust

The pre-Conquest sculptural tradition in Durham, in N. Coldstream and P. Draper (eds), *Medieval Art and Architecture at Durham Cathedral*, (Brit Archaeol Assoc Conference Trans for 1977, 3), 1–10, Leeds: BAA (reprinted in *Studies in Anglo-Saxon Sculpture*, 1992, 258–71)

Borders (Berwickshire): Coldstream, The Hirsel, 234, 247; in L. E. Webster and J. Cherry (eds), Medieval Britain in 1979, *Medieval Archaeol*, 24, 218–64

Excavations at The Hirsel, Coldstream, Berwickshire, *Univ Durham Newcastle Archaeol Rep for 1979*, 17–19

The Hirsel (Coldingham p): early medieval church, cemetery, medieval domestic structure, *Discovery Excav Scot 1980*, 1

Review of: B. Hope-Taylor, *Yeavering: an Anglo-British centre of early Northumbria*, London 1977, in *Antiquity*, 54, 63–5

1981

The Hermitage and Offshore Island (Second Paul Johnstone Memorial Lecture, Occasional Lecture 3, National Maritime Museum), London: National Maritime Museum

Borders (Berwickshire): Coldstream, The Hirsel, 180, 199; in S. M. Youngs and J. Clark (eds), Medieval Britain in 1980, *Medieval Archaeol*, 25, 166–228

Excavations at The Hirsel, Coldstream, Borders Region, *Univ Durham Newcastle Archaeol Rep for 1980*, 45–8

The Hirsel, Coldsteam (Coldingham p): early medieval church, cemetery, domestic structures, *Discovery Excav Scot 1981*, 1

Review of: V. I. Evison (ed) *Angles, Saxons and Jutes: studies presented to J. N. L. Myres*, Oxford 1981, in *British Book News*, 763

1982

The Viking image, in R. T. Farrell (ed), *The Vikings*, 8–19, London and Chichester: Phillimore

Borders (Berwickshire): Coldstream, The Hirsel, 217; in S. M. Youngs and J. Clark (eds), Medieval Britain in 1981, *Medieval Archaeol*, 26, 164–227

Excavations at The Hirsel, Coldstream, Borders Region, *Univ Durham Newcastle Archaeol Rep for 1981*, 33–7

The Hirsel (Coldstream p): early medieval church, cemetery, medieval domestic building, *Discovery Excav Scot 1982*, 1

Review of: D. Fossard, M. Vieillard-Troiekouroff and E. Chatel, *Recueil général des monuments sculptés en France pendant le Haut Moyen Age (IVe-Xe siècles), 1: Paris et son Département*, Paris 1978, in *Antiq J*, 62, 163–4

Review of: G. Nott, The origin of the so-called plan of St Gall, *Journal of Medieval History* 8, Amsterdam 1982, in *Archaeol J*, 141, 354–5

Review of: W. Rodwell, *The Archaeology of the English Church*, London 1982, in *Archaeol J*, 141, 355

Cramp, R. and Miket, R., *Catalogue of the Anglo-Saxon and Viking Antiquities in the Museum of Antiquities, Newcastle upon Tyne*, Newcastle upon Tyne: Museum of Antiquities, Department of Archaeology

1983

The Anglian sculptures from Jedburgh, in A. O'Connor and D. V. Clarke (eds), *From the Stone Age to the 'Forty Five: studies presented to R. B. K. Stevenson, former Keeper, National Museum of Antiquities of Scotland*, 269–84, Edinburgh: John Donald

Anglo-Saxon settlement, in J. C. Chapman and H. C. Mytum (eds) *Settlement in North Britain, 1000 BC to AD 1000: papers presented to George Jobey, Newcastle upon Tyne, December 1982* (Brit Archaeol Rep, Brit Ser, 118), 263–97, Oxford: BAR

The archaeologist's view - general, in G. D. Hart (ed), *Disease in Ancient Man: an international symposium*, 11–20, Toronto: Clarke Irwin

Pre-Conquest: Introduction, in F. H. Thompson (ed), *Studies in Medieval Sculpture* (Soc Antiq London, Occas Pap, new ser, 3), 1–2, London: Society of Antiquaries

Coldstream, The Hirsel, 221–2; in S. M. Youngs, J. Clark and T. B. Barry (eds), Medieval Britain in 1982, *Medieval Archaeol*, 27, 161–229

Excavations at The Hirsel, Coldstream, Borders Region, *Univ Durham Newcastle Archaeol Rep for 1982*, 57–60

1984

Corpus of Anglo-Saxon Stone Sculpture, 1, County Durham and Northumberland, Oxford: British Academy / Oxford University Press

Corpus of Anglo-Saxon Stone Sculpture: General Introduction, Oxford: British Academy / Oxford University Press

The Iken cross-shaft, 291–2; in S. E. West, N. Scarfe and R. Cramp, Iken, St Botolph and the coming of East Anglian Christianity, *Proc Suffolk Inst Archaeol Hist,* 35 (4), 279–301

The Hirsel (Coldstream p): prehistoric, Romano-British occupation, medieval church, burials, *Discovery Excav Scot 1984,* 1

1985

Anglo-Saxon Architecture and Anglo-Saxon sculpture, 309–12; in M. Biddle, R. Cramp, M. McC. Gatch, S. Keynes and B. Kjølbye-Biddle, *Anglo-Saxon Architecture* and Anglo-Saxon studies: a review, *Anglo-Saxon England,* 14, 293–317

Introduction, in J. M. Cronyn and C. V. Horie, *St Cuthbert's Coffin: the history, technology and conservation,* ix-xi, Durham: Dean and Chapter, Durham Cathedral

Coldstream, The Hirsel, 219–20; in S. M. Youngs, J. Clark and T. B. Barry (eds), Medieval Britain in 1984, *Medieval Archaeol,* 29, 158–230

Excavations at The Hirsel, Coldstream, Borders, *Univ Durham Newcastle Archaeol Rep for 1984,* 52–7

Review of: D. Whitelock, R. McKitterick and D. Dumville (ed), *Ireland in Early Medieval Europe: studies in memory of Kathleen Hughes,* Cambridge 1982, in *Antiq J,* 65 (1), 184–7

1986

Anglo-Saxon and Italian sculpture, in *Angli e Sassoni al di qua e al di là del mare, 26 aprile–1 maggio 1984* (Settimane di studio del Centro italiano di studi sull'alto Medioevo, 32), tomo primo, 125–40, Spoleto: Centro italiano di studi sull'alto Medioevo (reprinted in *Studies in Anglo-Saxon Sculpture,* 1992, 298–328)

Foreword, in J. Higgitt (ed) *Early Medieval Sculpture in Britain and Ireland* (Brit Archaeol Rep, Brit Ser, 152), 1–4, Oxford: BAR

The furnishing and sculptural decoration of Anglo-Saxon churches, in L. A. S. Butler and R. K. Morris (eds), *The Anglo-Saxon Church. Papers on history, architecture and archaeology in honour of Dr H. M. Taylor* (CBA Res Rep 60), 101–4, London: Council for British Archaeology (reprinted in *Studies in Anglo-Saxon Sculpture,* 1992, 289–97)

Northumbria and Ireland, in P. Szarmach with V. D. Oggins (eds), *Sources of Anglo-Saxon Culture* (Studies in Medieval Culture 20), 185–201, Kalamazoo, Michigan: Medieval Institute Publications (reprinted in *Studies in Anglo-Saxon Sculpture,* 1992, 272–88)

The Corpus of Anglo-Saxon Stone Sculpture, in P. Szarmach with V. D. Oggins (eds), *Sources of Anglo-Saxon Culture* (Studies in Medieval Culture 20), 431–2, Kalamazoo, Michigan: Medieval Institute Publications

Review of: R. Deshman, *Anglo-Saxon and Anglo-Scandinavian Art: an annotated bibliography,* Boston 1984, and M. Werner, *Insular Art: an annotated bibliography,* Boston 1984, in *Archaeol J,* 143, 390–1

1987

Cramp, R. J. and Daniels, R., New finds from the Anglo-Saxon monastery at Hartlepool, Cleveland, *Antiquity*, 61, 424–32

1988

Northumbria: the archaeological evidence, in S. T. Driscoll and M. R. Nieke (eds), *Power and Politics in Early Medieval Britain and Ireland*, 69–78, Edinburgh: Edinburgh University Press

Bailey, R. N. and Cramp, R., *Corpus of Anglo-Saxon Stone Sculpture, 2, Cumberland, Westmorland, and Lancashire North-of-the-Sands*, Oxford: British Academy / Oxford University Press

1989

(with contributions from C. Entwhistle), *Anglo-Saxon Connections*, Durham: Dean and Chapter, Durham Cathedral

The artistic influence of Lindisfarne within Northumbria, in G. Bonner, D. Rollason and C. Stancliffe (eds), *St Cuthbert, His Cult and His Community to AD 1200*, 213–28, Woodbridge: Boydell Press (reprinted in *Studies in Anglo-Saxon Sculpture*, 1992, 329–44)

1990

Review of: C. B. McClendon, *The Imperial Abbey of Farfa: architectural currents of the early Middle Ages*, London 1987, in *Antiq J*, 70 (1), 141–2

Cramp, R. and Cronyn, J., Anglo-Saxon polychrome plaster and other materials from the excavations of Monkwearmouth and Jarrow: an interim report, in S. Cather, D. Park and P. Williamson (eds) *Early Medieval Wall Painting and Painted Sculpture in England* (Brit Archaeol Rep, Brit Ser, 216), 17–30, Oxford: BAR

1991

Grammar of Anglo-Saxon Ornament: a general introduction to the Corpus of Anglo-Saxon Stone Sculpture, Oxford: British Academy / Oxford University Press

Anglosassoni: scultura, in *Enciclopedia dell'arte medievale*, 1, 753–4, Rome: Istituto della Enciclopedia Italiana

The Rt Hon The Lord Fletcher of Islington, LLD, FSA. Eric George Molyneaux Fletcher, 1903–1990, President of the British Archaeological Association 1960–1963, *J Brit Archaeol Assoc*, 144, v-vi

1992

Studies in Anglo-Saxon Sculpture, London: Pindar Press (including seventeen previously published papers, with Introduction, i-vi, and Additional Notes, 347–9)

1993

Aidan – the pioneer, in C. Yeates (ed), *A Christian Heritage: a collection of addresses in honour of the 900th anniversary of Durham Cathedral*, 9–15, Bangor: Headstart

The hall in Beowulf and in archaeology, in H. Damico and J. Leyerle (eds), *Heroic Poetry in the Anglo-Saxon Period: studies in honor of Jess B. Bessinger, Jr.* (Studies in Medieval Culture 32), 331–46, Kalamazoo, Michigan: Medieval Institute Publications

A reconsideration of the monastic site of Whitby, in R. M. Spearman and J. Higgitt (eds), *The Age of Migrating Ideas: early medieval art in northern Britain and Ireland*, 64–73, Edinburgh and Stroud: National Museums of Scotland/Sutton Publishing

1994

The Govan recumbent cross-slabs, in A. Ritchie (ed), *Govan and its Early Medieval Sculpture*, 55–61, Stroud: Alan Sutton Publishing

Conclusions from the Govan conference, in A. Ritchie (ed), *Govan and its Early Medieval Sculpture*, 133–7, Stroud: Alan Sutton Publishing

Monkwearmouth and Jarrow in their continental context, in K. Painter (ed), *'Churches Built in Ancient Times': Recent Studies in Early Christian Archaeology* (Soc Antiq London, Occas Pap 16, and Specialist Studies on the Mediterranean 1), 279–94, London: Society of Antiquaries and Accordia Research Centre, (reprinted in C. E. Karkov (ed), 1999 *The Archaeology of Anglo-Saxon England: Basic Readings* (Basic Readings in Anglo-Saxon England 7), 137–53, New York and London: Garland Publishing)

The sculpture, 106–17; in T. W. Potter and R. D. Andrews, Excavation and survey at St Patrick's chapel and St Peter's church, Heysham, Lancashire, 1977–8, *Antiq J*, 74, 55–134

Gladys Bettess, *Archaeol North*, 8 (winter 1994), 7–8

1995

The making of Oswald's Northumbria, in C. Stancliffe and E. Cambridge (eds), *Oswald: Northumbrian King to European Saint*, 17–32, Stamford: Paul Watkins

Nature redeemed, in D. Brown and A. Loades (eds), *The Sense of the Sacramental: movement and measure in art and music, place and time*, 122–36, London: SPCK

Whithorn and the Northumbrian Expansion Westwards (Third Whithorn Lecture, 17 September 1994), Whithorn: Friends of the Whithorn Trust

1996

The monumental stone, in A. Boddington, *Raunds Furnells: the Anglo-Saxon Church and Churchyard, Raunds Area Project* (English Heritage Archaeol Rep 7), 102–12, London: English Heritage

RAF Catterick 1966, 29–30; in P. R. Wilson, P. Carwell, R. J. Cramp, J. Evans, R. H. Taylor-Wilson, A. Thompson, and J. S. Wacher, Early Anglian Catterick and *Catraeth*, *Medieval Archaeol*, 40, 1–61

1997

The Insular tradition: an overview, in C. E. Karkov, R. T. Farrell and M. Ryan (eds), *The Insular Tradition* (SUNY Series in Medieval Studies), 283–99, Albany: State University of New York Press

Not Why But How: the contribution of archaeological evidence to the understanding of Anglo-Saxon England, in P. E. Szarmach and J. T. Rosenthal (eds), *The Preservation and Transmission of Anglo-Saxon Culture. Selected Papers from the 1991 Meeting of the International Society of Anglo-Saxonists* (Studies in Medieval Culture 40), 271–86, Kalamazoo, Michigan: Medieval Institute Publications

The window glass, in P. Hill, *Whithorn and St Ninian. The excavation of a monastic town 1984–91*, 326–32, Stroud: Whithorn Trust and Sutton Publishing

Obituary: Jim Lang, *British Archaeol*, 22 (March 1997), 13

Corfe, T. and Cramp, R., Bernicia before Wilfrid, in T. Corfe (ed), *Before Wilfrid: Britons, Romans and Anglo-Saxons in Tynedale* (Hexham Historian 7 (August 1997)), 57–64, Hexham: Hexham Local History Society

1998

Brixworth; Ecclesiastical architecture, early Anglo-Saxon; Kentish churches; Wearmouth-Jarrow: architecture; in P. E. Szarmach, M. T. Tavormina and J. T. Rosenthal (eds), *Medieval England: an Encyclopedia*, 145–6, 265, 392, 777–8, New York and London: Garland Publishing

Preface, 19, and Endnote, 26–7, in R. Cramp, T. Tatton-Brown, R. Gem and D. Parsons, St Mary's, Deerhurst - a retrospective, *Church Archaeol*, 2, 19–28

1999

The Anglo-Saxon church of Britford and the Italian connection, in *Arte d'Occidente: Temi et Metodi, I. Studi in onore di Angiola Maria Romanini*, 35–40, Rome: Edizione Sintesi Informazione

Architectural stone sculpture; Monkwearmouth (or Wearmouth) and Jarrow; in M. Lapidge with J. Blair, S. Keynes and D. Scragg (eds), *The Blackwell Encyclopedia of Anglo-Saxon England*, 43–4, 325–6, Oxford: Blackwell Publishers

Glasfenster aus Jarrow (Rekonstruktion), in C. Stiegemann and M. Wenhoff (eds) *799 - Kunst und Kultur der Karolingerzeit: Karl der Grosse und Papst Leo III. in Paderborn. Band 1, Katalog der Ausstellung Paderborn 1999*, 184–5, III. 95, Mainz: Phillipp von Zabern

The Northumbrian identity, in J. Hawkes and S. Mills (eds), *Northumbria's Golden Age*, 1–11, Stroud: Sutton Publishing

Index

Compiled by Arthur MacGregor